BEST MOUNTED POLICE STORIES

BEST
Mounted Police
STORIES

Edited by Dick Harrison

The University
of Alberta
Press

Lone Pine
Publishing

First published in this edition by:

The University of Alberta Press
141 Athabasca Hall
Edmonton, Alberta, Canada   T6G 2E8
   and
Lone Pine Publishing
206, 10426–81 Ave.
Edmonton, Alberta, Canada   T6E 1X5

Printed in Canada   5   4

ISBN 0–88864–054–4

Canadian Cataloguing in Publication Data

Main entry under title:
Best Mounted Police Stories

   ISBN 0–88864–054–4

   1. Canada. Royal Canadian Mounted Police—Fiction. 2. Short stories, Canadian. 3. Short stories, American. I. Harrison, Dick, 1937–
PS8323.M6B48   C813'.084   C78–002163–0
PR9197.32.B48

Printed by Friesens, Altona, Manitoba, Canada.
∞ Printed on acid-free paper.

Front cover: North West Mounted Police in the Yukon, 1898–99. (National Archives of Canada, PA 13422)
Title page and back cover: Corporal Bowler on horse "Bury Billy," 1904. (Glenbow Archives, NA–494–2)

COMMITTED TO THE DEVELOPMENT OF CULTURE AND THE ARTS

The publishers gratefully acknowledge the assistance of the Department of Canadian Heritage and the Canada Council.

To Irene, who helped me to choose these stories

CONTENTS

PART THREE
The Gold Rush and the North

PART FOUR
The Twentieth Century

ACKNOWLEDGEMENTS

The University of Alberta Press acknowledges the following sources for the stories included in this volume. The press is grateful to those who have granted permission for reprinting.

"The Taking of Fort Whoop-Up" from *Blackfoot Crossing* (1959) by Norma Sluman. Reprinted by permission of McGraw-Hill Ryerson Limited.

"Riding West from Duck Lake" from *The Scorched-Wood People* (1977) by Rudy Wiebe. Reprinted by permission of the author.

"O'Brien's Doom" by Joseph Gollumb, from *Scarlet and Gold*, XVIII, 1937. Reprinted by permission of the Royal Canadian Mounted Police Veterans' Association, Vancouver Division.

"The Wolfer" by Wallace Stegner, originally published in *Harper's Magazine* (1959). Reprinted by permission of Mrs. Mary Stegner.

"Main-teen Luh Droyt" from *The Meadowlark Connection* (1975) by Ken Mitchell. Reprinted by permission of Bella Pomer Agency Inc.

"The Detachment Man" by H.J. MacDonald, from *Maclean's Magazine* (July, 1972). Reprinted by permission of Maclean-Hunter Ltd.

"The Arrest of Wild Horse" from *Spirit of Iron* (1923) by Harwood E. Steele.

"Whiskey Smuggling" from *Raw Gold* (1907) by Bertrand W. Sinclair, Dillingham, New York.

"A North-West Mounted Police Party" from *Sinners Twain* (1895) by John Mackie, T. Fisher Unwin, London.

"A Strike on the Railroad" from *Corporal Cameron* (1912) by Ralph Connor (C.W. Gordon), Westminster, Toronto.

"The Siege of Fort Pitt" from *Annette, the Métis Spy* (1886) by Joseph Collins, Rose Publishing Co., Toronto.

"The Lean Man" from the collection *Tales of Western Life* (1888) by Roger Pocock, C.W. Mitchell, Ottawa.

"The Error of the Day" from the collection *Northern Lights* (1909) by Gilbert Parker, Copp Clark Co., Toronto.

"The Sun-Dance in the File Hills" from the collection *Sage Brush Stories* (1917) by Frederick Niven, Eveleigh Nash, London.

"Smoke" by Z.M. Hamilton from the pamphlet *Christmas in Regina* (1919), Roper, Regina.

"Routine Patrol" by James B. Hendryx, from *Great Tales of the American West* (1945), Henry E. Maule, ed., Modern Library, New York.

"The Law Versus the Man" from *Philip Steele of the Royal North-West Mounted Police* (1911) by James Oliver Curwood, Bobbs-Merritt Co., Indianapolis, reprinted as *Steele of the Royal Mounted* by Pocketbooks, Montreal, 1946.

"We Generally Don't" from *The Law-Bringers* (1913) by G.B. Lancaster (Edith Lyttleton), Musson Book Co., Toronto.

In addition to those whose names appear in this volume, I would like to acknowledge my debt to Bruce Peel, whose Bibliography of the Prairie Provinces to 1953 *led me to much of the fiction I canvassed for these stories, to Stan Horrall, the R.C.M.P. Historian, who encouraged me in my search for more, and to Don Walker of the University of Utah, who first drew my attention to Stegner's "The Wolfer."*

Introduction

Selling a Birth-Rite
For a Mass of Plottage

It is difficult to ask Canadian readers to look seriously at
fiction about the Mounted Police. They are too conscious
of the clichés and stereotypes that have attached to the figure
of the Mountie—the dry husks of a discredited glamour which
Canadians have been quick to despise but slow to understand.
This, too, is why it is hard to explain that the fate of the
Mounted Police story has been more complex and culturally
more significant than is realized. Quite aside from the peculiar-
ly Canadian development of the Mountie as fictional hero,
the Mounted Police story, in its fortunes and misfortunes,
stands as a typical example of the recent history of popular
culture in Canada.

The stories written about the Mounted Police in the early
Twentieth Century represent Canada's nearest approach to
an indigenous formula Western of the sort which has proven
so durable in American popular culture. The stories enjoyed
a similar popularity in their time; at least seventy-five volumes
of Mountie fiction were published by 1930, to say nothing
of juvenile stories and what appeared in magazines, newspapers, and other ephemeral forms. Many of these novels
had wide domestic and foreign circulation, especially those
by authors such as Gilbert Parker and Ralph Connor, who
both have selections in this volume. As a rough comparison,
Zane Grey is estimated to have sold over forty million copies
of his Westerns, while Connor sold five million of his novels.[1]
Since Connor published fewer titles and worked in a country
with less than one-tenth the population of America, his
popularity at home must have been comparable to Grey's.

Connor's stories in particular also held the place of a truly
popular fiction in Canadian culture in that they were read
widely enough to constitute a shared body of experience for
Canadian readers. In 1915, for example, a woman named

1

Elinor Marsden Eliot recorded her travels across the prairies in a book entitled *My Canada*. There she describes her first Mountie by reference to Ralph Connor:

> At Regina I saw my first Mounted Policeman. He was altogether beautiful, and I only hope that his nice shiny boots did not pinch him, and that he was not laced too tightly. "The red coats of the North-West Mounted Police"— what a Ralph Connorish thrill it gives one. . . .[2]

We can see in Ms. Eliot's remarks the irony with which Canadians have always liked to treat anything approaching glamour in their own country, but we can also see that her preconceptions of the Mounties are drawn from Canadian fiction and not from Rudolf Friml and Nelson Eddie, as they might have been a generation later.

Like the formula Western, many of the early Mountie tales were produced for consumption by a mass audience, and exhibited a predictable uniformity of character, situation, and plot. In the simplest possible terms, the Mountie could be expected to get his man.

To say that they were written to a discernible formula is not, however, to diminish the importance of these early Mounted Police stories. The individual stories may thus lose the literary importance we attach to unique creative expressions of an individual imagination, but as a type they acquire in the process an importance as a common expression of the culture which gave rise to them. John Cawelti, in his *The Six-Gun Mystique*, explains that the formula Western has endured because it is more than escapist entertainment. It is that, but it also has certain functions which in older, more cohesive societies were performed by game and ritual, among them "articulating and reaffirming the primary cultural values."[3] The early Mounted Police story had a similar potential for articulating those values which have given a distinctive shape to Canadian culture, though that potential has never been fully realized. The two types of fiction are, in fact, outwardly similar in many respects, but the differences in typical character, plot, and setting of the Mounted Police story say a good deal about the Canadian West and about the values of the nation which settled it.

The central character in both the Mounted Police story and the formula Western is a chivalric hero, a man on a horse, devoted to the assertion of law over lawlessness or savagery. Such similarities serve, conveniently, to sharpen the contrasts between the two types of fiction. The Western hero, as Cawelti says, is equipped to protect the civilized townspeople from the savages or outlaws who threaten them because he possesses "many of the qualities and skills of the savages."[4] Whether he be a mountain man like Jeremiah Johnson, a cowboy like Wister's Virginian, a Marshal Dillon, or a gunfighter like Schaefer's Shane, he is at home in the wild environment and has the mobility and mastery of violence of the savage as well as an understanding of the savage love of freedom which enables him to mediate between the two forces. The Mountie, by contrast, is more thoroughly identified with the civilized order and values than are the settlers themselves. He cannot stand between them and the savages in any but a physical way; rather than a mediator, he serves as an arbitrator in the dispute between savagery and civilization, imposing a solution based on higher authority.

The contrast is essential to an understanding of the Mounties' cultural significance, and it can be seen clearly only if we distinguish the "Canadian Mountie" from two contending images of the force which can be identified in the first hundred years of Mountie fiction. The first to appear was the British Mountie, represented here in selections by Roger Pocock, John Mackie, and G. B. Lancaster, and popular for years in the work of Harold Bindloss, Ridgwell Cullum, and other British adventure writers. He is usually a young adventurer, the black sheep of a good family, losing himself temporarily in the colonies. At the same time, he has the responsibilities as well as the privileges of his class, including a duty to uphold the flag of empire. For him, the empire is the cause to be served, and social caste is the true basis of authority in doing

3

it. The British Mountie declined along with the English market for romantic tales about the farther flung reaches of the empire, but he died hard. He is to be found as late as 1944 in stories printed in *Blackwood's Magazine* as "Experiences in the life of Dr. H. G. Esmonde told by Major George Bruce."[5] There he is still doing his colonial duty in the wilds of northern Canada, and falling into what sound suspiciously like East Indian tiger traps in the bush. Such survivals emphasize the fact that the British Mountie was never clearly distinguished from any other colonial soldier on police duty.

The Canadian fictional Mountie, as defined first by Ralph Connor, is obviously related to the British. He has strong imperial ties, but since he is permanently separated from Britain, they have become impersonal, almost abstract—a faith in an unseen order. He is civil and well-mannered, but gentility of birth is not important; he carries no personal authority by virtue of his birth or anything bred into him. Even physically he may give no impression of personal force, yet he can ride into a howling mob and arrest his prisoner without unholstering his gun because he upholds the law by moral rather than physical force and by a power which flows out of his selfless devotion to a remote ideal of civilized order. The Canadian Mountie can be found here in selections by Sluman, Sinclair, Steele, Connor, Wiebe, MacDonald, and others.

The American image of the Mountie is again superficially similar but profoundly different to the Canadian and British. James Oliver Curwood's *Steele of the Royal Mounted* provides an example as early as 1911. "Private" Philip Steele is tracking murder suspect William de Bar across the frozen North. In the chapter reprinted here, significantly entitled "The Law Versus the Man," they meet at the absolute end of their resources, fight to exhaustion, and then agree to postpone their dispute until they have reached shelter and food. In gallantly saving Steele's life, de Bar is rising above the purely official, legal differences which separate their common humanity. By agreeing to allow de Bar a fair fight for his freedom, Steele is setting aside his duty to the law for his private sense of fair play. And in Curwood's story, this is right, because these men are depicted as *larger* than the law—mere law, blindly imposed from a distance, must yield to justice as arbitrated by the individual conscience on the spot. Curwood is giving us essentially the morality of the U.S. frontier, one diametrically opposed to the spirit of the NWMP. In effect Curwood populates the North with US Marshals in red tunics.

Stories like Curwood's, which impose the values of the American Western on the story of a Mounted Policeman, accentuate some of the most important differences between the two. While both dramatize the assertion of law and order, they reflect the very different visions of order which informed the settlement of the two Wests. In Curwood's (essentially American) West, as in hundreds of Westerns, order is generated inductively from the particular needs of the situations at hand. By this process, as American tradition would have it, a new civilization is formed from the ground up, in keeping with the ideals of its members. Justice is often extra-legal, defined by a consensus of right-thinking individuals (sometimes constituting a vigilance committee), and the conscience of an honest man is superior to any established law. As the old judge in Wister's *The Virginian* says, the law comes originally from the people; when they take it back into their hands it is not a defiance but an assertion of the law.[6] Such fiction naturally articulates the basic frontier values of individualism, egalitarianism, and love of freedom. In its republicanism there also lurk the anarchic forces of innocence, primitivism, and violence. Such fiction and such a vision of order is consonant with the spirit of a nation created by revolution, based on the rights and freedoms of the individual, and dedicated to raising a new civilization out of the wilderness of the American continent. But when writers like Curwood impose that vision on the Canadian West—and many of them have—it becomes an alien and incongruous thing.

Canada, of course, is an anti-revolutionary nation formed by an act of the British Parliament in the interests of peace, order, and good government, and its characteristic vision of order, as embodied in the Mounted Police story, is hierarchical rather than democratic; order descends deductively from precepts which are beyond the view and questioning of the individual. The Mountie represents that faith in an established, unseen order which characterized the settlement of the Canadian West. There runs through all the early fiction a hazy identification of the human order of empire with the natural order and ultimately with the divine order. There is little room in such a vision for excesses of individualism, egalitarianism or freedom, and no room for the anarchic elements of innocence, primitivism, and violence. In the story by Frederick Niven included here, "The Sun-Dance in the File Hills," we find one of those rare exceptions which actually does prove a rule. The young constable sent out to disperse the Indians from a prohibited Sun-Dance has a proper British public school training, but is too receptive, too impressionable. Instead of breaking up the dance, he joins it. When his corporal finds him dancing around the centre pole with skewers through his flesh, it appears that the youngster has forsaken the order he is supposed to represent, gone native, embraced anarchy, freedom, and primitive violence. But as soon as the dance is over the young man sees the Indians again from entirely within the white culture: "And he felt a certain shame at his downfall, as a boy who thinks he is too old for toys may feel shame on being discovered at play with them." The lad is easily brought back because the lure of anarchic freedom and primitive reunion with nature which draws the American hero to the frontier has little place in the Canadian non-frontier West where freedom is a delusion, and the basic pioneer ideals of order, security, progress, prosperity, and refinement must be upheld.

All this does not mean that the Mountie's role is unheroic— simply that he is not a hero in the same sense that the central character in the Western is. A hero, to take a *Standard College Dictionary* definition, is "a man distinguished for exceptional courage, fortitude, or bold enterprise, especially in time of war or danger." Like the Western hero, the Mountie can answer to this description, but he can be more precisely defined as a *champion*, "one who fights for another or defends a principle or cause." The fictional Mountie, whose service motto is "maintain the right," is permanently dedicated to fighting for others, and even more conspicuously to defending a cause or principle. The Western hero may choose to fight for others, as when he defends the townspeople; he could even be said to espouse the cause of civilization, but for him these are voluntary and temporary choices. His belief in individualism and his passion for freedom prohibit any permanent commitment. As Cawelti says, "The hero's primary moral concern is to preserve himself with individual dignity and honour in a savage and violent environment."[7] So if both Mountie and Western hero are chivalric, the Western protagonist represents the medieval knight as individual hero, while the Mountie represents that figure more particularly as champion. The hero's principal expression, as we can see from Cawelti's remarks, is self-assertion; the champion's is self-abnegation, which may explain why international adventure writers like Curwood, and a hundred Hollywood directors, have never understood their Mountie heroes.

Canadian literature in general has been remarkably inhospitable to heroes.[8] Whenever a character does rise to heroic stature, he is usually—like the Mountie—the champion of some spiritual or temporal cause, a self-abnegating figure more remarkable for what he represents than for what he accomplishes. Consider Archibald Lampman's "Dulac" in "At the Long Sault," E. J. Pratt's heroic Jesuits in "Brebouf and his brethren," the figure of Jerome Martell in Hugh MacLennan's *The Watch That Ends the Night*, or Rudy Wiebe's characterization of the Cree chief Big Bear. All achieve a heroic dimension through surrendering themselves to a cause. A less noble but especially instructive example is James Potter in Sheila Watson's *The Double Hook*, a novel which has sometimes been described as an "anti-western." James attempts to cast off all responsibility, to seize his freedom and assert his individuality, to ride out of town like any adolescent Western hero. What he discovers, though, is that the freedom of irresponsibility is empty and meaningless. He is gratefully relieved of his freedom and returns to the com-

7

munity where he is no hero, but where he has some human meaning as a champion of the growth of a new generation. James is a quintessentially Canadian hero; even when he attempts to escape his role as champion, he cannot. The Mountie of popular fiction seems in this respect more consistent with the traditions of serious Canadian literature than is usually assumed.

Like the characters, the typical action of the Mounted Police story reflects what is different about the Canadian West. The formula of the American Western generates a considerable range of plots, but the most familiar involves a hero riding into a town threatened by savagery and saving the inhabitants by a salutary exercise of violence on their behalf. Again, Schaefer's *Shane* is a convenient example, though there is usually a pursuit through the savage environment leading to the violent showdown. Much has been made of the Freudian implications of the hand-gun, and of the Western's appeal to the reader's desire for vicarious violence, but for our purposes it is sufficient to see that the violence is a consistent ingredient, and that it is justified in the moral perspective of the story by the surgical precision with which the hero administers it and by the circumstance that it protects the townspeople.[9] As the selections in this anthology illustrate, the Mounted Police story is typically a narrative of pursuit, confrontation, and capture. It has several optional phases, including detective work, mystery and intrigue, romantic love interludes, and (only occasionally) gunplay. Pursuit, confrontation, and capture without violence are not surprising features in police stories of any kind, but their persistence in the Mounted Police story is consistent with the cultural implications of the Mountie as champion. In a narrative of pursuit, the villain is necessarily a fugitive and therefore not a serious threat to life and property. What the Mountie who pursues the fugitive across the prairie or the tundra is defending is not the townspeople but the law itself, order in the abstract, the "right." This is primarily what the villain threatens as long as he remains at large and unpunished. The Mountie, then, champions a principle or cause, and it is typical of our Canadian culture to be more concerned with order and the institutions which embody it than with individual human rights or destinies.

Like his cause, the Mountie's showdown is commonly bloodless; he resolves the conflict between civilization and savagery not by using violence but by denying it. Consider him at his most typical, say, in the character of Inspector Lief Crozier in Rudy Wiebe's *The Temptations of Big Bear* asserting his will in the face of the massed tribes of Big Bear's Plains Cree, fired up after the last great Thirst Dance. Or in the present collection, consider Bertrand Sinclair's constable emptying out the whiskey trader's keg while looking up the barrel of a six-gun, or Steele's Hector Adair arresting Wild Horse in the midst of a hostile Indian camp. In these nerveless confrontations with superior force the Mountie traditionally convinces the savages of at least three things: that his civilized values are more important than an individual life, that they have the power to raise a man above the threat of violence, and that their coming is so clearly inevitable that it does not depend on the success of the policeman himself. In effect, he resolves the conflict by persuading the savage side that no conflict is desirable or even possible.

The two most important elements of the Mountie formula, then, character and action, have a rich potential for articulating the "primary cultural values" of a non-violent, anti-revolutionary, hierarchical culture. The setting is even more predictably appropriate and distinctive. The wilderness through which the American Western hero rides is commonly more idyllic and pastoral than threatening; its savagery is almost totally expressed in the form of Indians and outlaws. By contrast, the non-human natural environment in the Mounted Police story is usually threatening. It can, in fact, become the major threat against which hero and villain struggle, to the point where in many of the tales with northern settings, including the Curwood story reprinted here, the interest in the pursuit gives way to an interest in wilderness adventure. So many of the tales have, in fact, been set in the North that the pursuit by dog-team across the tundra has become a minor convention of the genre. To judge the power of convention in the production of this type of fiction we need only look at Oscar Olson's *Mountie on Trial*, the work of a long-time member of the Force. Though the main action of his story takes place in relatively civilized areas of Saskatchewan, he has his main characters rush north and hire dog-teams in order, apparently, to complete the tale in a suitable fashion.

It is typically Canadian that the natural setting should be thus obtrusive and that it should be menacing. The forests and barren lands of the Mountie story are not, however, that metaphoric wilderness of the national soul of which Northrop Frye, Doug Jones, and Margaret Atwood have written. The wilderness of the Mounted Police story is not represented as the point at which "the unconscious terrors of nature and the subconscious horrors of the mind coincide."[10] It ordinarily remains an uncomplicated physical antagonist whose chief effect is to prove the manhood of the characters.

The history of the Mounted Police in the West and the North provides endless raw material for adventure romance which would reaffirm the "primary cultural values" of a nation devoted to principles of peace, order, and good government rather than to such revolutionary ideals as freedom and equality. The most familiar anecdote involves a single policeman walking into a camp of armed savages, but my ideal example comes from the North, where men fought their way through howling snowstorms to establish customs posts in the White and Chilkoot passes in February of 1898. Of these I especially like the men of Inspector Belcher's detachment who could not fit into his small, leaky customs house:

> Because of the hut's limited size, the rest of the Chilkoot detachment stayed in tents on Crater Lake, battered by a hurricane-force wind and driving snow for ten days non-stop. The conditions were appalling. Attempts to fetch firewood from the nearest source of supply seven miles away had to be abandoned because

it was dangerous to move more than a few feet
away from the tents. Those containing the
supplies were blown down and the others were
kept upright by teams of men taking it in turn
to cling grimly to the support poles. To make
things even more intolerable, the water began
to rise on top of the frozen lake; soon the tents
were six inches deep in water, blankets and
bedding were saturated and the police crouched
on sleighs above the water level trying to snatch
some sleep. But on 26 February, the first fine
day after the storm, the Union Jack was hoisted
and Customs collections began.[11]

Who else would suffer such hardships in order to stop a stream
of bewildered goldseekers in the middle of a frozen wilderness
and exact customs duties for a government several thousand
miles away which was paying them seventy cents a day to
supervise one of the richest gold rushes in history? There is
something emblematic, something richly, comically, tragically
Canadian about such episodes.

Why, then, has this rich potential for a popular literature
never been realized? Some of the reasons are external, historical, and obvious; others probably run deep into the grain
of Canadian character. If properly understood they might
explain why the nation has been unable to sustain a popular
culture.

The Mountie was, in a sense, a victim of his own popularity.
He quickly became the property of an international entertainment industry, providing stories for British and American
adventure writers. And despite the authenticity of the "Canadian" fictional Mountie, it was the American image that won
out in the 1930s. The time is significant because it marks the
rise of the motion picture industry, and Hollywood alone has
produced more than two hundred movies with Mounties in
them, including *North-West Mounted Police* (1940) with
Robert Preston and Gary Cooper, *Susannah of the Mounties*
(1939) with Shirley Temple and Randolph Scott, *McKenna*

11

of the Mounties (1932) with Buck Jones, and of course, *Rose Marie* (1936) with Nelson Eddy and Jeanette MacDonald. There was even a silent version of this Rudolf Friml musical starring Joan Crawford in 1928.[12] What novelist could hope to compete with such a cast, or with the image-making power of the screen? The Hollywood Mountie, reinforcing its predecessor in American fiction, left little room on the page for the authentic "Canadian" Mountie. Even Canadian writers such as W. Lacey Amy and Ralph Kendall began imposing the formula of the American Western on their police stories.

Hollywood must have cut into the traditional market of entertainment fiction everywhere, but in Canada its effect was dramatic. The domestic popular fiction industry, which had been sufficient to produce a Ralph Connor in the early years of the century, appears to have suffered permanent damage. By the mid-1930s Canada ceased to have a popular fiction in the full sense in which Connor's early work had been "popular." No doubt the industry was suffering various other economic pressures, but the movie industry must have been a major factor, and one which is particularly identifiable in the fate of that segment of the popular fiction dealing with Mounties. During the same period, writers of serious fiction in Canada were unlikely to do much to preserve an authentic image of the Force. The vogue of the Mountie movie happened to coincide with the rise of realism in Canadian fiction, represented in the West by writers such as Frederick Philip Grove and Sinclair Ross. There was little room in their stark vision of prairie life for a glamorous policeman, and the overblown romantic image of the Force generated by the movies was one most serious writers would prefer to avoid at any time. Occasional realistic depictions of Mounties appeared in the 1930s and 1940s, including the story by James B. Hendryx reprinted here, but for the most part they could be expected only from writers such as Joseph Gollomb, who were almost completely innocent of literary intent, and thought of themselves merely as delivering the facts in narrative form. Gollomb's "O'Brien's doom" (1937), included here, is a good example of this totally documentary realism.

The fate of the Mounted Police story is interesting as a chapter in the history of the entertainment industry and as a reflection of Canada's celebrated tendency to export raw materials and import finished products. But it also suggests something about Canadians' attitudes towards the West. Unlike the American people, Canadians have not accepted their own West as the country of their imaginative escape. They prefer the more remote and impersonal choice of the American West as the scene of their escapist entertainment. There may be something in the self-conscious constraint of Canadians that rejects the imperfect images of themselves which a popular culture can sustain. At a deeper level, Canadians have not accepted their West as the fabulous or mythic land of their imaginations. For more than a century Americans have envisioned the West as that area of their country in which their national ideals would be realized, their national character matured. The expression of that character has often been taken to be a main function of western literature. As Leonidas Payne said in his *History of American Literature*, "The expression of pure Americanism of the democratic spirit in its broadest significance, is the characteristic note of our Western literature."[13] In this respect, the Western has remained in the popular culture as a "foundation ritual," to use Cawelti's phrase, a re-enactment of the process by which Americans ceased to be European and became American. To Canadians the West has never been the setting in which they would demonstrate their distinctive nationhood, though it probably should have been. As Dave Godfrey has said, the West is the archetypal region of Canada. Quebec and Ontario were settled by the French and the English, but *we* settled the West.[14] The Canadian people might have developed a "foundation ritual" out of the settling of the West, including the Mounted Police, but they did not, and that choice is as basic to their culture as the difference between a revolution and an act of the British Parliament.

One result of the choice, ironically, has been to encourage the pervasiveness of American popular culture and the values implicit in it, engendering a new kind of cultural colonialism before the older British variety has quite worn off. For western Canadians in particular this leads to a species of cultural insanity, the delusion that they live in a northern extension of the Wild West so familiar to them through American Westerns. They fancy that their own West may have been quieter and more respectable than its American counterpart, but has expressed the same frontier values and enjoyed a similar significance in the growth of their nation.

The Mounted Police story can hardly be expected to realize its potential in Canadian popular fiction when no such thing exists, but the image of the Mountie has begun to reappear in serious fiction about the West, like Rudy Wiebe's Governor General's Award winning novel *The Temptations of Big Bear*. The popularity of the Mountie movie about coincided with the heyday of Hollywood itself, and since its decline the image of the Force has begun to cool off to the point at which novelists can make serious use of its significance in critically examining the values of their society. Here again the formula of the Mounted Police tale serves in a role analogous to that of the American Western. Serious literature of the American West in the twentieth century questions the frontier values embodied in the popular Western. The basic ideals of individualism and justice set up in Wister's *Virginian* or Schaefer's *Shane*, for example, are subjected to close scrutiny in Walter van Tilburg Clark's *The Oxbow Incident*. In a similar way, serious fiction about the Mounties in the twentieth century questions the values implicit in the pursuit narrative. In some stories the pursuit is seen ironically. The Mounties succeed in capturing or enforcing the law upon some defenseless, harmless person. Here they represent an abstract order which is seen as dehumanized and oppressive. In "Riding West from Duck Lake" reprinted here from Rudy Wiebe's new novel *The Scorched-Wood People*, the pursuit is seen from the opposite side and it ends in defeat, with the implication that the defeat is morally justified. Another of Wiebe's stories depicts the pursuit of Albert Johnson, in which the resourceful lone fugitive is pitted against Mounted Police equipped with dogs, provisions, radio communications, and a spotting aircraft. Yet another dramatizes the death of Almighty Voice, in which the traditional image of the lone Mountie riding into the Indian encampment and capturing his suspect without firing a shot is parodied in a scene where more than a hundred Police and civilian volunteers surround three Indian teenagers, and fire not only small arms but two field pieces. In the chapter of Ken Mitchell's *The Meadowlark Connection* reprinted here, the fugitive or elusive enemy is presumed to be imaginary. In a variety of ways, these writers are making use of the romantic image of the Mounted Police to comment ironically upon their own society.

We should not exaggerate how much these ironic and anti-heroic portrayals say about general Canadian attitudes toward the Mountie or the ideals he embodies. It is simply one of the functions of serious literature to scrutinize the prevailing values of its society. The great American dream of pulp fiction, for example, has always been accompanied by the American nightmare as seen by serious novelists from Hawthorne to Mailer. Canadians do not, as Margaret Atwood contends, prefer their heroes to be losers; they obviously love the heroes in American Westerns.[15] But serious literature in the Twentieth Century does not generate heroes. A glance at the best modern British and American literature would lead to a similar conclusion that Americans and Englishmen identify only with losers. Misleading as this conclusion is, it usually passes unchallenged when applied to Canada because there is no indigenous popular culture to breed specifically Canadian heroes. Thus an accident of literary history is presented as a national character trait. Profound and permanent effects may of course follow from this strange condition of having only a serious literature. One of the purely incongruous results is that a Canadian's heroes are likely to be foreign gunmen while his anti-heroes are domestic policemen, which begins to suggest what may become of the "primary cultural values" of a country which imports its popular culture.

The final story in this collection, "The Detachment Man," can be seen as a tragic view of the force. There is irony, again, in the disparity between the romantic image of the Mountie and the prosaic realities of police work. In the presence of that irony, how does one do justice to individual heroism? Mac-Donald makes it very clear that the real courage is needed, not for the dramatic showdowns, but because there is no show-down. His Corporal Willow must do a sometimes dangerous job while sustaining the tedious routine of an utterly un-glamorous little Saskatchewan town. Where Willow gains his touch of tragic dignity is in being very much *of* this prairie society which the Mounties have always had a difficult and essential part in building, so that the death of Willow is like the impending death of the town itself. The Mountie stands one last time as champion.

This book is an historical anthology in two senses. First, the stories are arranged in sequence by time of setting rather than time of composition, so that they form a loose fictional history of the Mounted Police. Second, I have tried to select the best examples of the types of Mountie fiction popular in different periods since 1886. The desire to be historically representative has not always been easily reconciled with the desire to offer a readable collection of tales. I have had to exclude a number of prolific writers of police stories who might be considered representative, either because they did not excerpt well (Harold Bindloss, Ridgwell Cullum, William Byron Mowery) or because they were so bad I could not inflict them on the reader (William Lacey Amy). I hope the result is a wide variety of enjoyable and sometimes accomplished writing which exemplifies what has been done with the image of the Mountie in fiction over the past hundred years.

Notes

1. John Cawelti, *The Six-Gun Mystique* (Bowling Green: Bowling Green University Popular Press, 1975), p. 2, and Edward McCourt, *The Canadian West in Fiction*, revised (Toronto: Ryerson, 1970), p. 25.
2. *My Canada* (Toronto: Hodder and Stoughton, 1915), p. 135.
3. Cawelti, p. 31.
4. Cawelti, p. 46.
5. "Experiences in the Life of Dr. H. G. Esmonde. Told by Major George Bruce," *Blackwoods* (Feb., 1944), pp. 105–110.
6. *The Virginian* (London: Macmillan, 1902), p. 430.
7. Cawelti, p. 49.
8. For an early explanation of this condition, see Robert McDougall's "The Dodo and the Cruising Auk," reprinted in *Contexts of Canadian Criticism*, ed. Eli Mandel (Chicago: Chicago University Press, 1971), p. 222.
9. I am again indebted to Cawelti's *The Six-Gun Mystique* for a great many of these generalizations about the Western.
10. Northrop Frye, "Canada and its Poetry," *Canadian Forum* (Dec., 1943), reprinted in *The Making of Modern Poetry in Canada*, ed. Louis Dudek and Michael Gnarowski (Toronto: Ryerson, 1967), p. 95. This early essay marks the beginning of a chain of ideas which extends down through D. G. Jones's *Butterfly on Rock* (1970) and Margaret Atwood's *Survival* (1972).
11. Ronald Atkin, *Maintain the Right* (London: Macmillan, 1973), pp. 331–32.
12. *Canadian Magazine*, (22 Sept., 1973), p. 10.
13. *History of American Literature* (Chicago: Rand McNally, 1919), p. 316.
14. Godfrey, interviewed by Allan Anderson in a radio series, "Aspects of the Canadian Novel," number 5, CBC National Network, 2 Dec., 1972.
15. *Survival* (Toronto: Anansi, 1972), passim.

ASTEND POST N.W.M.P. 1879

The Trek West and the Early Days

The Taking of Fort Whoop-Up

from *Blackfoot Crossing*
by Norma Sluman

In this chapter from her historical novel Blackfoot Crossing *(Toronto: Ryerson, 1959), Norma
Sluman presents one of the first realistic accounts in fiction of the North West Mounted
Police arriving in what is now southern Alberta
in 1874. Her picture of a ragged and exhausted
band of men may be surprising because the
historic "Trek" West was romanticized in so
much early popular fiction. Harwood Steele,
for example, wrote in 1923 that "In their trail
blossomed flowers of law and order. The wilderness became a Land of Promise as they passed."*

*In fact, the Force began its active life in near-
disaster. Miss Sluman draws her historical
detail from John Peter Turner's* The North
West Mounted Police 1873–1893 *(Ottawa:
King's Printer, 1950). Other historical treatments of the trek can be found in Ronald Atkin's*
Maintain the Right *(London: Macmillan,
1973),* Cecil Denny, The Law Marches West
*(Calgary: Herald Printers, 1905), and S. W.
Horrall, "The March West," in* Men in Scarlet,
*ed. Hugh Dempsey (Calgary: McClelland and
Stewart West, 1974). Miss Sluman has also
written a fictionalized biography of the Cree
chief Poundmaker:* Poundmaker *(Toronto:
Ryerson, 1967).*

Sikimi parted long grass and looked down for the first time
at the North-West Mounted Police. Although his face was
expressionless, there was a deadly glitter in his eyes. The

21

white men were completely vulnerable to attack; his own Black Soldiers might have wiped them out in an hour or two. Another pair of black eyes, a thin merciless smile behind a bush not far away, indicated that Bad Wound thought much along the same lines. These two had no need for words.

Then Sikimi shook his head and, as Bad Wound vanished again, he went back to assessing the straggling column. There were about two to three hundred men down there in a wide valley. They coaxed horses along that seemed to be at the point of death. The Red River carts squealed agonized protest with every revolution of their wooden wheels, and on them the half-breed drivers nodded and dozed. Dead stock and broken wagons lay along their back trail. It was apparent to these expert watchers that the force was really lost, that they persisted grimly in the push to the west, hoping now only to hit forage for the horses and water. Had they gone a few miles to the north, a little further to the south, they would have found these necessities; but Morriseau, their guide, either did not know this or had no intention of telling the police officers.

Word had gone around that he was really in league with the wolfers, but Sikimi had not seen him before, so could not know if this was true. Certainly the guide had done the force no favour by serving with them; that much must be obvious by now even to the white men! The column was spread out over a stretch of several miles, moving so slowly that Sikimi wondered if they could make more than five or ten miles a day at best. There was only one impressive thing about them, at least to the warrior. The policemen were dressed splendidly. Bright scarlet coats set off their white helmets; brass buttons and belt buckles sparkled. One of the men was bellowing out a song in a hoarse voice, and the laughter that followed was ribald laughter. It was the National Anthem, with improvisation:

> Confound their politics;
> Frustrate their knavish tricks,
> Get us out of this damned fix.
> God save all here.

Sikimi grew very thoughtful. Their obvious discipline and this evidence of good spirits were not lost on the leader of warriors who wore fur and feathers.

When they had finally gone by, Sikimi and the Black Soldiers followed the rutted back trail curiously. As he rode Sikimi amused himself by trying to imagine what would have happened if he and his warriors had chosen to show themselves to the pony soldiers. Armed to the teeth, riding swift, fresh horses, painted and decorated, they would have struck quick life into that battered line! But Crowfoot had forbidden them to reveal their surveillance.

Long Mane danced sideways. There on the trail were the bodies of five horses. Sikimi looked at them with regretful eyes. They were in such pitiful condition that yesterday's chill and cold rain had been enough to finish them.

Sikimi returned to Crowfoot with his report. He offered the veiled hint that the white men should be informed of the fact that they were now entering Blackfoot territory; but the Chief was adamant. "This is a serious business, my son. When the time comes we will meet. Until then we watch and wait. They are not far now from good water and grass. Let them rest."

Rest they did. They made camp on West Butte, where they found the water good and plenty of grass, even fuel from an outcropping of coal. Again Sikimi came home with information. While the main body remained, resting and recuperating, two of their leaders and a few men had set out on the trail to Fort Benton in Montana.

"They probably go there for supplies and fresh horses," said Bearchild to Crowfoot. After Sikimi had left them, the two old friends exchanged a few quiet words. It was agreed that Bearchild would go to Benton and take a look at these men. This parting was like the closing of a door. Crowfoot stood for a long time watching Bearchild ride away. When would he see him again? What would their meeting bring?

After a while the Chief became aware that Sikimi stood beside him, also watching. The older man knew that the young warrior was too astute not to know where Bearchild was

23

going. He put a hand on Sikimi's shoulder, leaning for a moment as though very tired, then he drew himself up straight and tall again. "Now we, like the pony soldiers on West Butte, will rest."

Commissioner French and Assistant Commissioner Mac-Leod had just about completed their trading for horses and fresh supplies. They had concluded arrangements for these supplies to be freighted north by the I. G. Baker Company under the supervision of Charles Conrad, the manager. There remained only the pressing matter of a guide for the Fort Whoop-up trail. "You would be getting the best man in the territory if you hired Jerry Potts," advised Conrad. "The man has a built-in compass in his head. He is not much to look at, he likes his whiskey, and he hates to waste talk on white men, but he is the best man for a job like the one you have ahead."

"I don't know," said French doubtfully. "A half-breed— after Morriseau—"

"Go look him up in the Dead Horse Saloon," insisted Conrad. "I heard he was in town. He would be worth ten other men to you."

French gave MacLeod the nod. The Conrad brothers were honest, respected merchants who had been of tremendous help to the two officers and their party. Accordingly Mac-Leod found himself in the notorious Dead Horse Saloon. The erect, stiffly correct man with the clipped moustache and the impeccable uniform was such an unexpected sight in this place that an utter silence fell over the crowd. Those too far back stood on chairs to see what was going on. There were a few jeering whistles, a couple of muttered comments, then the *habitués* turned back to their card playing and drinking and yarning. MacLeod was not over-sensitive. He stared around quite frankly. Perhaps in this very room some of the murderers of the Cypress Hills might be looking back at him; certainly agents of the northern wolfers would be here.

He draped his long, booted legs around a bar stool and struck up a conversation with a young lieutenant of the American Cavalry. The polite overtures and self introductions disposed of, MacLeod told the American that he was looking for Jerry Potts.

"That's funny, sir; he has been around asking questions about you people. Think you have a chance of signing him? He's a good man. Won't work for us though. Claims he can't work with the same outfit that protects the buffalo hunters."

When the silence lengthened, the young lieutenant flushed. "Look, sir, sure, the Indians don't like it. It's going to force them back to the reservations. But a starving man is not a fighting man, and when they quit fighting we can quit killing them—the Sioux I mean."

MacLeod's eyes were thoughtful. "I have not thought about it that way. Yet you will have to provision them when they *are* back on the reserves."

"Well, but once the country is safe the herds of beef cattle will start to come through."

MacLeod glanced around in annoyance as a wildly dressed man elbowed his way in beside him, coughing deep in his chest.

The American broke into a wide grin. "Colonel MacLeod, meet the hardest drinker, the worst liar, the unhealthiest character in the Northwest—Jerry Potts himself." This stumpy, bowlegged, seamy-faced figure looked like the worst reprobate in the saloon. He had to tilt back his head to look up at the officer from under his droopy-brimmed hat, and MacLeod would have thought the whole thing a joke if he had not found a pair of calm, very keen eyes meeting his own.

Potts took out his black pipe, lit up and began to puff, throwing out a cloud of strong smoke that made the officer blink and move back out of the way. Finally he spoke. "Maybe you and me got some talking to do."

"Right away, if you like," answered the policeman. "Come out to where we are camped. We can talk there."

They walked together out of the saloon. Every pair of eyes in the place watched them go.

Out at the police camp Potts was escorted to the command tent and introduced to Commissioner French, the punctilious and rather frosty leader of this remarkable expedition. They

25

inspected one another warily. Jerry found himself reasonably satisfied. These two men looked honest enough; they were certainly unusual men to have made that killing trek and then to have made it here to Fort Benton, showing very little sign of their ordeal. And now they were obviously going ahead with plans to face what lay ahead of them: five hundred forted whisky traders, six thousand formidable and well-armed Blackfeet. The more Jerry looked, the more he approved of what he saw, especially this man MacLeod with the hint of humour in his eyes, his jutting bearded chin and his lack of pomposity. It was to him he spoke. "What you want to know about Whoop-up, Spitzee, Slide-out and Stand-off, I tell you. Also about Blackfeet. But first you tell me. You will never lie to them, to Crowfoot who is Chief?"

Neither of his listeners showed indignation. They approved the sincerity behind the question. MacLeod answered. "We lie to no one, Jerry Potts. Never to you, never to our own men; nor will we lie to the Indians or the wolfers. We have orders to that effect. Whatever it may cost us, we will do or say nothing dishonourable as long as we are here. We are staking our lives and the lives of those with us on just that policy."

"Then I work for you," said Jerry simply.

Potts appeared to think the matter settled, and the two officers looked at one another both pleased and surprised.

"Blackfoot scouts watched you all the way from the Dirt Hills," Jerry volunteered suddenly. The other two were startled.

"We never saw a Blackfoot all the way."

"You never will, unless they wish it." He coughed and chuckled. "They reported to Crowfoot that you ran around like ants on anthill. They know about Morriseau, saw him lead you wrong; saw broken wagons, dead horses." There was a long uncomfortable silence. This was hardly reassuring!

Commissioner French stood up and began walking back and forth. His sumptuous sideburns and his waxed, high-pointed moustaches fascinated Potts.

"I have orders to leave here tomorrow. I must rejoin troops

26

'D' and 'E' to go back to Swan River, where our headquarters are being built. MacLeod here will take the remaining one hundred and fifty men to Fort Whoop-up, where they will engage the fort, capture the ringleaders and place them in charge."

The cold nerve of it, the assumption of success, delighted Potts, but he kept his smile from showing. "You know there are five hundred armed men in there?"

"So we have heard," answered MacLeod. "But we have also heard our orders. We have field guns and mortars, and more important, the finest young fellows who ever wore a uniform." His face softened for a moment. "With them I would say the odds are just about even."

"I bet you," said Jerry Potts.

*   *   *

The half-breed rode to the crest of a long slope and pointed. "Whoop-up down there."

James MacLeod sat quietly taking in the scene. The setting sun was reddening the waters of the Belly and St. Mary Rivers, in whose valley the fort rested. Everything was strangely quiet. The only movement was the flapping of the American flag insolently hoisted on the flagpole. Even as he watched, the shadows grew deeper. He gave his orders quickly, cautioning them all to silence.

The two nine-pounder muzzle-loading field guns were brought around into position; the brass mortars were un-limbered; there were clicks all around him as rifles were checked and loaded. In that moment MacLeod was inwardly assailed. Here he sat, with three troops of fifty men each, in this vast and soaring country that had literally swallowed them up. Behind him were thousands of Sioux on the war-path. Down below him was an infamous and dreaded fort. And somewhere out there in the deceptively peaceful and silent hills were more thousands of Blackfeet; he could almost feel them watching, waiting.

"We will not attack without warning," he said. "I must give them a chance to surrender without bloodshed." He announced this to an astounded Jerry Potts, and then as though riding to some routine parade, he cantered down the long slope. Potts recovered and rode hastily after him. In the midst of a deep and menacing silence they approached the gate to the stockade. It was open!

MacLeod dismounted, rapped sharply on the gate. The noise was shocking in the stillness, seeming to leave echoes hanging in the air. Jerry dismounted and came to stand beside him, peering into the shadows. MacLeod rapped again. There came a small, shuffling sound and a familiar grizzled head poked sleepily around the gate. "Dave Acker!" Potts' voice startled the echoes into life again.

The old, lame American surveyed MacLeod from the top of his gleaming white helmet to the toes of his polished boots. His mouth formed a soundless whistle of admiration. "It's all yours, Genrul. Ain't a soul here but me and my women. Welcome to Fort Whoop-up!"

It was true. And so the formidable fort was taken.

Whisky Smuggling

from *Raw Gold*
by Bertrand W. Sinclair

Whisky smugglers remained a prime responsibility of the NWMP, and in this episode from Raw Gold (*New York: Dillingham, 1907*), *Bertrand Sinclair is one of the first to dramatize the Mounties' legendary ability to prevail by the exertion of moral rather than physical force. The authentic atmosphere of his tale is not seriously marred by his bringing the first contingent West on a Missouri River steamboat and setting them down at Fort Walsh. He has them confused with the first reinforcements, who arrived in 1878—around the same time that Police Headquarters was shifted to Fort Walsh where a closer eye could be kept on Sitting Bull and his following of several thousand renegade Sioux. For historical accounts, see especially Paul Sharp,* Whoop-Up Country (*Minneapolis: University of Minnesota Press, 1955*), *R. C. McLeod,* The North West Mounted Police and Law Enforcement, 1873–1905 (*Toronto: University of Toronto Press, 1976*), *and John Peter Turner,* The North West Mounted Police 1873–1893 (*Ottawa: King's Printer, 1950*). *Sinclair wrote another novel featuring the NWMP,* The Land of Frozen Suns (*New York: Dillingham, 1909*), *and at least eleven others set in the northern bush, the American West, or on the British Columbia Coast.*

I expect nearly everybody between the Arctic Circle and the

Isthmus of Panama has heard more or less of the Northwest Mounted Police. They're changing with the years, like everything else in this one-time buffalo country, but when Canada sent them out to keep law and order in a territory that was a City of Refuge for a lot of tough people who had played their string out south of the line, they were, as a dry old codger said about the Indian as a scalp-lifter, naturally fitted for the task. And it was no light task, then, for six hundred men to keep the peace on a thousand miles of frontier.

It doesn't seem long ago, but it was in '74 that they filed down the gangway of a Missouri River boat, walking as straight and stiff as if every mother's son of them had a ramrod under his tunic, and out on a rickety wharf that was groaning under the weight of a king's ransom in baled buffalo-hides.

"Huh!" old Piegan Smith grunted in my ear. "Look at 'em, with their solemn faces. There'll be heaps uh fun in the Cypress Hills country when they get t' runnin' the whisky-jacks out. Ain't they a queer-lookin' bunch?"

They were a queer-looking lot to more than Piegan. Their uniforms fitted as if they had grown into them; scarlet jackets buttoned to the throat, black riding-breeches with a yellow stripe running down the outer seam of each leg, and funny little round caps like the lid of a big baking powder can set on one side of their heads, held there by a narrow strap that ran around the chin. But for all their comic-opera get-up, there was many a man that snickered at them that day in Benton who learned later to dread the flash of a scarlet jacket on the distant hills.

They didn't linger long at Benton, but got under way and marched overland to the Cypress Hills. On Battle Creek they built the first post, Fort Walsh, and though in time they located others, Walsh remained headquarters for the Northwest so long as buffalo-hunting and the Indian trade endured. And Benton and Walsh were linked together by great freight-trails thereafter, for the Mounted Police supplies came up the Missouri and traveled by way of long bull-trains to their destination; there was no other way then; Canada was a wilderness, and Benton with its boats from St. Louis was the gateway to the whole Northwest.

Two years from the time Fort Walsh was built the La Pere outfit sent me across the line in charge of a bunch of saddle-horses the M.P. quartermaster had said he'd buy if they were good. I turned them over the afternoon I reached Walsh, and inside of forty-eight hours I was headed home with the sale-money—ten thousand dollars—in big bills, so that I could strap it round my middle. I remember that on the hill south of the post the three of us, two horse-wranglers and myself, flipped a dollar to see whether we kept to the Assiniboine trail or struck across country. It was a mighty simple transaction, but it produced some startling results for me, that same coin-spinning. The eagle came uppermost, and the eagle meant the open prairie for us. So we aimed for Stony Crossing, and let our horses jog; there were three of us, well mounted, and we had plenty of grub on a pack-horse; it seemed that our homeward trip should be a pleasant jaunt. It certainly never entered my head that I should soon have ample opportunity to see how high the "Riders of the Plains" stacked up when they undertook to enforce Canadian law and keep intact the peace and dignity of the Crown.

We had started early that morning, and by the time we thought of camping for dinner we saw ahead of us what we could tell was a white man's camp. It wasn't far, so we kept on, and presently it developed that we had accidentally come upon old Piegan Smith. He was lying there ostensibly resting his stock from the hard buffalo-running of the past winter, but I knew the old rascal's horses were more weary from a load of moonshine whisky they had lately jerked into the heart of the territory. But he was there, anyway, and half a dozen choice spirits with him, and when we'd said "Howdy" all around they proceeded to spring a keg of whisky on us.

Now, the whole Northwest groaned beneath a cast-iron prohibition law at that time, and for some years thereafter. No booze of any description was supposed to be sold in that portion of the Queen's domain. If you got so thirsty you couldn't stand it any longer, you could petition the governing power of the Territory for what was known as a "permit," which same document granted you leave and license to have in your possession one gallon of whisky. If you were a person of irreproachable character, and your humble petition reached his excellency when he was amiably disposed, you might, in the course of a few weeks, get the desired permission—but, any way you figured it, whisky was hard to get, and when you got it it came mighty high.

Naturally, that sort of thing didn't appeal to many of the high-stomached children of fortune who ranged up and down the Territory—being nearly all Americans, born with the notion that it is a white man's incontestable right to drink whatever he pleases whenever it pleases him. Consequently, every mother's son of them who knew how rustled a "worm," took up his post in some well-hidden coulée close to the line, and inaugurated a small-sized distillery. Others, with less skill but just as much ambition, delivered it in four-horse loads to the traders, who in turn "boot-legged" it to whosoever would buy. Some of them got rich at it, too; which wasn't strange, when you consider that everybody had a big thirst and plenty of money to gratify it. I've seen barrels of moonshine whisky, so new and rank that two drinks of it would make a jack-rabbit spit in a bull-dog's face, sold on the quiet for six and seven dollars a quart—and a twenty-dollar gold piece was small money for a gallon.

All this, of course, was strictly against the peace and dignity of the powers that were, and so the redcoated men rode the high divides with their eagle eyes peeled for any one who looked like a whisky-runner. And whenever they did locate a man with the contraband in his possession, that gentleman was due to have his outfit confiscated and get a chance to ponder the error of his ways in the seclusion of a Mounted Police guard-house if he didn't make an exceedingly fast get-away.

We all took a drink when these buffalo-hunters produced the "red-eye." So far as the right or wrong of having contraband whisky was concerned, I don't think any one gave it a second thought. The patriarchal decree of the government was a good deal of a joke on the plains, anyway—except when you were caught defying it! Then Piegan Smith set the keg on the ground by the fire where everybody could help himself as he took the notion, and I laid down by a wagon while dinner was being cooked.

After six weeks of hard saddle-work, it struck me just right to lie there in the shade with a cool breeze fanning my face, and before long I was headed smoothly for the Dreamland pastures. I hadn't dozed very long when somebody scattered my drowsiness with an angry yelp, and I raised up on one elbow to see what was the trouble.

Most of the hunters were bunched on one side of the fire, and they were looking pretty sour at a thin, trim-looking Mounted Policeman who was standing with his back to me, holding the whisky-keg up to his nose. A little way off stood his horse, bridle-reins dragging, surveying the little group with his ears pricked up as if he, too, could smell the whisky. The trooper sniffed a moment and set the keg down.

"Gentlemen," he asked, in a soft, drawly voice that had a mighty familiar note that puzzled me, "have you a permit to have whisky in your possession?"

Nobody said a word. There was really nothing they could say. He had them dead to rights, for it was smuggled whisky, and they knew that policeman was simply asking as a matter of form, and that his next move would be to empty the refreshments on the ground; if they got rusty about it he *might* haze the whole bunch of us into Fort Walsh—and that meant each of us contributing a big, fat fine to the Queen's exchequer.

"You know the law," he continued, in that same mild tone. "Where is your authority to have this stuff?"

Then the clash almost came. If old Piegan Smith hadn't been sampling the contents of that keg so industriously he would never have made a break. For a hot-tempered, lawless sort of an old reprobate, he had good judgment, which a man surely needed if he wanted to live out his allotted span in the vicinity of the forty-ninth parallel those troubled days. But he'd put enough of the fiery stuff under his belt to make him touchy as a parlor-match, and when the trooper, getting no answer, flipped the keg over on its side and the whisky trickled out among the grass-roots, Piegan forgot that he was in an alien land where the law is upheld to the last, least letter and the arm of it is long and unrelenting.

"Here's my authority, yuh blasted runt," he yelled, and jerked his six-shooter to a level with the policeman's breast. "Back off from that keg, or I'll hang your hide to dry on my wagon-wheel in a holy minute!"

The policeman's shoulders stiffened, and he put one foot on the keg. He made no other move; but if ever a man's back was eloquent of determination, his was. From where I lay I could see the fingers of his left hand shut tight over his thumb, pressing till the knuckles were white and the cords in the back of his hand stood out in little ridges.

There was a minute of nasty silence. Smith glowered behind his cocked pistol, and the policeman faced the frowning gun, motionless, waiting for the flutter of Piegan's eye that meant action. The gurgling keg was almost empty when he spoke again.

"Don't be a fool, Smith," he said quietly. "You can't buck the whole Force, you know, even if you managed to kill me. You know the sort of orders we have about this whisky business. Put up your gun."

Piegan heard him, all right, but his pistol never wavered. His thin lips were pinched close, so tight the scrubby beard on his chin stood straight out in front; his chest was heaving, and the angry blood stood darkly red under his tanned cheeks. Altogether, he looked as if his trigger finger might crook without warning. It was one of those long moments that makes a fellow draw his breath sharp when he thinks about it afterward. If any one had made an unexpected move just then, there would have been sudden death in that camp. And while the lot of us sat and stood about perfectly motionless, not daring to say a word one way or the other, lest the wrathful

35

old cuss squinting down the gun-barrel *would* shoot, the policeman took his foot off the empty cause of the disturbance, and deliberately turning his back on Piegan's levelled six-shooter, walked calmly over to his waiting horse.

Smith stared after him, frankly astonished. Then he lowered his gun. "The nerve uh the darned—Say! don't go off mad," he yelled, his anger evaporating, changing on the instant to admiration for the other's cold-blooded courage. "Yuh spilled all the whisky, darn yuh—but then I guess yuh don't know any better'n t' spoil good stuff that away. No hard feelin's, anyhow. Stop an' eat dinner with us, an' we'll call it square."

The policeman withdrew his foot from the stirrup and smiled at Piegan Smith, and Piegan, to show that his intentions were good, impulsively unbuckled his cartridge-belt and threw belt and six-shooters on the ground.

"I don't hanker for trouble with a *hombre* like you," he grunted. "I guess I was a little bit hasty, anyhow."

"I call you," the policeman said, and stripping the saddle and bridle from his sweaty horse, turned him loose to graze.

The Arrest of Wild Horse

from *Spirit-of-Iron*
by H. E. R. Steele

*Harwood Steele's hero, Hector Adair, is a
thoroughly idealized Mountie, probably based
on the author's own father, the remarkable Sam
Steele, who enjoyed a long, colourful, and distinguished career in the Force. But despite
Steele's romantic proclivities, he has drawn the
present incident from Police records. His Constable "Chester" is Constable Marmaduke
Graburn, the first member of the Force to be
killed by an Indian. Graburn was murdered
in 1879 near Fort Walsh while searching, like
Chester, for a forgotten axe. Six months later,
some Indians charged with horse stealing said
a fellow Blood named Star Child had done the
killing, and Star Child was eventually arrested
in an Indian camp by Corporal Robert Patterson and three other policemen. The flourish of
imperial pride with which Steele ends his tale is
ludicrous today, but the circumstances of the
arrest are faithfully reported. Historian Ronald
Atkin describes Star Child's arrest in his* Maintain the Right (*London: Macmillan, 1973*): *"As
his friends tried to pull him free, Patterson
grabbed Star Child by the throat, snapped
handcuffs on his wrists, swung into the saddle
with the half-choked Indian under his arm and
shouted to his colleagues, 'Ride, boys.'"* The
Graburn murder can also be found in John
Peter Turner's The North West Mounted Police
1873–1893 (*Ottawa: King's Printer, 1950*). *Harwood Steele has published several volumes of
fiction about the Mounted Police, including*

Spirit-of-Iron (*Toronto: McClelland and Stewart, 1923*), The Ninth Circle (*New York: Burt, 1927*), To Effect and Arrest (*Toronto: Ryerson, 1947*), I Shall Arise (*London: Hodder and Stoughton, n.d.*), Ghosts Returning (*Toronto: Ryerson, 1950*), The Red Serge (*Toronto: Ryerson, 1961*), *and* The Marching Call (*Toronto: Thomas Nelson, n.d.*).

Hector was in charge of the Police herd-camp a few miles from the fort. One morning the detachment shifted to a new site. Chester was a shy, retiring sort of youngster, newly joined. During the move Hector placed him in charge of the tools. As a result, the only axe was left behind. At dusk the loss was discovered and Hector sent the boy off to get it, promising to follow him and aid the search himself.

Darkness fell while he was still some distance from his objective. He caught himself wondering why he did not meet Chester. Reassuring himself with the thought that the boy had perhaps encountered some unforeseen difficulty, he pushed on. But no sign of Chester greeted him. All about the old camp was lifeless and silent.

Returning to camp as rapidly as possible, he hoped to find the missing man there before him. The cook's anxious enquiry disillusioned him:

"Is that you, Chester? And have you got the axe?"

"Turn out, the lot of you," said Hector. "Chester's lost."

Lanterns were lighted and the whole party made an extended search on foot. The results were disappointing. The discovery of the axe added to their alarm.

Hector reported the affair to Inspector Denton, at the fort, who promised to send out a large search party at dawn. To continue the hunt at night would have been futile.

Next morning, in a little hollow as yet untouched by the wind, they found the first clue—a sprinkle of blood, among jumbled hoof-prints—and a wide cast revealed Chester's hat in a clump of bushes. They searched the woods. More evidence of a foreboding character was then quickly gathered and the reason why Chester's horse had not returned was made clear.

Hector himself found the horse. It had been led into the woods, tied to a tree and shot.

And then they found Chester himself. The body was lying in the bottom of a deep ravine, where it had been thrown. The foulest of foul work had been done, for he had been shot in the back at short range.

In the days and weeks that followed, they exhausted every resource, but the murder remained an unsolved mystery.

II

"Beg pardon, sir," said MacFarlane, waylaying Inspector Denton as he passed the guard-room. "The In'juns say they'll talk now. And they want you, with the interpreter, sir, and Sergeant Adair."

The Inspector wheeled quickly.

"Good! Splendid!" he exclaimed. "Is Brent back? Then send a man for 'em right away."

Twenty-four hours previously, Hector had carried out the arrest of a gang of Indian horse-thieves, accused of stealing stock from the 'Lazy G,' an 'outfit' in Montana. They had refused to talk, however, having apparently decided to say nothing whatever until the day of trial. Martin was away and the best linguists in the division had been able to produce no effect. MacFarlane's announcement relieved the Inspector's mind considerably.

When all four—the Inspector, Hector, Martin and MacFarlane—were assembled, they held a consultation outside the guard-room.

"Why in—ah—heavens," said the Inspector, "wouldn't they talk before?"

"Yes—what was the idea?" Hector agreed. "I made everything clear to them. But they wouldn't speak a word."

Martin laughed. He knew the Indian mind better than any of them.

"They got what chaplain call 'guilty conscience,'" he declared. "One thing—they either 'fraid say a word, fear give themselves away, or other thing—they think you have um for bigger job than horse-steal but you won't let on. You bet your boots, that it! They either make confession or give some other feller away. That why they want me an' Inspector. You see—damn quick."

To a number of a dozen, villainous-looking warriors every one of them, the Indians rose to their feet as the Inspector came in. A good deal of parleying then resulted in Bear Sitting Down, who was their leader, being elected to speak for them all. And Martin began.

"Why did you not say what you have to say to Sergeant Adair?"

The Indian looked uncomfortable.

"We would rather talk to you," he said.

"Well, what have you to say?"

Bear Sitting Down glanced nervously 'round the room. The other Indians watched him intently.

"Come," Martin said in his most commanding voice. "Answer quickly. What have you to say?"

Bear Sitting Down shuffled his feet, cleared his throat and at last exclaimed desperately, with the air of a man goaded to action:

"We did not do it. We know we have been arrested on that account. But we had no hand in it."

"No hand in it?"

"No hand in it—none!"

The spokesman's companions seconded him with anxious monosyllables of approval.

Martin's keen eyes flickered.

"Why didn't you tell the Sergeant so when he arrested you?" he asked.

"He told us he was arresting us for horse-stealing. But we know better. We have stolen horses, yes. But we had no hand in the killing of the pony-soldier."

Martin quivered like a dog on an unexpected scent. Otherwise he betrayed no emotion.

"You are *known* to have killed him," he said calmly, "and you will all be hanged."

The shot in the dark flashed home.

"No—no—no!" exclaimed Bear Sitting Down. The Indian fear of the rope was evident in his face and he trembled in every limb. "You will not hang us if we tell you who killed him?"

"Not if you speak truth."

Inwardly, Martin was still completely puzzled, but he went on bluffing cleverly.

"I will tell all," said Bear Sitting Down. "The man who did it was Wild Horse. He came to us that night and he said, 'I have killed one of the Shagalasha. I killed his horse also and I threw the body into the ravine.' If you arrest Wild Horse, you will find that this is so."

The mystery solved—at last!

Martin turned swiftly to the other Indians.

"Is this true?" he asked.

"Yes, yes!" they answered eagerly. "It is true—true!"

"Come 'long outside," said Martin to the Inspector, with as much excitement as it was possible for him to show at any time.

"That feller," Martin declared very impressively, "He think you lie, Sergeant. He think you take him up, not for horse-steal—just bluff, that—though he say it true he steal horses, but for murder Constable Chester last spring. An' he say—all say—did not murder Chester. 'You no hang me if I tell who did it?' he ask. 'No hang you.' I say. 'Then,' he say, 'I tell you. Wild Horse kill him!'"

III

A fortnight elapsed before Hector was able to attempt the arrest of Wild Horse. The Indian had taken alarm with the apprehension of the horse-thieves and had left the reserve. Sooner or later, Hector knew, he would return, thinking the storm blown over. It behooved the Police to be ready to take him when that time came. They placed the reserve under the observation of Liver-eating John, a half-breed scout, whose orders were immediately to report to Hector any news concerning the whereabouts of Wild Horse.

So the fortnight dragged by. Then, in great haste, one afternoon, came Liver-eating John.

"Wild Horse, he sneak in 'bout noon," he told Hector. "Me see um—self. He be there p'raps two days. Hide in brother's lodge. Go, get him, quick!"

Within fifteen minutes, Hector and his men were on the trail.

It was raining when they turned out, a thin, penetrating, all-day drizzle, and the sky, just lightening, was heavy with an unbroken pall of dense grey cloud. Such weather, all in all, was admirable for their purpose. Half an hour's careful scouting brought them within sight of the teepees they sought —a ghostly group in the wet desolation. The question was— in which lodge was Wild Horse?

At this moment, they found an Indian boy, who willingly pointed out the teepee occupied by The Gopher, headman of the band. In order to comply with the custom of the Police it was necessary that Hector should inform The Gopher of his intentions.

The Gopher was instantly at the door when Hector sent the small boy into the teepee to awaken him. Speaking the Indian's own tongue, Hector rapidly explained his mission and was relieved to find that The Gopher, far from offering any objection, took the matter philosophically and himself pointed out the lodge in which Wild Horse was hiding.

"Keep everyone in their teepees," Hector went on, "until we go. Then there will be small likelihood of trouble."

The Gopher agreed. Hector ordered the constable with the horses up to a position close to Wild Horse's lodge. The others he placed one on each side, ready to seize the murderer should he attempt escape by crawling under the flap. For the last time, obedient to one of the greatest principles of the Mounted Police, he cautioned the men on no account to draw their revolvers. Then, removing his great-coat, he boldly entered the teepee alone.

For a moment unable to see anything, he shortly became

aware of the presence of at least a dozen Indians, who sat up in their blankets and stared at him anxiously.

"What do you want?" one of them asked, bristling defiance.

Hector pushed back the door of the lodge still further. The cold light, streaming in, clearly revealed his uniform.

"I have come for Wild Horse," he answered.

The wanted Indian glared shiftily at the speaker over the edge of his blanket.

"You hear me, Wild Horse?" Hector queried. "I say I have come for you. You know what that means. I am waiting."

"I will not come," answered Wild Horse.

"What do you mean?" said Hector sternly.

The Indians had learned to dread that tone. They stirred uneasily.

"I will not come!" repeated Wild Horse.

The others broke into a loud murmur of applause. Some of the bolder threw off their blankets and reached for their rifles. Hector caught the sound of angry voices at his back. A hostile crowd was gathering outside. The Gopher had failed, either through weakness or treachery, to maintain control. Hector remembered that they were only four white men among at least a hundred Indians. The least misstep, lack of tact or wavering in courage, might have fatal consequences.

He fixed the murderer with penetrating eyes.

"I say that you are to come," he said. "Do not look so at me—I will not have it. And do not attempt to resist or it will be the worse for you."

In reply, Wild Horse bounded suddenly to his feet, a knife in his hand. The other Indians, muttering fierce threats, stood up behind him. A row of levelled rifles confronted Hector.

"Get out of this lodge!" said Wild Horse.

Instantly Hector closed. A wrench twisted the knife from the Indian's hand. Seizing him, he exerted a supreme effort of his great strength, whirled him off his feet and threw him bodily out of the lodge. Before the murderer's friends could pull a trigger, Hector was also outside.

But it was 'out of the frying-pan into the fire.'

A crowd apparently representing every grown man in camp, to say nothing of women and boys, was thickly clustered round the teepee. The men were all armed and many of them were actually covering the two constables.

One glance revealed all of this to Hector; another, that Wild Horse had been promptly and efficiently handcuffed by his men, who held the murderer between them.

What now?

"Take him out of this," Hector ordered coolly. To the crowding Indians, he gave the stern command, "Stand back!"

They answered with a wild yell and one overwhelming rush.

In the furious struggle that resulted, only the intervening bodies of the nearest Indians prevented the policemen from being shot. To hang on to Wild Horse and to beat their assailants off without drawing a weapon—these two thoughts occupied Hector's mind exclusively. He could trust his men—through it all, they clung to Wild Horse like grim death. Meanwhile, all three were knocked down a dozen times, trampled on, beaten with rifles, bitten, throttled, kicked. When opportunity offered, Hector gathered his failing breath and bellowed for The Gopher.

"Give us Wild Horse!" yelled the Indians, pulling and dragging at the policemen. "Let him go!"

"He is our prisoner," answered Hector. "Where is The Gopher?"

So, like a football scrum, the three undaunted redcoats carried the crowd with them to the horses. The mob raved on. The crash of their carbines pierced the uproar.

"Put up your gun, will you!" Hector bawled, as the constable in charge of the horses, a young fellow and inexperienced, drew his revolver.

Then suddenly, at this crisis, came comparative quiet and The Gopher pushed his way forward.

"Where have you been?" Hector demanded. "What do you mean by allowing this to go on?"

The Gopher pretended not to hear. Instead, he bent his energies towards quelling the riot. Presently Hector found himself beside his horses, the prisoner and escort with him, the crowd, visibly subdued, falling back with lowered rifles and the shamefaced Gopher at his side.

"They know they've done a serious thing," Hector thought.

His troubles were obviously over. What plain men call sheer 'guts' had carried the day, as they so often do—as, with savages, they always do.

Hector struck while the iron was hot.

"Now that you've recovered your senses," he said to the hangdog assembly, "I have a word to say to you. You have committed a grave crime. You have tried to stop the arrest of one of your number by a Mounted Policeman. That is wrong, as you know. And it is also quite useless. You see that we are not afraid of you. When the Mounted Police come for any man, white or red, he has got to come, and we will see that he does come, let a thousand rifles come between. Wild Horse will get a fair trial, you know that. As for you," here he turned to The Gopher, who hung his head, "you have disgraced yourself. Instead of helping us with your authority, you stood aside. The Mounted Police have always treated you well—and this is how you repay us! You are unworthy of your trust. Is it not so?"

"It is so," The Gopher muttered sullenly.

"If you have any explanation to make, you must come to Fort Macleod. And let us have no more of this because, I tell you again, when the Mounted Police come for any man, he has got to come and it is no use resisting."

A moment later, with Wild Horse between them, Hector and his little party rode slowly out of the camp. In recognition of their superior authority, courage and determination, the Indians fell back before them as they passed, lowering their rifles with a gesture that was a salute.

A North-West Mounted Police Party

from *Sinners Twain*
by John Mackie

This excerpt from the novel Sinners Twain
(*London: Unwin, 1895) is not a narrative but a
character sketch. At the same time, it reveals
how the Force looked to one of the many British
adventurers who enlisted in the early days.
Mackie was a writer who served in the NWMP
from 1888 to 1893, and later set at least six of
his adventure romances in the Canadian West.
He was evidently very class-conscious, and from
the tone of his description we can guess that he
may himself have smarted under the authority
of someone he considered his social inferior.
Mackie's other western Canadian novels include* The Devil's Playground (*London, Unwin,
1894*), The Heart of the Prairie (*London: Nis-
bet, 1899*), The Prodigal's Brother (*London:
Jarrold, 1899*), The Rising of the Red Man
(*London: Jarrold, 1904*), and* Canadian Jack
(*Toronto: Bell and Cockburn, 1913*).

The most important individual in the party referred to, not
only in his own eyes, but by virtue of rank, was a commis-
sioned officer of Mounted Police. His eyes were dark, and his
whole facial expression might be summed up in three words—
red, round, and vulgar. Indeed, he enjoyed the sobriquet of
"Pudding-face Jamie," from the supposed resemblance of
the facial features aforesaid to that popular but homely article
of diet. He had at one time been a private holding some sub-
ordinate "staff job" in the force, but, having the necessary
influence at his back, had secured a commission. Those of
his old chums in the force, who had expected that when Jamie

became an officer he would at least have some consideration for his old comrades, were grievously disappointed; for, true to the old adage regarding the putting of a beggar on horseback, when he tasted power he rode rough-shod over the unfortunates under him. Fortunately, most of his brother officers (the exception being those drawn from his own substratum of society) were gentlemen by birth and education, splendid, all-round, good-hearted fellows as one could wish to meet, so they, providentially, kept such characters as Jamie in check, and saved many a gently-nurtured youth from a martyrdom of petty but galling annoyances. For in the Mounted Police a few years ago, a very large percentage of the men belonging to the rank and file were gentlemen. Of course Jamie resented the presence of gentlemen: they offered too great a contrast to his own condition—a condition which not even a gold crown on the collar of his serge, and goodness knows how many yards of gold lace besides, could ever ameliorate. This was where the shoe pinched with Jamie. No wonder that the milk of human kindness was somewhat soured in his composition. The three others present were a police sergeant, a private, and a French quarter-breed scout named Pierre, a short, stout, dark-eyed and pleasant looking individual upon the whole. He had a weakness for saying what were meant to be funny things, while at the same time his face bore a look of preternatural gravity. But just then the fact that Jamie had informed him that he would recommend the Commissioner to discharge him on the completion of the trip, had somewhat damped Pierre's natural cheerfulness. The sergeant was a smart, dark, handsome fellow, and like many more in his position, seemed born for better things. Even now although his face was unshaven, although the stump of an old briar pipe protruded from between his lips, and his seedy old buffalo coat was buttoned up to his chin, one could see at a glance that Harry Yorke was a gentleman. The fourth man of the party seemed rather a young individual to be a policeman. He was the son of a younger son—some army officer with a large family and limited means who was only too glad to get one of his boys disposed of, even if it were in the ranks of the

North-West Mounted Police; for then the youth would be self-supporting and would give no further trouble. As it was, Dick Townley, like many more young men in a like position, found the life was not exactly a bed of roses—when, for instance, an officer like Jamie ordered him while in the post to gather bones in a gunny-sack, round the Barrack-Square, which had been deposited there by other people's dogs, or to remove the refuse from behind the officers' quarters, in close proximity to an Indian who was ornamented with a ball and chain attached to one leg. Doubtless, so far as the Indian was concerned, the punishment was not undeserved, for he had, probably, got six months for appropriating another Indian's squaw, and breaking his rival's head when politely remonstrated with. As for the unfortunate private—well, somebody had to do the scavenger's work. It was not, perhaps, then to be wondered at that his speech partook of a certain cynical and sarcastic tone when the conversation referred to his superior officer. Indeed, it might be almost said to savour of his disloyalty; but then, in the often circumscribed and lonely life of the trooper, there were things said, done, and tolerated, that would not have been dreamt of under different conditions. In the ranks of the Mounted Police, partly on account of that subtle affinity of class, and conscious necessity of mutual help and encouragement in a life which is to a certain extent one of exile, there was a healthful spirit of *camaraderie*, the like of which, perhaps does not exist in any other force of the kind in the world. Between the non-commissioned officers and privates there was a mutual understanding and good feeling, that made the duties of the former comparatively easy and pleasant.

A Strike on the Railroad

from *Corporal Cameron*
by Ralph Connor

The Reverend Charles Gordon, "Ralph Connor," did more to create the literary image of the Mountie than any other writer, probably because he had a gift for telling uncomplicated adventure stories. In this episode from Corporal Cameron (*New York: Hodder and Stoughton, 1912*) *his fictional hero, Constable Cameron, is involved in a real incident. In the Kickinghorse Pass in 1885, Sergeant Billy Fury arrested the ringleaders of a strike which was blocking the construction of the CPR. The circumstances were very like those Connor describes, and the police Inspector who rose from his sick bed to terrorize the mob and hold the bridge was the redoubtable Sam Steele. A factual account of the incident can be found in Sam Steele's memoir,* Forty Years in Canada: Reminiscences of the Great North-West (*1915; rpt. Toronto: Coles, 1973*). *Because no police records of the case survive, all historians' accounts are taken from Steele's memoir. Connor's western novels include* Black Rock (*Toronto: Westminster, 1898*), The Sky Pilot (*Toronto: Westminster, 1899*), The Foreigner (*Toronto: Westminster, 1909*), Corporal Cameron (*Toronto: Westminster, 1912*), Patrol of the Sun Dance Trail (*Toronto: Westminster, 1914*), The Major (*Toronto: McClelland and Stewart, 1917*), *and* To Him That Hath (*Toronto: McClelland and Stewart, 1921*).

"Constable Cameron," said the Sergeant in a voice of sharp command, "there's a row on. Constable Scott has been very badly handled in trying to make an arrest. You are to report at once for duty."

The strikers had indeed broken loose, supported by the ruffianly horde of camp followers who were egging them on to violence and destruction of property. At present they were wild with triumph over the fact that they had rescued one of their leaders, big Joe Coyle, from Constable Scott. It was an exceedingly dangerous situation, for the riot might easily spread from camp to camp. Bruised and bloody, Constable Scott reported to Superintendent Strong lying upon his sick bed.

"Sergeant," said the Superintendent, "take Constables Cameron and Scott, arrest that man at once and bring him here!"

In the village they found between eight hundred and a thousand men, many of them crazed with bad whiskey, some armed with knives and some with guns, and all ready for blood. Big Joe Coyle they found in the saloon. Pushing his way through, the Sergeant seized his man by the collar.

"Come along, I want you!" he said, dragging him to the open door.

"Shut that there door, Hep!" drawled a man with a goatee and a moustache dyed glossy black.

"All right, Bill!" shouted the man called Hep, springing to the door; but before he could make it Cameron had him by the collar.

"Hold on, Hep!" he said, "not so fast."

For answer Hep struck hard at him, and the crowd of men threw themselves at Cameron and between him and the door. Constable Scott, who also had his hand upon the prisoner, drew his revolver and looked towards the Sergeant who was struggling in the grasp of three or four ruffians.

"No!" shouted the Sergeant above the uproar. "Don't shoot—we have no orders! Let him go!"

"Go on!" he said savagely, giving his prisoner a final shake. "We will come back for you."

There was a loud chorus of derisive cheers. The crowd opened and allowed the Sergeant and constables to pass out. Taking his place at the saloon door with Constable Scott, the Sergeant sent Cameron to report and ask for further orders.

"Ask if we have orders to shoot," said the Sergeant.

Cameron found the Superintendent hardly able to lift his head and made his report.

"The saloon is filled with men who oppose the arrest, Sir. What are your orders?"

"My orders are, Bring that man here, and at once!"

"Have we instructions to shoot?"

"Shoot!" cried the Superintendent, lifting himself on his elbow. "Bring that man if you have to shoot every man in the saloon!"

"Very well, Sir, we will bring him," said Cameron, departing on a run.

At the door of the saloon he found the Sergeant and Constable white hot under the jeers and taunts of the half drunken gang gathered about them.

"What are the orders, Constable Cameron?" enquired the Sergeant in a loud voice.

"The orders are, Shoot every man in the saloon if necessary!" shouted Cameron.

"Revolvers!" commanded the Sergeant. "Constable Cameron, hold the door! Constable Scott, follow me!"

At the door stood the man named Hep, evidently keeping guard.

"Want in?" he said with a grin.

For answer, Cameron gripped his collar, with one fierce jerk lifted him clear out of the door to the platform, and then, putting his body into it, heaved him with a mighty swing far into the crowd below, bringing two or three men to the ground with the impact of his body.

"Come here, man!" cried Cameron again, seizing a second man who stood near the door and flinging him clear off the platform after the unlucky Hep.

Speedily the crowd about the door gave back, and before

they were aware the Sergeant and Constable Scott appeared with big Joe Coyle between them.

"Take him!" said the Sergeant to Cameron.

Cameron seized him by the collar.

"Come here!" he said, and, clearing the platform in a spring, he brought his prisoner in a heap with him. "Get up!" he roared at him, jerking him to his feet as if he had been a child.

"Let him go!" shouted the man with the goatee, named Bill, rushing up.

"Take that, then," said Cameron, giving him a swift half-arm jab on the jaw, "and I'll come back for you again," he added, as the man fell back into the arms of his friends.

"Forward!" said the Sergeant, falling in with Constable Scott behind Cameron and facing the crowd with drawn revolvers. The swift fierceness of the attack seemed to paralyse the senses of the crowd.

"Come on, boys!" yelled the goatee man, bloody and savage with Cameron's blow. "Don't let the blank blank blank rattle you like a lot of blank blank chickens. Come on!"

At once a roar rose from eight hundred throats like nothing human in its sound, and the crowd began to press close upon the Police. But the revolvers had an ugly appearance to those in front looking into their little black throats.

"Aw, come on!" yelled a man half drunk, running with a lurch upon the Sergeant.

"Crack!" went the Sergeant's revolver, and the man dropped with a bullet through his shoulder.

"Next man," shouted the Sergeant, "I shall kill!"

The crowd gave back and gathered round the wounded man. A stream lay in the path of the Police, crossed by a little bridge.

"Hurry!" said the Sergeant, "let's make the bridge before they come again." But before they could make the bridge the crowd had recovered from their momentary panic and, with wild oaths and yells and brandishing knives and guns, came on with a rush, led by goatee Bill.

Already the prisoner was half way across the bridge, the

Sergeant and the constable guarding the entrance, when above the din was heard a roar as of some animal enraged. Looking beyond the Police the crowd beheld a fearsome sight. It was the Superintendent himself, hatless, and with uniform in disarray, a sword in one hand, a revolver in the other. Across the bridge he came like a tornado and, standing at the entrance, roared,

"Listen to me, you dogs! The first man who sets foot on this bridge I shall shoot dead, so help me God!"

His towering form, his ferocious appearance and his well-known reputation for utter fearlessness made the crowd pause and, before they could make up their minds to attack that resolute little company headed by their dread commander, the prisoner was safe over the bridge and well up the hill toward the guard room. Half way up the hill the Superintendent met Cameron returning from the disposition of his prisoner.

"There's another man down there, Sir, needs looking after," he said.

"Better let them cool off, Cameron," said the Superintendent.

"I promised I'd go for him, Sir," said Cameron, his face all ablaze for battle.

"Then go for him," said the Superintendent. "Let a couple of you go along—but I am done—just now."

"We will see you up the hill, Sir," said the Sergeant.

"Come on, Scott!" said Cameron, setting off for the village once more.

The crowd had returned from the bridge and the leaders had already sought their favourite resort, the saloon. Straight to the door marched Cameron, followed by Scott. Close to the counter stood goatee Bill, loudly orating, and violently urging the breaking in of the guard room and the release of the prisoner.

"In my country," he yelled, "we'd have that feller out in about six minutes in spite of all the blank blank Police in this blank country. *They* ain't no good. They're scairt to death."

At this point Cameron walked in upon him and laid a compelling grip upon his collar. Instantly Bill reached for his gun, but Cameron, swiftly shifting his grip to his arm, wrenched him sharply about and struck him one blow on the ear. As if held by a hinge, the head fell over on one side and the man slithered to the floor.

"Out of the way!" shouted Cameron, dragging his man with him, but just as he reached the door a heavy glass came singing through the air and caught him on the head. For a moment he staggered, caught hold of the lintel and held himself steady.

"Here, Scott," he cried, "put the bracelets on him."

With revolver drawn Constable Scott sprang to his side.

"Come out!" he said to the goatee man, slipping the handcuffs over his wrists, while Cameron, still clinging to the lintel, was fighting back the faintness that was overpowering him. Seeing his plight, Hep sprang toward him, eager for revenge, but Cameron covering him with his gun held him in check and, with a supreme effort getting command of himself, again stepped towards Hep.

"Now, then," he said between his clenched teeth, "will you come?" So terrible were his voice and look that Hep's courage wilted.

"I'll come, Colonel, I'll come," he said quickly.

"Come then," said Cameron, reaching for him and bringing him forward with a savage jerk.

In three minutes from the time the attack was made both men, thoroughly subdued and handcuffed, were marched off in charge of the constables.

"Hurry, Scott," said Cameron in a low voice to his comrade. "I am nearly in."

With all possible speed they hustled their prisoners along over the bridge and up the hill. At the hospital door, as they passed, Dr. Martin appeared.

"Hello, Cameron!" he cried. "Got him, eh?" Great Cæsar, man, what's up?" he added as Cameron, turning his head, revealed a face and neck bathed in blood. "You are white as a ghost."

"Get me a drink, old chap. I am nearly in," said Cameron in a faint voice.

"Come into my tent here," said the doctor.

"Got to see these prisoners safe first," said Cameron, swaying on his feet.

"Come in, you idiot!" cried the doctor.

"Go in, Cameron," said Constable Scott. "I'll take care of 'em all right," he added, drawing his gun.

"No," said Cameron, still with his hand on goatee Bill's collar. "I'll see them safe first," saying which he swayed drunkenly about and, but for Bill's support, would have fallen.

"Go on!" said Bill good-naturedly. "Don't mind me. I'm good now."

"Come!" said the doctor, supporting him into the tent.

PART TWO
The North-West Rebellion and After

The Siege of Fort Pitt

from *Annette, the Métis Spy*
by Joseph Collins

*Joseph Collins was probably the first writer to
introduce Mounties into his novels. His fiction
is now entertaining chiefly because of its comic
absurdity, but it reveals how anxious writers
were from the outset to make heroes of the
NWMP at any cost. Collins's "Inspector Dick-
en" is Francis Dickens, who was in command of
Fort Pitt at the time of the North-West Rebellion. The son of the great English novelist, he
was a total incompetent, whose father had sent
him first to India and then to Canada, apparently to be rid of the sight of him. When Francis
once asked his father for £15, a horse and a rifle
to set himself up in the colonies as a gentleman
farmer, Charles's comment was, "The first consequence of the £15 would be that he would be
robbed of it—of the horse that it would throw
him—and of the rifle that it would blow his head
off." His police Commissioner, A. G. Irvine,
seems to have been no better pleased with
Francis: "I consider this officer unfit for the
Force—he is lazy and takes no interest whatever
in his work. He is unsteady in his habits. I am of
the opinion that his brain is slightly affected."
Dickens withdrew from Fort Pitt without offering any serious resistance, and while he was a
man more to be pitied than blamed, he was certainly not one to be made a hero. All of Collins's
historical references are equally unreliable.
They could be corrected by reference to R. C.
McLeod's entry on Francis Dickens in the*
Dictionary of Canadian Biography, *vol. XI,*

63

> *and to Ronald Atkin,* Maintain the Right *(London: Macmillan, 1973), and Vernon LaChance, "The Diary of Francis Dickens,"* Queens Quarterly, *XXXVII (Spring 1930), on which all subsequent accounts are based. Collins, an Ontario journalist, set only two romances in the Northwest:* The Story of Louis Riel, the Rebel Chief *(Toronto: Rose, 1885) and* Annette, the Metis Spy *(Toronto: Rose, 1886).*

All over the territory, I may say, the Indians had now begun to sing and dance, and to brandish their tomahawks. Their way of living during late years has been altogether too slow, too dead-and-alive, too unlike the ways of their ancestors, when once at least in each year, every warrior returned to his lodge with scalp locks dangling at his belt.

Les Gros Ventres for the time, forgot their corporosity, and began to dance and howl, and declare that they would fight, till all their blood was spilt with M. Riel, or his adjutant M. Marton.

The Blackfeet began to hold pow-wows, and tell their squaws that there would soon be good feasts. For many a day they had been casting covetous eyes upon the fat cattle of their white neighbours. Along too, came the feeble remnant of the once agile Salteaux, inquiring if it was to be war; and if so, would there be big feasts?

"Oh, big feasts, big feasts" was the reply. "Plenty fat cattle in the corrals; and heaps of mange in the store." So the Salteaux were happy, and, somewhat in their old fashion, went vaulting homewards.

Tidings of fight, and feast, and turmoil reached the Crees, and they sallied out from the tents, while the large-eyed squaws sat silent, marvelling what was to come of it all.

High into the air the Nez Perce thrust his nostril; for he had got scent of the battle from afar. And last, but not least, came the remnant of that tribe whose chief had shot Custer in the Black Hills. The Sioux only required to be shown where the enemy lay; but in his enthusiasm he did not lose sight of the fat cattle grazing upon the prairies.

But we return for a time to Captain Stephens and his party. When their deliverer, the Indian boy, departed, they rode along the bank of the Saskatchewan, according to the lad's instructions, and in half an hour were in sight of Pitt. Inspector Dicken was glad enough to receive this addition to his little assistance; and informed Captain Stephens that he had resolved to fight it out against the forces menacing him.

"What is the number of the enemy?" enquired Stephens.

"About a hundred armed braves I should judge," Inspector Dicken replied. "Big Bear accompanied by a dozen wives came under the stockade this morning, and invited me to have a talk. With the coolest effrontery he informed me that if I would leave the fort, surrender my arms, and accompany him, with my men, into his wigwams, that he would give me a guarantee against all harm. If I refused these terms, he said he would first let his young men amuse themselves by a couple of days firing at our forces; and that afterwards he would burn the Fort and put the inmates to death.

I expostulated with the greasy, swaggering ruffian, but he only swore, and reiterated his threats. Then I told him to be gone for an insolent savage, and that if I found him prowling about the Fort again, I should send my men to take charge of him. Thereat his squaws began to jeer, and cut capers; and squatting upon the sod in a row they made mouths, and poked their fingers at me. Then they arose yelling and waving their arms, and followed the savage. It appears that after the chief left me, he went to the people of our town and proposed the same terms; for an hour later, to my horror, I saw the chief factor of the Hudson Bay Company, his wife and daughters, and several others following the Indian to his wigwams. Had these people put themselves under our protection, and the men aided us in defence, we might have laughed defiance at the five score of the enemy who threaten."

"But," returned Stephens, "I fear that you do not count at its full the force preparing itself to attack. From all I can gather a hundred or so of Plain Crees will come here to-day under Tall Elk; while the total strength of the Stonies, who will rise at Big Bear's call, cannot be less than five hundred."

Inspector Dicken looked grave; but he was a brave man and busied himself in making preparations. The total number of his force, including mounted police and civilians was 24; and each man had a Winchester and about twenty rounds of ammunition.

"Two of my scouts are abroad," he said, "reconnoitering; they should be here by this time." While he was yet speaking a storm of yelling came from the wigwams of Big Bear, and three or four score of braves were seen pouring from their tents, like bees bundling out of a hive. Each one had a gun in his hand, and a hatchet in his belt. The cause of this sudden commotion was soon apparent: about half a mile distant, two police scouts were riding leisurely along the plain towards the Fort, and evidently not suspecting the danger which menaced them. They advanced to a point about two hundred yards from the stockades; then a yell went up from a body of prostrate savages, and immediately half a hundred rifles were discharged. One of the men fell from his horse, dead, upon the prairie; but the other rode through the storm of lead to the Fort, and entered struck by half a dozen bullets.

"The devils have begun!" muttered the Inspector, and he quivered from head to foot, but not with fear.

The first taste of blood set the savages in a high state of exultation. They gathered yelling and dancing, and flashing their weapons in the sun around the door of the chief. Big Bear pulled off his feathered cap and threw it several times in the air. Then turning to his wives he told them to make ready for a White Dog feast; and he bade his braves go and fetch the animals.

So a large fire was built upon the prairie, a short distance from the chief's lodge, and the huge festival pot was suspended from a crane over the roaring flames. First, about fifteen gallons of water were put in; then Big Bear's wives, some of whom were old and wrinkled, others being lithe as fawns, plump and bright-eyed, busied themselves gathering herbs.

Some digged deep into the marsh for "bog-bane," others searched among the knotted roots for the little nut-like tuber that clings to the root of the flag, while a few brought to the pot wild parsnips, and the dried stalks of the prairie parsley. A coy little maiden whom many a hunter wooed, but failed to win, had in her sweet little brown hands a tangle of wintergreen vines, and maidenhair.

Then came striding along the young hunters with the dogs. Each dog selected for the feast was white as the driven snow. If a black hair, or a blue hair, or a brown hair was discovered anywhere upon his body he was taken away; but if he was *sans reproche* he was put into the pot just as he was, with head, and hide, and paws, and tail, his throat simply having been cut.

Six dogs were thrown in, and the roots and stalks of the prairie plants, together with salt, and bunches of the wild pepper-plant, and of swamp mustard, were added for seasoning. Through the reserves round about for many miles swarthy heralds proclaimed that the great Chief Big Bear was giving a White Dog feast to his braves before summoning them to the war-path. The feast was, in Indian experience, a magnificent one, and before the young men departed they swore to Big Bear that they returned only for their war-paint and arms, and that before the set of the next sun they would be back at his side.

True to their word the Indians came, hideous in their yellow paint. If you stood to leeward of them upon the plain a mile away you could clearly get the raw, earthy smell of the ochre from their hands and faces. Some had black bars streaked across their cheeks, and hideous crimson circles about their eyes. Some, likewise, had stars in pipe-clay painted upon the forehead, and others were diabolical in the figures of horrid beasts, painted with savage skill upon their naked breasts.

The beleaguered could notice all these preparations with their glasses; and the men spoke to each other in low tones. Savages seemed to be gathering from all points of the compass, and massing upon the plateau round about the camps of the

Cree Chief. But several bands were stationed around the Fort, in such a manner as to cut off retreat from the stockades should escape be attempted.

Close to the fort was the shining, yellow Saskatchewan; and for miles, with a glass, you could see the bright coils of its leisurely waters, as that proud river pierced its way through the great stretch of plain till it became lost in the haze of the distance.

"If you were only upon the river in yonder flat boat," said Captain Stephens, "you might drop quietly down to Battleford. The reinforcement would come quite opportunely to Morrison."

"I do not care to leave here without giving the rebels a little of our lead," the Inspector replied. "But even though I desired to do so, now, the thing as you see is impossible."

Night fell, and when it came there was not a star in the sky. A heavy mass of indigo-coloured cloud had risen before the set of sun, in the south east, and crept slowly over the whole heavens, widening its dark arms as it came. So when night fell there was not a point of light to be seen anywhere in the heavens.

"It would seem," murmured one, "as if God were going to aid the savages with His darkness."

Shortly after dark the wind began to wail like a tortured spirit along the plain; and in the lull between the blasts the cry of strange night-birds could be heard coming from each little thicket of white oak or cottonwood.

Louder and louder grew the screaming of the tempest, and it shrieked through the ribs of the stockade, like a Titan blowing through the teeth of a giant comb.

Inspector Dicken, with Captain Stephens at his side, was standing at the edge of the stockade. Not a sound came from the plateau, and not a glimmer of light appeared in the darkness. Then the great, wide, black night suddenly opened its jaws and launched forth an avalanche of blinding, white light. The two men bounded in their places; then came a roll of mighty thunder, as if it were moving on tremendous wheels and destroying all the heavens.

No enemy yet!

But the besieged had hardly breathed their breath of relief, before there arose upon the dark air, a din of sound so diabolical that you might believe the gates of hell had suddenly been thrown open. From every point around the fort went up a chorus of murderous yells, and then came the irregular flash and crack from rifles.

The Inspector ran hastily back among his men:

"Don't waste your ammunition," he said, "in the dark. Part of their plan is to burn the fort. Wait till they fire the torches, and then blaze at them in their own light."

Every man clenched his rifle, and the eyes of the brave band glimmered in the dark.

Crack! crack! crack! went the rifles of the savages, and now and again a sound, half like a snarl, and half like a sigh, went trailing over the fort. It was from the Indians' bullets.

"Keep close, my men," shouted the Inspector; "down upon your faces."

Drawn off their guard by the silence of the besieged, the enemy became more reckless, and lighting flambeaux of birch-bark, they began to wave them above their heads. The sputtering glare showed scores of savages, busy loading and discharging their rifles.

"Now, my men; ready! There, have at them." Crack, crack, crack, went the rifles, and in the blaze of the torches several of the enemy were seen writhing about the plain in their agony. Together with the exultant whoop, came cries of pain and rage; and perceiving the mistake that they had made, in exposing themselves to the guns of the garrison, the savages threw down their torches and fled for cover.

The conduct of some of the savages who received slight wounds was exceedingly ludicrous. One who had been shot, *in running away*, began to yell in the most pitiable way; and he ran about the plain in the glare of the light kicking up his heels and grabbing at the wounded spot.

Thereafter the enemy's firing was more desultory, but it was kept up for several hours, during which not a rifle flash came from the Fort. Then there arose the sharp yelp of a wolf through the night, and instantly the firing ceased. Not a sound could be heard anywhere, save the uneasy crying, and the occasional howls of the wind.

"The attack is to commence in right earnest now," Stephens whispered to Mr. Dicken; but in what shape the hovering assault was to come would be hard to guess.

They were not to be kept long in suspense, however. The pandemonium cry again went suddenly through the night and the storm; and an assault of axes was heard against the stockades.

"That is their game is it?" muttered the Inspector. "Now then, my lads, get your muzzles ready;" for the Indians had lighted a couple of torches for the benefit of those engaged chopping.

"Fire carefully, picking them off singly. Off you go!" Away went the rifles, and three more savages sprawled in the light of the torches. But others came into their places and chopped, and hacked, and smote like fiends, yelling, jumping, and frequently brandishing their axes above their heads; their eyes all the while gleaming with the very light of hell!

"Pick away at them boys," cried the Inspector; "they must not be allowed to get through." But the men needed no urging; each one loaded nimbly, fired with deliberation, and hit his man. This part of the contest continued for fully ten minutes, but sturdy as were the posts, it was plain that they must soon give way. Sometimes, it is true, the savages would draw rearward from their work, terrified at the heap of dead and wounded now accumulating about them; but it was only to return, as the waves that fall from the beach on the sea-shore come back to strike, with added fury. Meanwhile a number of lights had begun to appear upon the plateau, and the Inspector, turning to Captain Stephens said in a low grave voice:

"It cannot last much longer. See, they are coming with torch and faggot." Scores of Indians were revealed in the blaze, hastening down the hill; and troops of squaws were perceived dragging loads of brush wood. Then one of the posts gave way;

and another was seen to totter. In the gloom of the Fort, the paling of many a brave man's cheek was noticed.

"They will be here instantly, my lads," said Inspector Dicken in the same calm, firm voice. "But we will sell our lives like men. Hurrah!"

Riding West from Duck Lake

from *The Scorched-Wood People*
by Rudy Wiebe

*In the North-West Rebellion of 1885, the
NWMP played only a limited and undistin-
guished part. They encountered the Métis in
force only once, at Duck Lake, when Superintendent Leif Crozier led about a hundred police
and civilian volunteers in an attempt to recover
supplies commandeered by the Métis. They
were routed by a larger force under Riel and
Gabriel Dumont, and subsequent judgment
held that Crozier should have waited for the
force of NWMP under Commissioner Irvine
to join him at Fort Carleton. After Crozier's
defeat, the entire garrison withdrew to Prince
Albert where they spent the rest of the war
waiting to be called into action by General
Middleton. The following excerpt from Rudy
Wiebe's* The Scorched-Wood People *(Toronto:
McClelland and Stewart, 1977) portrays all of
that encounter, but from the unfamiliar view-
point of the Métis insurgents. The tension
evident in this selection between Dumont's
practical generalship and Riel's spiritual leader-
ship of the Métis nation was characteristic of
the entire campaign.*

*For historical accounts of the Battle of Duck
Lake, see Desmond Morton,* The Last War
Drum *(Toronto: Hakkert, 1972), R. C. McLeod,*
The North West Mounted Police and Law En-
forcement 1873–1905 *(Toronto: University of
Toronto Press, 1976), G. F. G. Stanley,* Louis
Riel *(Toronto: Ryerson, 1963), George Wood-
cock,* Gabriel Dumont *(Edmonton, Hurtig,
1975).*

Rudy Wiebe has published one other novel set during the North-West Rebellion, The Temptations of Big Bear *(Toronto: McClelland and Stewart, 1973) as well as a number of short stories in which the Mounted Police appear.*

From the veranda of Nolin's house that afternoon Riel and Gabriel alternately called out the names they had agreed upon; the Métis shouted their approval of each "Exovedate." Pierre Parenteau was President, Phillipe Garnot French and Henri Jaxon English Secretary; Gabriel Dumont Adjutant-General. Riel himself had no formal position; he needed none and when Nolin objected not only to the expropriation of his house but to the Provisional Government as a whole and the seemingly military direction of the Exovedate in particular, Riel accused him of treason and called for trial next day; Nolin was locked in his former bedroom, a guard at the door. Gabriel organized his captains and sent them off to recruit men; daily now he heard reports on the progress of Irvine's column; he had cut the telegraph at Humboldt and was expropriating supplies in all the stores on the east side of the river. Riel sent a long letter to the English halfbreeds and on the day of Nolin's trial "Gentleman Joe" McKay arrived from Crozier now commanding at Carlton; for a time Riel lost his temper. McKay was exactly the kind of halfbreed the Saskatchewan did not need: a man who used his Cree wits and his Cree body to carry about negotiation demands for the police. The Exovedate fed McKay, let him sleep off his long ride and sent him back; when Nolin, outfaced by Riel's accusations and sentenced by the twelve to be shot, quickly recanted, he was given the chance to prove his loyalty by carrying a message to Crozier:

> The councillors of the Provincial Government of the Saskatchewan...require you to give up completely the situation which the Canadian Government have placed you in, together with all government properties. In case of non-

acceptance, we will attack you, a war of extermination upon all those who have shown themselves hostile to our rights. Major, we respect you. Let the cause of humanity be a consolation to you for the reverses which governmental misconduct has brought upon you.

Nothing but a white proclamation came of that: Crozier called on everyone who remained loyal to the Queen to come in to Carlton and receive police protection; but Riel had decided they should take the Fort. Gabriel agreed.

"It's like Fort Garry, it means Company and Government both," Riel said.

"I wish it was Fort Garry," Gabriel said. "Stone walls with bastions and cannon on the corners. But here I could sit on the river bank with my rifle and no rat could crawl across the square without losing its head."

"It's what it means to the people, Clarke and Crozier!"

"I know, I know, but for headquarters it's useless."

"There was no Crozier in Fort Garry," Charles Nolin said, "with policemen and Prince Albert volunteers."

"We'll take the Fort without spilling blood," Riel said curtly.

Nolin rode silently between them in the cold morning; Napoleon Nault was nudging his horse forward on the narrow trail when Riel twisted in his saddle.

"You think we won't do that?" Riel barked at Nolin. "There are two curses on this country, the Company and the Government, and you're still thinking about the third—the Roman priests!"

"Louis, I'm not thinking about anything," said Nolin hastily, "like that . . . but you've seen Crozier's proclamation, do you think he'll give up Carlton?"

He was looking at Gabriel, who shrugged.

"What does it matter? We'll take it."

"I don't want any bloodshed," Riel said fiercely. Between the bare trees and willows of the creek valley they could see

74

horsemen flicker on either side; behind them sleighs filled with men. "We take Carlton and Macdonald will give in like he did in Manitoba. A threat, that's all he needs."

"You know Macdonald," Gabriel said, "I know Crozier. He'll give up nothing."

"We have established the threat," Riel said, "and we must push it until they have no way out. Here," he was groping in his inner pocket, "four hundred and fifty-five signatures from the English halfbreeds say either the government agrees with us, or there's war!"

"That paper's okay," said Gabriel, "okay, but I want those guys who write so good to pick up their rifles and ride with us."

"They'll ride," Riel said, "it's just they're English and Protestant, they catch on slower."

Gabriel and Napoleon roared; even Nolin grimaced in what might have been amusement.

"It's that Irvine coming," said Napoleon after a moment, "If they get those Ninetieth Rifles marching out of Winnipeg—"

"We just keep them in small groups," said Gabriel. "Who can't handle ninety men and sixty-six horses? Irvine didn't dare come through us to join Crozier, did he?"

"But he got around us to Prince Albert, and he'll just come down the river to Carlton from the north."

"What does that matter?" Gabriel said, and suddenly laughed at Napoleon's dogged argument written on his young face still stiff in the morning cold. "You got too impressed at that Winnipeg parade grounds, jerking a rifle around, shoulder, ground, shoulder, snap! snap! that don't mean nothing in this bush country."

Saddles creaked, and behind them in the sleighs a voice began an old French marching song.

"Anyway, who knows," Gabriel said. "Right now we're between them, and we've got to stay there till we get the Duck Lake and Carlton supplies. If the shooting starts," he shrugged. "They're all here anyway, there's not that many left anywhere else."

On that cold thought they emerged into the wider cold of the open prairie where the sun was just breaking through clouds on the horizon. And a horse galloping towards them: "Isidore," Gabriel said instantly, and so it was, with a scouting report: Inspector Gagnon and Gentleman Joe McKay with twenty men and sleighs from Fort Carlton were heading for Duck Lake as well, probably to get the provisions at Mitchell's store. Gabriel swore and signalled out four companies of ten and followed Isidore to intercept. The police sleighs huddled immediately when they appeared on the trail; soon McKay rode forward.

"We thought we were meeting men," Gabriel yelled at him, "where are they? You're just a blockhead who won't listen."

After shouting and threats McKay returned to the sleighs and in a moment the entire group turned on their soggy trail and trotted away, to the derisive laughter of the Métis. Having set scouts again, Gabriel and troop rode to join Riel at the Duck Lake store. Hillyard Mitchell had refused to accept that Riel could commandeer his huge stock and so the Métis helped themselves, taking knives, rifles, ammunition, bullets, flour, salt pork, lard, even thin muskrat spears none of them would have any time to use properly that spring, and stowing them in their sleighs or saddle bags while Mitchell and his partner watched, sullenly enraged.

"We'll pay you when we succeed," Riel told them, touching nothing. "And if we don't, send Sir John the bill."

"Right now," Gabriel said, waving his men in, "you're our prisoners."

"God damned if we are," Mitchell glared from one to the other.

"Sure. We're the Provisional Government here," Gabriel was already turning away. "If you aren't with us you're against us."

They were feeding the horses in the deserted livery stable yard when a galloping horse interrupted them; and a shout, "The police are coming!"

It was Isidore again. "Gagnon sent a fast rider back, and Crozier's coming now, about a hundred men mostly in sleighs."

"How many left in Carlton?" Gabriel asked.

"Maybe fifty, sixty, with Gagnon. They've got about eighty volunteer whites from Prince Albert."

"We've got the supplies here," Riel said, "if we could circle these we could take Carlton."

Gabriel shook his head. "If we had enough horsemen, but forty's nowhere enough."

"They're bringing a seven pounder gun on one sleigh," Isidore said.

"By god no!" Gabriel laughed, incredulous. "We can take that damn Carlton any time, but Crozier's come out with his horses and gun—he's stupid! We'll pick our spot and take them all prisoner."

Within moments they were riding west, the scouts already ahead, the forty riders clustered up front near Gabriel and Isidore, and the sleighs filled with men in a long straggling line behind. The empty cabins of Duck Lake echoed, the small vacant windows caught their blurred shadows an instant. Riel looked at the deserted church and Gabriel thought, This is all too cold for him; the chance of blood, he's within a minute of saying no, we won't do this. Complete surprise and he would be completely in it but now . . . Riel was looking at him, face bunched up almost in pain and he swung his horse close so that whatever it was he alone would hear it, argue that they all had known it would come to something like this, how once they talked of 'Provisional Government' and 'war of extermination' there was nothing but push ahead and—

"We should have brought a priest," Riel said very quietly. "Paquette here ran away with the rest of the whites."

In his surprise Gabriel could say nothing for a moment, then Napoleon Nault came crashing through the crusted snow along the line of sleighs, plowing up to them. He offered Riel a long cross, a tiny twisted Jesus nailed to its brown wood.

"It's from the church," Napoleon said. "I was going to ask the priest but he isn't there now, so I took this, for you."

Riel silently studied the cross in his hand but Gabriel could have laughed aloud, kissed Napoleon for joy. Then he said very clearly, for he knew the men around him were listening,

"You are our priest. There's your blessed cross, big enough to see. When we fought the Sioux on the Missouri Couteau Father De Smet made a huge cross out of wagon poles, he could hardly lift it, and he walked behind us in the trenches praying aloud, back and forth and the Sioux got so scared of him they ran away."

"I don't think," Isidore said, "Gentleman Joe prays much."

"Then today we'll make him!" Gabriel laughed, and the men laughed with him. But not as easily as he would have liked; they were so young some had never hunted buffalo, leave alone been shot at. They needed something, a sign to help them know, and Riel was not yet giving it. When would the Spirit catch him, again? He looked so bleak, still in the warm air hazed grey. And then as they had crossed the frozen marsh north of the lake and the trail bent between first stunted poplars they saw riders; Gabriel twisted to Isidore,

"What?"

"It's Patrice, he's with them," Isidore said, "with Indians."

Beside young Tourond rode Chief Beardy and behind them about thirty-five horses, some carrying double riders and all armed with carbines or shot guns or clubs or sticks, anything; Gabriel almost laughed.

"We heard the police ran back to the fort when you stopped them," Beardy smiled through his tremendous paint. "That made your tobacco even sweeter. Now they have more coming, so we want to help you make them run back faster."

Gabriel roared, "Good brother! We have all the Duck Lake supplies and maybe we can use your land to set our trap?"

Beardy's few straggly whiskers shook with laughter. "We would be very, very happy," he said, "to see Hardass Crozier run off our land."

"You are welcome," Riel said slowly after the laughter was over, and whether his tone was simply the dignity appropriate between two chiefs or his apprehension Gabriel could not decide. "Gabriel is our general, and we have agreed we will not shoot first."

Beardy looked steadily from one to the other, then at his oldest councillor Asseyewin; who nodded. So they all rode west together with the sleighs crunching behind until in a few moments that seemed like hours stretching into the ever-brightening day the trail bent down over a low hill with a rotting cabin on the far left and Gabriel said to Isidore,

"Here?"

"Yes."

"Good, this is good, stop here."

For Gabriel and Isidore knew this place, could see like a bird flying what was past the spot where the trail bent away into the trees, and the land hidden so featurelessly as it seemed in snow. The sleighs would stay behind this small hill and Crozier would never know how many there were; the snow was too deep and crusted soggy to maneuver horses, they and the riders could be held in reverse in the shallow ravine behind and the men on foot sent forward on either side, the best shots with their buffalo guns into the empty cabin on the left and strung out in a line beyond that through the hollows and the sparse trees on that side, the ones with poorer weapons along the better hollow and denser bush to the right where they could get in close. Gabriel sat motionless, concentrated, and he saw how the grouped police must come, their scouts ahead and the loaded sleighs behind riders and if his men stayed low in the snow and worked ahead there on both wings they could have them surrounded, Crozier would be forced to . . . but he did not think beyond that, or he would destroy himself by hemming himself into what should happen but might not on the snow beginning to glitter in grey sunlight, the men and horses behind him, waiting. He could see the trail though, already run over twice that day and fourteen miles of it hard on winter-fed horses, as clearly as if he were a raven winging over the white and spidery brush. There they would come, and stop, so he gave his orders; Moise Ouellete to command the sharp-shooters and advance on the left, his younger brother Edouard Dumont on the left; and when these promptly started to move forward a flurry in among the rear sleighs brought Michel Dumas galloping through the snow, brandishing his rifle in his right hand above an exhausted horse: he had heard of the police trying for Duck Lake that morning and had brought

79

a hundred and fifty men and fifty-four horses; was anything happening? One Arrow was with him, come in from his reserve with forty men. Gabriel greeted him with a hug and sent some to the wings immediately, the tension settling tighter and tighter into him like a steel trap being slowly spread for bear. The men moved swiftly now and the emptied sleighs stretched out of sight behind him on the hill; he could not care now that if he had known Michel was coming he would have sent him around to Carlton, for he had over three hundred men now and he was certain Crozier could be destroyed. Crozier must be made certain of it too.

"Remember," he said as his captains passed, "we do *not shoot first*. But if we have to, shoot as fast as you can, and keep it *low*. You'll be down in the snow and you'll want to shoot high so keep it low, legs we want, legs."

"I want them to surrender," Riel repeated, his eyes gleaming with sudden excitement, "I want them to surrender, without bloodshed, Gabriel."

"Yes, yes!" Gabriel said, and saw Riel would be all right, that was clear as lightning in the cold air. "When they come around that bend and see us here, they'll stop. That's when I ride forward with a white flag, to parley. They have to surrender, we've got them sur—"

"Not you," Riel said. "No."

Into the sudden silence Charles Nolin spoke, who had said nothing at all since Duck Lake.

"Why not?" Nolin's voice sounded unfamiliar, thin on that little hill. "A parley's no good unless the men are trustworthy, and Crozier knows Gabriel."

Nolin had helped himself efficiently enough at the store but he did not look very happy; Gabriel knew immediately for him to ride forward was bad.

"No," Isidore said, "I'll go. If something happens to you right away we're in trouble."

"I'm old," the soft Cree voice of Asseyewin said behind them. "I have no weapon, I can carry a white flag well."

They did not have long to wait; really, it was barely enough time for half the men to get in position on the wings but it seemed long to Gabriel, as it always did though he could and had waited endlessly, motionless so often when it was necessary, hunt or battle. Soldiers spend nearly all their time waiting. The police came in 1875 he had had no battles whatever and strangely enough now the first policeman he had ever met twelve years before was the first he would confront with a gun. But he felt only a tense happiness; this was inevitable, between Wolseley's betrayal at Red River and the police coming he had known that somewhere in his bones and had said so three times in five years in useless petitions to Macdonald:

> Having so long held this country as its masters and so often defended it against the Sioux and Blackfeet at the price of our blood, we consider it not asking too much to request that the Government allow us to occupy our lands in peace.

André's writing but his own, hard words.

Riel was praying. He held the cross high, facing first right, then left, then to the horsemen and the men on foot beside the forward sleighs all waiting, spread out on their knees and praying perhaps too as they tried to peer between the riders clustered on the small hill with Gabriel at the center. Gabriel turned now, said quietly to Riel,

"That's good," in the tone of 'enough,' and loudly, so the men behind him could hear, "they're here, the police. Down now, and quiet."

Two scouts had come around the bend of the trail and stopped; immediately one wheeled, rode back and in a moment the lead party was there. The tall fur hats, the bright colors of the police sparkled under fur coats opened to the noon sun. Crozier sat on a bay horse; come forward, come, but Crozier erect as a tree would not move another inch. The sleighs were crowding up behind him, that was good, and Gabriel leaned forward, rubbed down his horse's forehead between his ears, again and again: move Edouard, move

81

Moise, if they won't come any more you get around them, all the way around, yes, but Crozier was signalling back and quickly the police were piling forward, fanning to their right across the bare snow toward the cabin; their horse sleighs were pulling up into a long barricade on their left. It was incredible, Crozier drawing more and more men forward and in nothing but another few minutes Edouard and Moise would have their wings opposite the center of his position.

"That's Lawrence Clarke," Napoleon said, "the wildcat hat with the tail."

"Isidore," Gabriel said between his teeth, "if there's shooting, either you or I kill him. For sure."

"There's the gun," Isidore said and Gabriel laughed aloud, not because he was amused but because the men around him were staring so intently; none of them had ever seen such a monstrous iron.

"All you do is get the gunner," he said loudly, "that thing doesn't shoot by itself. Isidore..."

"When?" Isidore said.

"Now, I think now, and slow as you can. Let them see you, think a little, it'll give us more time."

Their right line was extending nicely, no uniforms, that must be the Prince Albert volunteers, skirmish position, the men wallowing after the officer in the snow; the police were un-hitching horses from bunched sleighs: Crozier's tried and true bluff tactics. He'll come forward now, demand the supplies, maybe Riel.

Gabriel said over his shoulder to Nolin, "Give Asseyewin your white handkerchief." Nolin's face is grey mud he thought, scared shitless, but he had no time to look around and laugh in the coward's face. There's no government contract here.

"God protect you, my brothers," Gabriel said.

Riel was praying; lifting his cross over the two as they rode at a walk down the slope towards the police. The old Indian holding the handkerchief high, Isidore empty-handed, his Winchester stuck in his saddle.

When a rifle is taken from the wall and loaded deliberately, eventually it will have to be fired; Gabriel had always known that, and so did Riel though now he was praying fervently against it. Nevertheless, the first deaths are always the worst: until that point there is always hope despite rage and hatred and the furious momentary joy of an anticipated destruction of enemies. Now as Gabriel had known he would, Crozier rode forward alone, stopped, then gestured back. "Gentleman Joe" MacKay moved his horse beside him.

"McKay's on a fresh horse," Gabriel said. "He's been riding for two days, he'll be jumpy."

Crozier was looking to his right, suddenly shouted something in English, and then McKay yelled at Isidore and Asseyewin in Cree so loud they understood him on the hill.

"Get those men back! Back!"

They've seen Moise's men advancing, Gabriel thought. Now he knows we're no Cree at Cutknife Hill or Blackfeet at the Crossing, he can't bluff us with his uniform and gun we've got him and we'll take him, we're the People here, tell him Isidore, tell him so he never forgets.

The four riders were very close now in the blank center of the sparkling snow; McKay was nudging Crozier over so that old Asseyewin with the handkerchief was between them and Isidore who held both his empty hands high though his rifle butt stuck up in front of him. That was bad, bad, and Gabriel standing rigid in his stirrups now concentrating himself completely on those four men shifting on horses throwing their heads violently, hardly controllable by the nervous shouting men—Gabriel understood with a jolt he had sent his wings too far forward, Crozier and McKay would not permit themselves to be surrounded and Isidore, Asseyewin were . . .

For an instant everything happened at once: old Asseyewin leaned across McKay towards Crozier, the handkerchief extended in his hands a white splotch against Crozier's scarlet uniform and McKay suddenly jerked as if he snatched something, jerked and a pistol fired and Crozier spun so fast Gabriel's heart leaped but the policeman was enraged, screaming at McKay and it was Isidore on the outside who was sinking, clearly gutshot, Isidore get your rifle, Isidore!

Gabriel had his rifle up, his horse under him steady as a rock, but old Aseeyewin was blocking the center there, wrestling for McKay's pistol and Crozier wheeled around, his arm high and smoke puffed here and there behind the sleighs, a bullet shrieked high over the hill. Isidore slid dead to the snow, his horse wheeling frantic and the rifles across the brow of the hill behind Gabriel burst into roar as Riel screamed there,

"In the name of God, return their fire!"
but Gabriel had already fired. The instant Crozier's head was clear of the two still held together as in a bending, swaying weld and then the Indian was hurled from his horse as if clubbed and in that instant Gabriel's sights caught Crozier's head and he fired, fired again and saw Crozier's right hand leap to his face—jesus he was galloping, two inches and he'd have no face—the police bullets were too close now and the gun muzzle rising ponderously. Gabriel hauled his horse back among his men, leaped off, threw Napoleon the reins.

"Get Crozier, McKay," he yelled, "and low, shoot low!"
The center was empty now except for the two bodies; and the two horses lunging, hurling themselves about the snow in terrified circles. As he waded back to the front of his line Gabriel saw the gun puff smoke for the first time and Isidore's horse arching itself in another desperate lunge seemed to explode into spray, its head and withers one enormous splotch of brownish red while its hindquarters still erect in the snow gathered themselves as if to leap for a long moment and the thunder of the gun rolled over the hills.

"God," Gabriel muttered, "they're using shrapnel." He yelled to Lépine, Carrière, old Ouellette on the ridge right, their long buffalo guns curling smoke in the cold air. "Get the gunners, those gunners!"

Clarke had disappeared but Crozier was very conspicuous on his bay among the overturned sleighs. The police there were firing steadily but the skirmish line of volunteers extending far right had almost bogged down in the snow, unprotected against the halfbreed fire there. Especially Captain Morton still untouched apparently, still waving his men

ahead with his sword though none of them moved. Crozier
swung to his gun captain.

"Howe!" he shouted. "Take out the cabin, a shell on the
right! Shell!"

A bullet pinged on the gun barrel, sang away as all the crew
except Howe flung themselves in the snow.

"Our men are extended there, sir," Howe said. "I may fire
into them."

"What do you think's happening to them now? Shoot
through them, or they'll all be killed!"

"Your orders, sir," the captain said. "Load with shell, boys,
com'mon." The men scrambled up again as Howe began
cranking the gun around. "If you hear a Sharps bullet like
that," he explained to his powderman, "you can be sure it
hasn't hit you."

"Gabriel," Riel rode up on the hill, "this is useless. We
should advance, forward."

Gabriel was reloading his Winchester swiftly, "No, no, we're
no English square, and not half of us would get to their
sleighs." He slammed the bolt up, put his hand up on the
horse's withers.

"You're kinda high up there," he grinned, "fur hat and all."

"They won't hit me," Riel said.

"Just carry your cross, high so the men can see it. But you're
right, we should move, they've got Moise pinned—"

The gun sounded again, but strangely, and the men on the
hill cheered. Napoleon yelled,

"It exploded, the gun's finished, finished!"

"What?" Gabriel wheeled toward the sleighs, the grey smoke
drifting up there. Like the fireworks in Fort Garry, the February night of the Provisional Government.

"It exploded!"

"God be praised! We have to get around them, right,
through that draw, right!"

Crozier was bending over Howe and cursing under his
breath. "Are you hit bad?" he asked.

"Right leg's numb, I don't know," Howe grunted in pain.
"A Métis bullet, not the gun."

"What the hell happened?"

"They rammed in the ball, before, the powder."

"Can you fix it?"

"It'd take a day," Howe grimaced.

Crozier wheeled away, wiping his still bleeding face, cursing; McKay galloped up. "How far are they?"

"They're starting around on the left again," McKay reported. "Down that draw, riders now too."

"How many?"

"At least two hundred there, sixty, seventy horses."

"Christ. If they circle us..."

"Should we pull the Volunteers back on the right? There're seven to ten dead, I think."

Crozier hauled his horse around on its haunches, "Get the teams hitched!" he yelled. "Retreat. Watch the left flank. Officers, orderly retreat, all the wounded and killed on the sleighs! Retreat."

Gabriel had led the riders at a hard gallop around his right through the belly-deep snow, wide around the copse where Edouard and the men on foot still struggled forward, firing, but the police sleighs were already retreating across the next clearing when he arrived, their blazing rifles protruding over the sides of the boxes. The ride was violent, beautiful, Gabriel's horse leaping through the crusted drifts and the rider behind him hallooing like a run for buffalo down in snow and he charged straight at the frantic sleighs, screaming,

"Come on! We'll make the red coats jump!"

firing two shots each time his horse hung momentarily solid between leaps forward, stationary they would have been easier picking than squirrels off a spruce tree, never more than one bullet for a head shot, but suddenly his head! As if a hammer had smashed him, the snow lunged up into his face and his horse's heels, its belly torn one long red, an axe-chop through it and guts about to burst, over him Joseph Delorme's worn face, his mouth open, screaming,

"Gabriel, Gabriel!"

"Shut up Joe!" Gabriel blinked. The world washed red,

the snow red diamonds, and he sat up, "I've still got my head, I can't be dead yet! Feel it."

But his hand slid aside warm as grease, the snow tilted black over him, a sheet, and then a crucifix was there crossed on the bright sky so startlingly blue and the white clouds puffed like giants breathing on a cold day, it was so soft on the—a small tortured Jesus twisted on wood dear god they should take him off there after all these years as long as he could remember nailed on so crooked, and a nail, it drove into him, a nail spiked into his head just above the eyes and he roared with pain sitting up, he was on his knees again:

"Keep shooting! I'm okay, I can feel everything, don't let them get away! Cut them off!"

Riel was holding his shoulders, his huge grey-streaked beard against his shoulder and his cousin Auguste Laframboise tipped over him too, the few blond hairs on his cheek streaked black with powder.

"Little cousin, use my rifle," Gabriel found it still in his right hand, thrust it forward. "It's good to 800 yards, just lead them a little, as they move. Twelve shots . . . ten now . . . then you have to reload . . ."

He could hear the sharp crack of his rifle again, good, he opened his eyes to Riel's face so close and hunched almost to tears,

"I'm okay, just let me lie, you go with your cross, show yourself."

"Gabriel," Riel's eyes were flaming black, bending.

"Go! You have to, tell Edouard to lead them, go!"

He lay perfectly still on his back a moment surrounded by the fighting, heard shots, screams, the terrified horses of the police still struggling to get by on the ruined trail, and he felt a kind of peace; he knew he would not die, not yet. It was a cut, nothing broken, a cut much deeper than he got Crozier but the snow would hold the bleeding and the sky was so blue there was even a bird, yes it was a bird flying so high he could barely see it, could not distinguish any colour at all but its lazy motion.

"Uncle... Uncle..."

A small voice, a child? But it was Auguste, the rifle no more than inert iron in one hand now, his left clutching himself; face contorted in agony. Gabriel lunged up, began crawling, called to him,

"Courage, my little cousin... courage, the good Lord..."

He was beside him in the snow, the boy's eyes already glazing and he wanted to lift his arm and make the cross over him but his right shoulder and arm, they weren't there, nothing and he strained his left arm up and lost his balance and fell face down beside Auguste in the stinging snow and the groan shuddered against his left hand fallen across the ripped, sodden jacket and he heaved desperately on his dead shoulder, got his head up and almost laughing a little for shame of his body's betrayal before the last terrifying distance that the boy's eyes suddenly fixed open before him. Saying lightly, so dreadfully ashamed,

"Auguste, I want to pray, but I'll... have to owe it..."

but he was praying. His prayer, even while he continued in this last moment the silly joking words he had always spoken with his many cousins who stared after him and listened as if to God, the many words which he could not have changed now in the face of death, his own head throbbing prayer, "Lord, strengthen my courage and my honor and my faith," the prayer he thought every morning and every evening since he had knelt with Riel he would pray it forever and recognized a tree like a gallows and Father take him Auguste was certainly painless now, dead. Give him peace, so young, eternal peace.

He hoisted himself over and peeled the fingers from his Winchester; someone else would have to use it. Edouard. Edouard was there, above him, and he could sit up suddenly. Across the clearing the last police sleighs were dragging away, frantic horses whipped by frantic drivers and the Métis spread like a fan after them, shooting yes but not moving. Yelling in derision.

"They're getting away for god's sake! You let them get away!"

Edouard was screaming back, his coat ripped open to a long

slash down his left side, face dripping sweat and gunpowder and melted snow,

"We could have wiped them out and got the gun, killed them all—"

"No!" Riel was whirling Edouard around, voice tight as wound steel, "in the name of God, there has been enough bloodshed!"

"But their gun, ammunition, and hostages and Clarke—"

"Isn't Crozier at the back?" Gabriel groaned, "get Crozier at least, he's worth all—"

"He stopped us," Edouard tore himself from Riel. "All these people killed and hurt and noth—Guilliame!"

He was charging across the snow but he was too late; the Métis soldier had already pulled the trigger and volunteer Captain Morton jerked out stiff in the snow. They both looked down at him for a moment; the twitching stopped.

"He was screaming and screaming," Guilliame said at last. "His back was broken. Anyway, he killed Baptiste and Joseph Montour."

"Both?"

"By the cabin. He could really shoot."

Napoleon Nault joined them as they walked back to Gabriel, a fancy fur hat stuck on the point of his gun.

"That big mouth Lawrence Clarke," he muttered.

Edouard said, "I saw him run out from under it."

"His head should be in it, nothing else just his yapping head."

There were five sleighs and eight unwounded police horses left behind, thirteen rifles and a little ammunition, and nine dead Prince Albert volunteers, most of them near the cabin. All the dead policemen, three at least Edouard reported, maybe four, had been removed in the retreat. They tied Gabriel on a horse and carrying their own dead, four since Aseeyewin was taken by Beardy and his warriors back to their camp on the reserve, they rode back the way you do from a fight: both happy and sad, you cannot tell which. In Duck Lake prisoner Hillyard Mitchell dressed Gabriel's wound in his own house with his own medical supplies.

89

"Your skull is thick. Like a buffalo's," Mitchell said, "that bullet just glanced off the top."

"It feels like horns, yeah." Gabriel sat rigid, head propped on his hands, "like it was split in half."

The blackness rolled out and returned in waves; he knew they should be doing things quickly because if they annihilated the police quickly now the Indians would rise with them, the half breeds at Battleford and Bresaylor and Pitt and Victoria and perhaps even St. Albert and Lac St. Anne and Lac la Biche and—God grant such a miracle—all the Brelands and Bonneaus in Cypress Hills and Willow Bunch not standing in line for police guide money but picking up their guns for The Nation, listen: the intrepid, totally invincible North-West Mounted Police who in ten years have never killed so much as one Métis or Indian but forced hundreds behind stone walls to come out just before they die to avoid delivering a body to a family, who never back down, almost any officer of which would dare to kick Sitting Bull out of his own lodge or demand a warrior from Big Bear and Little Pine as if he had made the world and every pebble in it, these mighty police blundered into both Métis and Indian and were stopped dead and Superintendent Crozier, toughest of the tough, has lost a quarter of his men and had his own face nicked and run for Carlton and the dignity of Commissioner Irvine himself, small stiff man always mounted on a large stiff horse, with one hundred and eight men on forced march from Prince Albert arriving on the bluffs overlooking the so-called fort which is nothing but several wooden Company buildings surrounded by a spruce palisade, arrived just in time to see them haul the last of their wounded behind the huge, useless gate and all their volunteer dead, but no police dead of course, left behind for the coyotes. Patrice Tourond reported this late to Gabriel that night; he had it from Ambroise Desjarlais who was driving a sleigh for Irvine, and Gabriel had to laugh a little, drinking whiskey and holding his bound head in his hands. What stories these were to laugh around a campfire! And he tried to convince Riel for he had seen Irvine's thick cropped beard, and walk as if he had not bent knee or elbow in forty years. He could not imagine the report in officialise:

> It appears to me a matter of regret that with the knowledge that both myself and command were within a few miles of and *en route* to Carlton, Superintendent Crozier should have marched out as he did in the face of what had transpired earlier, but I am led to believe that this officer's better judgement was overruled by the impetuousness of both police and volunteers and Factor Clarke to go and take the stores and, if necessary, fight for them,

though he could very well imagine Crozier's total humiliation, the demand for three different reports each longer and each stating again and again: "with prompt action I certainly expected to succeed ... I admit I was deceived as to their strength ... how the prestige of the rebel half-breeds would have suffered and ours gained among the Indians had I succeeded in getting the provisions ..." for Crozier was, Gabriel knew, destroyed in the force; he could not remain in it, leave alone become the Commissioner as he certainly wanted. It would be several years before he saw Crozier again, close enough to see the white diamond on the right cheek which would be all that remained then of the passage of his bullet, but he would have enjoyed destroying Irvine even more and he easily might have if he could have convinced Riel.

"Can't you understand! They have to leave Carlton, all of them, they have to protect the women and children in Prince Albert."

"We're not fighting women and children," Riel said, "what—"

"They won't think that, we're savages, all those volunteers, god my head," Gabriel dared not clutch it though he longed to tear it off his shoulders. "Stiff on the snow and the rest shivering in Carlton, they think we're just riding like hell to

rape their goddam women. Carlton isn't defensible, the police
...look, we send Michel and Edouard with the horsemen,
they didn't get much today, on the Prince Albert trail there's
a dozen places, ambush...a few men..."

The room tilted, swam like fish diving; the whiskey thundered in his head, almost spilled.

"That does you no good," Riel said anxiously.

"Send them, destroy Irvine," he muttered.

"Gabriel, we don't want to destroy people, I have nothing
against the police or the volunteers—"

"They were killing us...pretty good...today."

"The invincible police are destroyed, you did that today!
We don't have to kill any more, Macdonald will listen, he has
to. We've got the guns like you said, remember? At Red River?
You've given me the guns again and they'll listen to me now.
They have to!"

"I wish we had that gun," Gabriel groaned, but he was past
caring just then. And so that night everyone pulled out of
Carlton, police, volunteers, Company shortly after midnight
and the fort burst into flame just as they were leaving and
Patrice Tourond with his watching scouts galloped in, saved
some burning stores as the last of the sleighs disappeared
above the cemetery ridge. They would have salvaged more
had they waited in the darkness of the spruced ravines and
picked off driver after driver as the sleighs crawled through
single file; they might have even captured the three big guns
and the ammunition to go with them which the police now
dragged up and down the snow-iced hills to Prince Albert
but Riel had forbidden them what had always been their
greatest military strength, ambush, and they had to content
themselves with fighting burning buildings with snow and
discovering kerosene-soaked flour intact, some rat-gnawed
bacon. Riel was right of course, Sir John was listening now,
very carefully indeed, but he had not considered well that Sir
John also had guns; a great many. That they, rather than
negotiation, might be his answer was not in Riel's mind as
he organized the march back to Batoche next day and the

funeral there of the four men fallen so gloriously in battle for the sake of the New Nation and the high calling of the Métis.

The Lean Man

by Roger Pocock

Captain Roger Pocock, founder of The Legion of Frontiersmen, sought out adventure all over the British Empire. In Canada he worked on farms and on the construction of the CPR before joining the NWMP in 1884. Three years later he was discharged because of severe frostbite to his feet, suffered during the North-West Rebellion. Pocock later wrote at least one novel and a number of stories from his experience in the Force. The ironic tone of "The Lean Man" suggests the urbane world adventurer, but the ending reveals a concern for the Indian which was unusual in 1887. The story was published in a collection entitled Tales of Western Life (*Ottawa: C. W. Mitchell, 1888*). *Pocock's novel,* The Cheerful Blackguard (*Indianapolis: Bobbs-Merrill, 1915*), is also concerned with the NWMP.*

Chapter 1

When "The Lean Man" entered his lodge at nightfall, and saw his young squaw adorning her cheeks with vermillion, and braiding her straight black hair in tails after the enlightened manner of the Palefaces; when she had made him a robe for his comfort at night of the skins of over 200 rabbits; when she welcomed him at the door of his tent with good things earned or stolen from the white men: no wonder that the young husband felt that the Great Spirit had been good to him in giving "medicine" to ward off evil times, and to provide for his modest wants during the long winters.

He didn't say much about it however; but, relieved of a great anxiety after the risky perpetration of early marriage, settled down to a life of honorable theft and genteel idleness, leaving "Turkey Legs" to manage his worldly affairs in the shape of a daily meal, which that lady never failed to produce in good season.

"The Lean Man" used to spend much of his time admiring his red blanket, for which he had wisely traded something that did not belong to him; and in meditating upon the obtuseness of the "Shermogonish" in arresting "the party of the second part" in that transaction instead of himself. For that ingenuous youth, "The-Man-Who-Bites-His-Nails," had been arrested on the information of the Indian agent at "Big Child's" reserve; and was now in the guard room at the barracks, and like to be tried for larceny. Our friend was a Sioux; and had come from Montana to the far Saskatchewan after an escapade on the part of his tribe that did not meet with the approval of the United States authorities. This was the glorious victory of "Sitting Bull" over "The Sun Child," Gen. Custer, who, with some four hundred American soldiers, had been slain in a coulee by only about 1400 Sioux. They had come to the land of the Great Mother, where the white Okemow told them, to their great surprise, that their conduct was wicked and disreputable; though, even after the usual largesse of tea and tobacco, they still retained some scepticism about the peculiar views of the white men. Gradually this little band had drifted to the Saskatchewan; and, providing the Great Mother didn't bother them about reserves and treaty—even with the loss of flour and other emoluments—they were fairly content. True, it was a great shame that they couldn't get "treaty payments" like the Crees, without being corralled on a reserve; but they were better off than when badgered and hunted in the south because of their natural proclivities for lifting the wandering cattle on the prairie, such as they had eaten from time immemorial, and which were their rightful prey.

And even if these poor wanderers could not overthrow the hosts of Pharaoh, as they tried to do last year, they could at least have the satisfaction of spoiling individual Egyptians, and so gain a precarious but honest livelihood in default of larger game.

And so it was that our hero went out to take the air one fine summer morning and walked down the main trail on the river bank with his blanket held about him with inimitable grace, while he fanned himself with the bedraggled old wing of a crane in great peace and dignity. For in truth it was a hot day, and the sun burned down on the dusty road. He wore his great hat, the abandoned top-hat of a departed Jesuit missionary, from which he had cut the crown, and after cutting battlements from the raw edge, adorned it with a feather and three brass nails. His leggings were of embroidered bead work, beautifully designed by his squaw. He had also well-fitting moccasins and a pipe-tomahawk. Altogether, despite that he felt it was foolish to expose himself to such a hot sun, he was delighted to feel that he looked his best, and that his new "fire bag" showed to perfection. He saw a white man cursing a team in one of the adjoining fields, and felt that his Race was able to look with superior calmness upon the irritable and too talkative whites.

But as he strode leisurely down the trail and was nearing the Hudson Bay Company's Post, he saw a cloud of dust beyond and the glitter of helmets above it. "By the Great Horn Spoon of the Pale-faces," he soliloquised, "here come the Shermogonish," and he went and hid himself. When "The Lean Man" had effaced himself he continued to gaze at the approaching horsemen from a secluded corner. And presently there came up the trail a gallant troop of Mounted Police, their accoutrements and scarlet tunics, their white helmets and rifles across the saddle, resplendent in the sunlight. First came the videttes, then twenty mounted men, followed by the rumbling transport. The waggons, loaded with provisions and bedding, carried each three men; and, at the trot, sent clouds of dust to leeward. Then came the rear guard of mounted men; and the commanding officer, the sergeant-major, and the bugler rode beside them. It was a stirring sight to see those splendid horses, the hardy sensitive bronchos of Alberta with their sun-burnt young riders; and all the eclat of military usage, and all the power of good rule over the great land-oceans of the far west.

The Indian followed the party with wistful eyes: these proud careless masters of the plains—these robbers of his people's heritage, who had driven away the buffalo and sent disease among the tribes, to slowly blight his kindred until they were all dead.

And they went on through the Mission, and out on the rolling prairie beyond, to patrol the country that had last year been the seat of war—when the restless wandering peoples had made one last useless stand against the tide that was overwhelming them. Their leader, Louis Riel, who had seemed their only friend, had turned out but a self-seeking adventurer, and a traitor to them; and now he was dead, and the whites were more powerful than ever.

But "The Lean Man" was not a politician or a sociologist, but only a poor Sioux, who, not knowing the meaning of events, was moderately happy. He went to the barracks, where he knew that the troop, having broken up camp, must have left many treasures in the shape of brass buttons, scarlet cloth and old boot-legs, among the refuse. But by the time he arrived at the barracks the camp had been cleared by a fatigue party, and he had to resort to the ash heaps. He was not challenged, save by a half-kindly, half-disdainful, "A wuss nitchie—get away out of this," from the cook; and in the evening he returned homewards laden with spoil. Now it happened that Const. Anstaye, being on pass that evening, was proceeding up town to see Her, when he remembered that his washing was not contracted for. He therefore turned into a tepee by the wayside and sat down. He knew four words of the language, and pronounced two of these wrong; but had little difficulty in making himself understood, and presently left the tent. So "The Lean Man" saw from the distance a young soldier coming out of his tent, and with his boots flashing in the sunlight, his forage cap balanced on the traditional three hairs, and his white gauntlets and switch and other finery, proceed gaily towards the Mission. Then "The Lean Man's" heart was filled with bad! When he came to the tent he disregarded the vacuous

97

broad smiles of welcome that greeted him, and said to himself that these were full of guile (although they certainly did not look it,) and he sat on the robes and sulked.

Later in the evening he crossed the river to where a bright fire burned amid the tents under the pine trees; and the usual pow-wow made the evening hideous, and continued with the gayest of howling and the most festive treatment of the tom-tom until a late hour. But there were speeches besides the music that night: the young Chief "Four Sky" made an oration, in which he said he would go to Carrot River—to the land of rabbits, and stray cattle, and hen roosts, and settlers, and every other kind of game—to the land of good water, and lots of fish, and all kinds of idleness. Then "The Lean Man" made a long and very stupid speech in which he said he would go too. Upon which the ancient and venerable big Chief "Stick-in-the-Mud," aided and abetted by "Resting Bird," the mother of "The Lean Man," made deprecations, and platitudes, and objections—all of which were overruled by the young men. "The Resting Bird," a few days after, retired in great gloom to a meadow some six miles up the river, with her brave and some other fogies.

Upon the morrow "Four Sky," with "The Lean Man," "Little Egg" with his son "Would not-go-out," "Wandering Mule" and "Sat On," with their horses, their squaws, their dogs, their children, their dignity, and all that they had, went down to Carrot River to sojourn.

A short time afterwards, "Would not-go-out," the son of "Little Egg," was returning from an unsuccessful hunt after a lost *cayuse*, when he was overtaken by a settler driving an empty waggon, and asked for a lift. The white man grumbled out a surly refusal, which so far incensed the lad that he climbed up into the waggon from behind, and carried out the traditions of his name by refusing to climb out again. Thereupon the settler, greatly to the annoyance of his passenger, lashed out behind with the whip, and "Would-not-go-out" became very angry, and pointed his "shooting stick" at the enemy. Happening to remember that the old flintlock gun was not loaded, he relented, and proceeded to have satisfaction with a threat. He told the white man that he wouldn't trouble to kill him now, "Because we are going to kill all you whites in a few days anyhow." Having delivered himself of this very silly remark, and perceiving that he was now close to the tents, he jumped out of the waggon and walked home. But the settler went about with information "on the very best authority" that there was to be a general massacre of the whole settlement, and so much alarmed were the neighbors that a deputation was sent to beg for a detachment of Police.

The little group of lodges were placed among the aspens by a lake, in a sheltered, shadowy hollow in the plain. The wide rolling prairie whose yellow grass, starred with flowers, melted towards the greys and softest azures that lay against the sky; the beautiful still waters where the young ducks swam; the delicate shimmering poplars; the smoke shaded lodges, and ponies grazing in the meadow—this was the lovely scene where the Red Men dwelt the happy abundant plain that the Good Spirit had given them.

In due course there came to the settlement a sergeant and four constables of the Mounted Police, bringing with them a tent or two in the waggon, and a general impression that they had come to stay. The people had seldom had the soldiers among them, and there was some idea among the women that they were queer animals with red coats and bad habits. The "Riders of the Plains," however, used, even as recently as that, to travel like bandits, often indeed being mistaken for horse-thieves; and soon won the hearts of the good wives by their liberal purchase of milk, eggs, and butter, by their quiet good humor and tendency towards a chat. To any one tired of the prosaic life of the cities of the East the very sight of these men would have been refreshment. Picturesque, liberal, unconventional, often highly educated, the Shermogonish have no flavor of the old tiresome life of the umbrella and the table-cloth, and I wish no man a better medicine than their company. Of course an early and rigorous examination was made into the causes that had given rise to such uneasiness among the people. Sergeant Monmouth had a chat with "Four Sky," whose people were found busy skinning rabbits; but there was some delay in producing the settler who had raised the alarm, he having gone to Fort a la Corne, from whence he could not be expected for a day or two. In the meantime nothing could be done, and there was no pressing necessity for action because everything was quiet.

Upon the third day some of the police were sitting in the little general store having a comfortable growl for want of something better to do. Steen having lit a very bad cigar, sat down on a barrel, and with his broad slouch hat jammed down on the back of his head, opened a discussion.

"Oh! it's all right," he said in reply to a general observation on the part of the storekeeper concerning the state of the country. "It's all right, if it warnt for them miserable 'nitchies' —who are no use anyhow—running the whole 'shebang' with their confounded monkey business. 'Sif thar wasn't enough drills and fatigues to keep the whole darned outfit on the keen jump without their fooling around the country stealing horses, and killing cattle, and raising rackets from one year's end to another; and now there's that damn fool Garnett robbing the mails, and he'll give enough trouble by the time he's hanged to keep half the troop busy hunting him. I—" He was interrupted by Sergt. Monmouth; "Look here, I'll bet anyone a month's pay that there'll be a mounted escort for every mail in the country within this month—you jest see if there ain't!"

Constable Mercer took up the growl at this point, and made out a very bad case against the Canadian Government "for running a poor——of a buck policeman 'sif he was a nigger or suthin' worse."

Here Le Soeur broke in: "There was—wot you say— General Ordaire? Yes, General Ordaire, jest befor' we come away —er—"

Sergt. Monmouth: "O, give us a rest, "nitchie"—go away back to your reserve, man!"

At this moment Constable Anstaye burst into the store with a joke that could not be kept back a minute, but in a sad dilemma that he had not breath to tell it. The substance of his tale was gathered in the course of a few minutes, and was to the effect that he had been in one of the tepees talking to a squaw when a "nitchie" came in, and, when he saw him, looked as black as thunder and went out. Presently he heard a racket outside, and found the same Indian unmercifully thrashing a boy; but he was interrupted by "Four Sky" and another, who dragged him off and looked about as cheerful as a blizzard on a cold day.

"But which 'tepee' were you in—and what were you up to?"

"Oh, I dunno, it was the one next the trail, and the chap that raised the row was that lanky young cuss in a red blanket, and a top hat with the crown out."

Monmouth strolled down to the camp, but on his return said that everything was quiet enough there. No further notice was taken of the affair, and the next day it was forgotten; but Anstaye noticed that whenever he went down to the camp the Indian with the red blanket scowled upon him.

In course of time the man Brown, who had raised the alarm, returned from Fort a la Corne; and was taken by Sergt. Monmouth to the Indian camp. He felt uncomfortable about the result of his assertions; and being a mean man determined that instead of an open confession that he had been needlessly scared, he would justify himself at all costs. Unfortunately it happened that "Would-not-go-out" was absent; and when all the braves in the little band were brought before him, and he was asked to produce the bloodthirsty savage who had, as he said, attempted to murder him, the white man hesitated, and tried to excuse himself, and make light of it all in the most generous manner, saying that he would be very sorry to get the poor fellow into trouble.

"Come on—no fooling!" said Monmouth. Brown asked in Sioux whether all the band were there: and the Chief replied that they were all there except a lad who was not even full grown, and could scare nobody with any spirit.

Monmouth: "Well, which was it?"

Brown: "Oh, I don't want to get a poor miserable nitchie in jail!"

Monmouth: "Well, you're a pretty specimen, having us sent pretty near 200 miles to take the man who was going to kill you. You say that he attempted murder—by Jove, I'll arrest you if you don't take care, for trying to screen a murderer!"

Brown was now thoroughly cowed, and felt that he must do a dirty crime to save himself from public contempt. Pointing to a tall, surly-looking young man in a red blanket he said: "That one."

Monmouth asked the Chief what character the accused bore; and the reply was sorrowfully expressed that of late the evil spirit had been upon "The Lean Man," for only two days ago he had wantonly attacked and thrashed a lad in camp, named "Would-not-go-out," for no cause.

And so it came about that the detachment returned to Headquarters, and carried away "The Lean Man" a prisoner.

Chapter II

It was a pleasant sight to see a party of Mounted Police ride in from some command, bronzed, dusty and travel-stained, their harness rusted with the rough usages of the camp, their eyes bright with the reflected breath and freedom of the plains, while the horses pricked their ears to hear the whinny of a colt in the corrall, as they foresaw the quietude of the dim stables, or the sunny upland where the herd was grazing. Thus came home the party from Carrot River, and drew up sharp before the Guard House. The prisoner was sent into his allotted cell, the waggon unloaded at the Quartermaster's Store, the horses led to water, the bedding taken to the barrack rooms, the cook urged to be ready with the provisions. The arrivals shed their prairie dress, while a rapid discussion took place on the current news; and a Guard was told off, and having got into uniform its members made their way to the Guard House, growling not a little that a single prisoner should cause so much extra work. Until then the picquet, had gone on solitary night rounds with his lantern, and dozed away the spare hours in the Guard Room; but this was only a pleasant reminiscence now. But the Indian, the restless unthinking child of the plains, had come to the weariness of an imprisoned spirit, and sank into the heavy lethargy of despair. The log walls of his prison, the iron bars of the door, the soldier sitting at the little table beyond, and what might be seen through a loop-hole in the wall, were now exchanged for the glorious horizon, with all the sweet sounds and sights of nature that people the broad tent of day. That loop-hole, pierced during the war, was now his only consolation, and he would sit for hours before it looking out upon the world. The sadness of his spirit seemed to weigh the atmosphere, for the air was dense for days with the smoke of prairie fires; and once at night he saw the sharp lines of flames coming down over the hills into the river flat, and hoped against hope that these would come down to release him.

"The Lean Man" was examined by the officer in command, but he was found so sullen and intractable that no evidence of his innocence could be come at: so he was committed for trial. One thing that he said to the interpreter was beyond the man's powers of translation, but was several times repeated among the men on the detachment in the words in which it was rendered: "The Good Spirit gave me the prairie for a bed, the trees to shelter me—but you Shermogonish have given me cold boards." And afterwards he said to Sergeant Monmouth, "You are going to kill me because I fought against you; be quick—kill me now—I am tired of waiting to die." He thought of the past—when he had gone through the tortures of the Sun Dance to come forth from the ordeal a warrior; he thought of all the excitement of the war, how he had seen the red flames of Fort Carlton leap up against the night, and had fought in the rifle pits of Batoche under Gabriel Dumont; he thought of his short happy married life before the dark cloud settled down upon him; and he brooded over what the Interpreter had said to him: "You will be tried next month."

Weeks passed outside the Guard House; and Change sat as usual on the wings of Time. The Mission people had ever since the war been as prompt in the matter of alarms as a fire brigade; and the Carrot River "scare," added to contemporary fictions about the Indians, had caused a general feeling of alarm. This was by no means mitigated by the departure of the Troop for the south by forced marches, to meet a great dignitary in the neighborhood of Long Lake; and by the rumored outbreak of an Indian war at Wood Mountain.

The band of "Four Sky" returned from Carrot River bringing the bereaved "Turkey Legs," who would sit for hours on the ground outside of the Guard House waiting for a casual glimpse of her lord; and comforted him much by her silent sympathy.

In due course the great dignitary returned to the East; and the Troop came home again, to the infinite regret of the little garrison, who by no means yearned for drill and discipline. The summer was ended, the harvest was gathered in, the winter began to send forth scouts to feel the way, and the full ripe year was waning to its close. And still "The Lean Man" knelt at the loop-hole, or made his little daily excuses for access to the free air of heaven. He lay through the long nights wondering what would be done to him after the trial, and feeling in his numbed sensibilities only the one terror—Disgrace. And he said within his heart, and whispered it to himself, and heard the winds whisper the words at night: "I will not be tried."

Three days after he arrived at this determination some of the men were spending a spare hour in the large barrack room engaged in "bed fatigue," and between the whiffs of a quiet smoke carrying on a desultory conversation. Burk, who was on guard that day, a tall, handsome, good-natured Englishman, sat on the edge of his bed fumbling in a kit-bag underneath for some tobacco, having permission to leave the Guard House for a few minutes.

"Well, Geometry," said Anstaye, "has the Nitchie been up to any of his games to-day?"

Burk: "I should just think he was! Why, I was just taking him over to the kitchen for the guard dinner at noon, when he made a break and got clean away past the Hospital."

Sergeant Monmouth: "Well, I hope you shot the—"

"Oh, it was no use shooting him; I just hollered out to the others and skinned after him."

"That is, you made use of your compasses, Geometry?"

"Oh shut up, Tribulation," said Burk; "Well, I caught up

close to the Riding School and nabbed him. And then I ran him off to the kitchen and made him lay hold of the big tea pot without any more fooling."

"And did he buck?"

"I saw buck! No, you bet he was as quiet as—as—er—death. That's the third bolt he's made to-day; he must have a pretty bad conscience."

Indeed, "The Lean Man" had made several attempts to escape, but his escorts had each time seized him, and taken no extra precautions other than to show him the butt of a revolver or set forth some counsel. That evening, however, before he was sent with an escort for supper, he was shackled with a "ball and chain," an instrument intended to restrain the most volatile of captives should he become too retiring. It must not be imagined that the prisoner was treated harshly, for if there is one virtue possessed by the rough soldiery of the prairies, it is their invariable kindness to the criminals committed to their charge.

"The Lean Man," thwarted in his attempts to escape, brought to the humiliation of chains, and filled with the darkest forebodings of evil, came to the black shadows of utter despair; and then, as man can do in the immediate presence of death, transcended his poor life as the day transcends night; he forgot the degradation of his people, and fought with all the magnificent courage and haughty endurance of his barbaric forefathers. He stood in the door of his cell when the time came that it was to be locked for the night, and, with his eyes aflame; his body trembling with the excitement, fought with the fury and the strength of madness for liberty. The whole guard hardly sufficed to cope with him, and it was only after a long and furious struggle that the Indian, overwhelmed with the weight of numbers, fell back into the cell utterly exhausted. He had cast aside the dross that had come over the Indian character from ruinous contact with the ruling race; he had asserted for once the inalienable rights of heredity, the greater and manlier past. The change in him was interpreted by the authorities as insanity.

Night deepened down upon the world, and the dim after-light waned through long hours into the north. The air was misty with smoke from the prairies; and, chilled in the shadowy, day night of Indian summer, all the valley lay in mysterious silence.

The Indian sat long brooding in the intense stillness. Through the barred aperture in the door a stream of golden light poured into the cell; and under the lamp in the Guard Room the Sergeant of the Guard sat at the table writing. The two men off duty lay asleep on the sloping dais at the other side of the room, still in complete uniform, and wearing their heavy side-arms as they took their brief, uneasy hours of rest. There was no sound save their breathing, and the steady scratching of the Sergeant's pen, as he proceeded with his letters. Presently the "picket" came in for the stable keys, saying that "the buckskin mare and Bulkeley's horse broke loose in the long stable—I can manage all right." Then he went out, and the prisoner watched him through the loophole as he went swinging his lantern towards the "corralls."

"The Lean Man" slowly unbound the sash from his waist, and knotted the ends together—he thrust the knot through the loophole—he drew the sash sharply back, catching the knot against the sides of a narrow gap between two logs—he pulled hard to make sure that the knot would hold. Then he sat a few moments in silence, and covered his face with his hands. He looked about him—the Sergeant of the Guard had taken a book and lay on the trestle bed beside his table reading, and the night around was infinitely still. Holding the loop of the sash the prisoner looked up towards heaven and prayed; then he placed his head within the loop and crouched down, leaning heavily with his throat against the sash. The Sergeant of the Guard was still reading—the two men were breathing quietly in their sleep—the "picquet" came out from the stables and went and stood on the bank of the river near by—the mist lay over the valley, and all was still.

The cold autumn day broke upon the world, and reveillé echoed from the wooded sides of the little valley, and rang melodiously against the banks of the broad river; the sun rose triumphant over the mists, and the waters were resplendent before his slanting rays—but the Indian had gone to the place of his fathers, and his sad stern eyes were closed forever in sleep. This man had dared the long agonies of torture in utter silence, had crushed with determined hands the life within him, and had gone down to the grave triumphant, without one sound to tell the watchful soldier, who was actually in the same room with him that the last tragedy was being transacted in a lingering anguish of suffocation.

They buried him on the bank of the river, and one of the soldiers made two laths into a cross during an idle moment and set it over the grave. The Indian lay under the prairie flowers in the shadow of the cross; on the one side of him Humanity rattled down the long dusty trail, and on the other lay the still expanses of silver, the broad, silent waters of the great Saskatchewan.

The Error of the Day

from *Northern Lights*
by Gilbert Parker

Gilbert Parker, by 1909, was a member of the British Parliament, writing stories about the Canadian North-West and publishing them in the New York Independent. *Though he was born in Canada, he had no first-hand experience of the Canadian West or of the NWMP; his setting evidently owes more to the American West, with which he would have had at least a literary familiarity. But for all that, Parker was a talented story-teller, and "The Error of the Day" includes the first attempt in literature to create a Mountie hero of any psychological complexity. It was published in a collection of Parker's stories entitled* Northern Lights (*Toronto: Copp Clark, 1909*). *The NWMP appear in many of Parker's other stories about the sly half-breed, Pretty Pierre, in* Pierre and His People (*Chicago: Stone and Kimball, 1894*), An Adventurer of the North (*London: Methuen, 1895*), A Romany of the Snows (*Toronto: Copp Clark, 1898*).

The "error of the day" may be defined as "The difference between the distance or range which must be put upon the sights in order to hit the target and the actual distance from the gun to the target."—*Admiralty Note.*

A great naval gun never fires twice alike. It varies from day to day, and expert allowance has to be made in sighting every time it is fired. Variations in atmosphere, condition of ammunition, and the wear of the gun are the contributory causes to the ever-varying "error of the day."

"Say, ain't he pretty?"
"A Jim-dandy—oh, my!"
"What's his price in the open market?"
"Thirty millions—I think not."
Then was heard the voice of Billy Goat—his name was
William Goatry—

"Out in the cold world, out in the street;
Nothing to wear, and nothing to eat,
Fatherless, motherless, sadly I roam,
Child of misfortune, I'm driven from home."

A loud laugh followed, for Billy Goat was a popular person
at Kowatin in the Saskatchewan country. He had an inimitable
drollery, heightened by a cast in his eye, a very large mouth,
and a round, good-humoured face; also he had a hand and arm
like iron, and was altogether a great man on a "spree."
There had been a two days' spree at Kowatin, for no other
reason than that there had been great excitement over the
capture and the subsequent escape of a prairie-rover, who had
robbed the contractor's money-chest at the rail-head on the
Canadian Pacific Railroad. Forty miles from Kowatin he
had been caught by, and escaped from, the tall, brown-eyed
man with the hard-bitten face who leaned against the open
window of the tavern, looking indifferently at the jeering
crowd before him. For a police officer he was not unpopular
with them, but he had been a failure for once, and, as Billy
Goat had said, "It tickled us to death to see a rider of the plains
off his trolley—on the cold, cold ground, same as you and me."
They did not undervalue him. If he had been less a man
than he was, they would not have taken the trouble to cover
him with their drunken ribaldry. He had scored off them in
the past in just such sprees as this, when he had the power to
do so, and used the power good-naturedly and quietly—but
used it.
Then, he was Sergeant Foyle of the Royal North-West
Mounted Police, on duty in a district as large as the United

Kingdom. And he had no greater admirer than Billy Goat, who now reviled him. Not without cause, in a way, for he had reviled himself to this extent, that when the prairie-rover, Halbeck, escaped on the way to Prince Albert, after six months' hunt for him and a final capture in the Kowatin district, Foyle resigned the Force before the Commissioner could reproach him or call him to account. Usually so exact, so certain of his target, some care had not been taken, he had miscalculated, and there had been the Error of the Day. Whatever it was, it had seemed to him fatal; and he had turned his face from the barrack-yard.

Then he had made his way to the Happy Land Hotel at Kowatin, to begin life as "a free and independent gent on the loose," as Billy Goat had said. To resign had seemed extreme; because, though the Commissioner was vexed at Halbeck's escape, Foyle was the best non-commissioned officer in the Force. He had frightened horse thieves and bogus land-agents and speculators out of the country; had fearlessly tracked down a criminal or a band of criminals when the odds were heavy against him. He carried on his cheek the scars of two bullets, and there was one white lock in his brown hair, where an arrow had torn the scalp away as, alone, he drove into the Post a score of Indians, fresh from raiding the cattle of an immigrant trailing north.

Now he was out of work, or so it seemed; he had stepped down from his scarlet-coated dignity, from the place of guardian and guide of civilisation, into the idleness of a tavern stoop.

As the little group swayed round him, and Billy Goat started another song, Foyle roused himself as though to move away— he was waiting for the mail-stage to take him south—

"Oh, father, dear father, come home with me now,
The clock in the steeple strikes one;
You said you were coming right home from the shop

As soon as your day's work was done.
Come home—come home——"

The song arrested him, and he leaned back against the window again. A curious look came into his eyes, a look that had nothing to do with the acts of the people before him. It was searching into a scene beyond this bright sunlight and the far green-brown grass, and the little oasis of trees in the distance marking a homestead, and the dust of the waggon-wheels out on the trail beyond the grain-elevator—beyond the blue horizon's rim, quivering in the heat, and into regions where this crisp, clear, life-giving, life-saving air never blew.

"You said you were coming right home from the
    shop
As soon as your day's work was done.
Come home—come home——"

He remembered when he had first heard this song in a play called *Ten Nights in a Bar-room*, many years before, and how it had wrenched his heart and soul, and covered him with a sudden cloud of shame and anger. For his father had been a drunkard, and his brother had grown up a drunkard, that brother whom he had not seen for ten years until—until——
He shuddered, closed his eyes, as though to shut out something that the mind saw. He had had a rough life, he had become inured to the seamy side of things—there was a seamy side even in this clean, free, wide land; and he had no sentimentality; though something seemed to hurt and shame him now.

"As soon as your day's work was done.
Come home—come home——"

The crowd was uproarious. The exhilaration had become a kind of delirium. Men were losing their heads; there was an element of irresponsibility in the new outbreak likely to breed some violent act, which every man of them would lament when sober again.

Nettlewood Foyle watched the dust rising from the wheels of the stage, which had passed the elevator and was nearing the Prairie Home Hotel far down the street. He would soon leave behind him this noisy ribaldry of which he was the centre. He tossed his cheroot away. Suddenly he heard a low voice behind him.

"Why don't you hit out, sergeant?" it said.

He started almost violently, and turned round. Then his face flushed, his eyes blurred with feeling and deep surprise, and his lips parted in a whispered exclamation and greeting.

A girl's face from the shade of the sitting-room was looking out at him, half-smiling, but with heightened colour and a suppressed agitation. The girl was not more than twenty-five, graceful, supple, and strong. Her chin was dimpled; across her right temple was a slight scar. She had eyes of a wonderful deep blue; they seemed to swim with light. As Foyle gazed at her for a moment dumfounded, with a quizzical suggestion and smiling still a little more, she said:

"You used to be a little quicker, Nett." The voice appeared to attempt unconcern; but it quivered from a force of feeling underneath. It was so long since she had seen him.

He was about to reply, but, at the instant, a reveller pushed him with a foot behind the knees so that they were sprung forward. The crowd laughed—all save Billy Goat, who knew his man.

Like lightning, and with cold fury in his eyes, Foyle caught the tall cattleman by the forearm, and, with a swift, dexterous twist, had the fellow in his power.

"Down—down, to your knees, you skunk," he said in a low, fierce voice.

The knees of the big man bent,—Foyle had not taken lessons of Ogami, the Jap, for nothing—they bent, and the cattleman squealed, so intense was the pain. It was break or bend; and he bent—to the ground and lay there. Foyle stood over him for a moment, a hard light in his eyes, and then, as if bethinking himself, he looked at the other roisterers, and said—

"There's a limit, and he reached it. Your mouths are your own, and you can blow off to suit your fancy, but if anyone thinks I'm a tame coyote to be poked with a stick——!" He broke off, stooped over, and helped the man before him to his feet. The arm had been strained, and the big fellow nursed it.

"Hell, but you're a twister!" the cattleman said with a grimace of pain.

Billy Goat was a gentleman, after his kind, and he liked Sergeant Foyle with a great liking. He turned to the crowd and spoke.

"Say, boys, this mine's worked out. Let's leave the Happy Land to Foyle. Boys, what is he—what—is—he? What—is—Sergeant Foyle—boys?"

The roar of the song they all knew came in reply, as Billy Goat waved his arms about like the wild leader of a wild orchestra—

> "Sergeant Foyle, oh, he's a knocker from the West,
> He's a chase-me-Charley, come-and-kiss-me tiger from the zoo,
> He's a dandy on the pinch, and he's got a double cinch
> On the gent that's going careless, and he'll soon cinch you:
> And he'll soon—and he'll soon—cinch you!"

Foyle watched him go, dancing, stumbling, calling back at him, as they moved toward the Prairie Home Hotel—

> "And he'll soon—and he'll soon—cinch you!"

His under lip came out, his eyes half-closed, as he watched them. "I've done my last cinch. I've done my last cinch," he murmured.

Then, suddenly, the look in his face changed, the eyes swam as they had done a minute before at the sight of the girl in the room behind. Whatever his trouble was, that face had obscured it in a flash, and the pools of feeling far down in the depths of a lonely nature had been stirred. Recognition, memory, tenderness, desire swam in his face, made generous and kind the hard lines of the strong mouth. In an instant he had swung himself over the window-sill. The girl had drawn away now into a more shaded corner of the room, and she regarded him with a mingled anxiety and eagerness. Was she afraid of something? Did she fear that—she knew not quite what, but it had to do with a long ago.

"It was time you hit out, Nett," she said, half shyly. "You're more patient than you used to be, but you're surer. My, that was a twist you gave him, Nett. Aren't you glad to see me?" she added hastily, and with an effort to hide her agitation.

He reached out and took her hand with a strange shyness, and a self-consciousness which was alien to his nature. The touch of her hand thrilled him. Their eyes met. She dropped hers. Then he gathered himself together. "Glad to see you? Of course, of course, I'm glad. You stunned me, Jo. Why, do you know where you are? You're a thousand miles from home. I can't get it through my head, not really. What brings you here? It's ten years—ten years since I saw you, and you were only fifteen, but a fifteen that was as good as twenty."

He scanned her face closely. "What's that scar on your forehead, Jo? You hadn't that—then."

"I ran up against something," she said evasively, her eyes glittering, "and it left that scar. Does it look so bad?"

"No, you'd never notice it, if you weren't looking close as I am. You see, I knew your face so well ten years ago."

He shook his head with a forced kind of smile. It became him, however, for he smiled rarely; and the smile was like a lantern turned on his face; it gave light and warmth to its quiet strength—or hardness.

"You were always quizzing," she said with an attempt at a laugh—"always trying to find out things. That's why you made them reckon with you out here. You always could see behind things; always would have your own way; always were meant to be a success."

She was beginning to get control of herself again, was trying hard to keep things on the surface. "You were meant to succeed—you had to," she added.

"I've been a failure—a dead failure," he answered slowly. "So they say. So they said. You heard them, Jo."

He jerked his head toward the open window.

"Oh, those drunken fools!" she exclaimed indignantly, and her face hardened. "How I hate drink! It spoils everything."

There was silence for a moment. They were both thinking of the same thing—*of the same man*. He repeated a question. "What brings you out here, Jo?" he asked gently.

"Dorland," she answered, her face setting into determination and anxiety.

His face became pinched. "Dorl!" he said heavily. "What for, Jo? What do you want with Dorl?"

"When Cynthy died she left her five hundred dollars a year to the baby, and——"

"Yes, yes, I know. Well, Jo?"

"Well, it was all right for five years—Dorland paid it in; but for five years he hasn't paid anything. He's taken it, stolen it from his own child by his own honest wife. I've come to get it—anyway, to stop him from doing it any more. His own child—it puts murder in my heart, Nett! I could kill him."

He nodded grimly. "That's likely. And you've kept Dorl's child with your own money all these years?"

"I've got four hundred dollars a year, Nett, you know; and I've been dressmaking—they say I've got taste," she added, with a whimsical smile.

Nett nodded his head. "Five years. That's twenty-five hundred dollars he's stolen from his own child. It's eight years old now, isn't it?"

"Bobby is eight and a half," she answered.

"And his schooling, his clothing, and everything; and you have to pay for it all?"

"Oh, I don't mind, Nett, it isn't that. Bobby is Cynthy's child; and I love him—love him; but I want him to have his rights. Dorl must give up his hold on that money—or——"

He nodded gravely. "Or you'll set the law on him?"

"It's one thing or the other. Better to do it now when Bobby is young and can't understand."

"Or read the newspapers," he commented thoughtfully.

"I don't think I've a hard heart," she continued, "but I'd like to punish him, if it wasn't that he's your brother, Nett; and if it wasn't for Bobby. Dorland was dreadfully cruel, even to Cynthy."

"How did you know he was up here?" he asked.

"From the lawyer that pays over the money. Dorland has had it sent out here to Kowatin this two years. And he sent word to the lawyer a month ago that he wanted it to get here as usual. The letter left the same day as I did, and it got here yesterday with me, I suppose. He'll be after it—perhaps to-day. He wouldn't let it wait long, Dorl wouldn't."

Foyle started. "To-day—to-day——"

There was a gleam in his eyes, a setting of the lips, a line sinking into the forehead between the eyes.

"I've been watching for him all day, and I'll watch till he comes. I'm going to say some things to him that he won't forget. I'm going to get Bobby's money, or have the law do it—unless you think I'm a brute, Nett." She looked at him wistfully.

"That's all right. Don't worry about me, Jo. He's my brother, but I know him—I know him through and through. He's done everything that a man can do and not be hanged. A thief, a drunkard, and a brute—and he killed a man out here," he added hoarsely. "I found it out myself—myself. It was murder."

Suddenly, as he looked at her, an idea seemed to flash into his mind. He came very near and looked at her closely. Then he reached over and almost touched the scar on her forehead.

"Did he do that, Jo?"

For an instant she was silent and looked down at the floor. Presently she raised her eyes, her face suffused. Once or twice she tried to speak, but failed. At last she gained courage and said—

"After Cynthy's death I kept house for him for a year, taking

116

care of little Bobby. I loved Bobby so—he has Cynthy's eyes. One day Dorland—oh, Nett, of course I oughtn't to have stayed there, I know it now; but I was only sixteen, and what did I understand! And my mother was dead. One day—oh, please, Nett, you can guess. He said something to me. I made him leave the house. Before I could make plans what to do, he came back mad with drink. I went for Bobby, to get out of the house, but he caught hold of me. I struck him in the face, and he threw me against the edge of the open door. It made the scar."

Foyle's face was white. "Why did you never write and tell me that, Jo? You know that I——" He stopped suddenly.

"You had gone out of our lives down there. I didn't know where you were for a long time; and then—then it was all right about Bobby and me, except that Bobby didn't get the money that was his. But now——"

Foyle's voice was hoarse and low. "He made that scar, and he—and you only sixteen—— Oh, my God!"

Suddenly his face reddened, and he choked with shame and anger. "And he's my brother!" was all that he could say.

"Do you see him up here ever?" she asked pityingly.

"I never saw him till a week ago." A moment, then he added, "The letter wasn't to be sent here in his own name, was it?"

She nodded. "Yes, in his own name, Dorland W. Foyle. Didn't he go by that name when you saw him?"

There was an oppressive silence, in which she saw that something moved him strangely, and then he answered, "No, he was going by the name of Halbeck—Hiram Halbeck."

The girl gasped. Then the whole thing burst upon her. "Hiram Halbeck! Hiram Halbeck, the thief,—I read it all in the papers—the thief that you caught, and that got away. And you've left the Mounted Police because of it—oh, Nett!" Her eyes were full of tears, her face was drawn and grey.

He nodded. "I didn't know who he was till I arrested him," he said. "Then, afterwards, I thought of his child, and let him get away; and for my poor old mother's sake. She never knew how bad he was even as a boy. But I remember how he used to steal and drink the brandy from her bedside, when

117

she had the fever. She never knew the worst of him. But I let him away in the night, Jo, and I resigned, and they thought that Halbeck had beaten me, had escaped. Of course I couldn't stay in the Force, having done that. But, by the heaven above us, if I had him here now, I'd do the thing—do it, so help me God!"

"Why should you ruin your life for him?" she said, with an outburst of indignation. All that was in her heart welled up in her eyes at the thought of what Foyle was. "You must not do it. You shall not do it. *He* must pay for his wickedness, not you. It would be a sin. You and what becomes of you mean so much." Suddenly with a flash of purpose she added, "He will come for that letter, Nett. He would run any kind of risk to get a dollar. He will come here for that letter—perhaps to-day."

He shook his head moodily, oppressed by the trouble that was on him. "He's not likely to venture here, after what's happened."

"You don't know him as well as I do, Nett. He is so vain he'd do it, just to show that he could. He'd probably come in the evening. Does anyone know him here? So many people pass through Kowatin every day. Has anyone seen him?"

"Only Billy Goatry," he answered, working his way to a solution of the dark problem. "Only Billy Goatry knows him. The fellow that led the singing—that was Goatry."

"There he is now," he added, as Billy Goat passed the window.

She came and laid a hand on his arm. "We've got to settle things with him," she said. "If Dorl comes, Nett——"

There was silence for a moment, then he caught her hand in his and held it. "If he comes, leave him to me, Jo. You will leave him to me, Jo. You will leave him to me?" he added anxiously.

"Yes," she answered. "You'll do what's right—by Bobby?"

"And by Dorl, too," he replied strangely.

There were loud footsteps without.

"It's Goatry," said Foyle. "You stay here. I'll tell him everything. He's all right; he's a true friend. He'll not interfere."

The handle of the door turned slowly. "You keep watch on the post-office, Jo," he added.

Goatry came round the opening door with a grin.

"Hope I don't intrude," he said, stealing a half-leering look at the girl. As soon as he saw her face, however, he straightened himself up and took on different manners. He had not been so intoxicated as he had made out, and he seemed only "mellow" as he stood before them, with his corrugated face and queer, quaint look, the eye with the cast in it blinking faster than the other.

"It's all right, Goatry," said Foyle. "This lady is one of my family from the East."

"Goin' on by stage?" Goatry said vaguely, as they shook hands.

She did not reply, for she was looking down the street, and presently she started as she gazed. She laid a hand suddenly on Foyle's arm.

"See—he's come," she said in a whisper, and as though not realising Goatry's presence, "He's come."

Goatry looked as well as Foyle. "Halbeck—the devil!" he said.

Foyle turned to him. "Stand by, Goatry. I want you to keep a shut mouth. I've work to do."

Goatry held out his hand. "I'm with you. If you get him this time, clamp him, clamp him like a tooth in a harrow."

Halbeck had stopped his horse at the post-office door. Dismounting he looked quickly round, then drew the reins over the horse's head, letting them trail, as is the custom of the West.

A few swift words passed between Goatry and Foyle.

"I'll do this myself, Jo," he whispered to the girl presently. "Go into another room. I'll bring him here."

In another minute Goatry was leading the horse away from the post-office, while Foyle stood waiting quietly at the door.

119

The departing footsteps of the horse brought Halbeck swiftly to the doorway, with a letter in his hand.

"Hi, there, you damned sucker!" he called after Goatry, and then saw Foyle waiting.

"What the hell——!" he said fiercely, his hand on something in his hip pocket.

"Keep quiet, Dorl. I want to have a little talk with you. Take your hand away from that gun—take it away," he added with a meaning not to be misunderstood.

Halbeck knew that one shout would have the town on him, and he did not know what card his brother was going to play. He let his arm drop to his side. "What's your game? What do you want?" he asked surlily.

"Come over to the Happy Land," Foyle answered, and in the light of what was in his mind his words had a grim irony.

With a snarl Halbeck stepped out. Goatry, who had handed the horse over to the hostler, watched them coming.

"Why did I never notice the likeness before?" Goatry said to himself. "But, gosh! what a difference in the men. Foyle's going to double cinch him this time, I guess."

He followed them inside the hall of the Happy Land. When they stepped into the sitting-room, he stood at the door waiting. The hotel was entirely empty, the roisterers at the Prairie Home having drawn off the idlers and spectators. The barman was nodding behind the bar, the proprietor was moving about in the backyard inspecting a horse. There was a cheerful warmth everywhere, the air was like an elixer, the pungent smell of a pine-tree at the door gave a kind of medicament to the indrawn breath. And to Billy Goat, who sometimes sang in the choir of a church not a hundred miles away—for people agreed to forget his occasional sprees—there came, he knew not why, the words of a hymn he had sung only the preceding Sunday:

"As pants the hart for cooling streams,
When heated in the chase——"

The words kept ringing in his ears as he listened to the

120

conversation inside the room—the partition was thin, the door thinner, and he heard much. Foyle had asked him not to intervene, but only to stand by and await the issue of this final conference. He meant, however, to take a hand in, if he thought he was needed, and he kept his ear glued to the door. If he thought Foyle needed him—his fingers were on the handle of the door.

"Now, hurry up! What do you want with me?" asked Halbeck of his brother.

"Take your time," said ex-Sergeant Foyle, as he drew the blind three-quarters down, so that they could not be seen from the street.

"I'm in a hurry, I tell you. I've got my plans. I'm going South. I've only just time to catch the Canadian Pacific three days from now, riding hard."

"You're not going South, Dorl."

"Where am I going, then?" was the sneering reply.

"Not farther than the Happy Land."

"What the devil's all this? You don't mean you're trying to arrest me again, after letting me go?"

"You don't need to ask. You're my prisoner. You're my prisoner," he said in a louder voice—"*until you free yourself.*"

"I'll do that damn quick, then," said the other, his hand flying to his hip.

"Sit down," was the sharp rejoinder, and a pistol was in his face before he could draw his own weapon.

"Put your gun on the table," Foyle said quietly. Halbeck did so. There was no other way.

Foyle drew it over to himself. His brother made a motion to rise.

"Sit still, Dorl," came the warning voice.

White with rage, the freebooter sat still, his dissipated face and heavy angry lips looking like a debauched and villainous caricature of his brother before him.

"Yes, I suppose you'd have potted me, Dorl," said the ex-sergeant. "You'd have thought no more of doing that than you did of killing Linley, the ranchman; than you did of trying to ruin Jo Byndon, your wife's sister, when she was sixteen years old, when she was caring for your child—giving her life for the child you brought into the world."

"What in the name of hell—it's a lie!"

"Don't bluster. I know the truth."

"Who told you—the truth?"

"She did—to-day—an hour ago."

"She here—out here?" There was a new cowed note in the voice.

"She is in the next room."

"What did she come here for?"

"To make you do right by your own child. I wonder what a jury of decent men would think about a man who robbed his child for five years, and let that child be fed and clothed and cared for by the girl he tried to destroy, the girl he taught what sin there was in the world."

"She put you up to this. She was always in love with you, and you know it."

There was a dangerous look in Foyle's eyes, and his jaw set hard. "There would be no shame in a decent woman caring for me, even if it was true. I haven't put myself outside the boundary as you have. You're my brother, but you're the worst scoundrel in the country—the worst unhanged. Put on the table there the letter in your pocket. It holds five hundred dollars belonging to your child. There's twenty-five hundred dollars more to be accounted for."

The other hesitated, then with an oath threw the letter on the table. "I'll pay the rest as soon as I can, if you'll stop this damned tomfoolery," he said sullenly, for he saw that he was in a hole.

"You'll pay it, I suppose, out of what you stole from the C.P.R. contractor's chest. No, I don't think that will do."

"You want me to go to prison, then?"

"I think not. The truth would come out at the trial—the whole truth—the murder, and all. There's your child Bobby. You've done him enough wrong already. Do you want him— but it doesn't matter whether you do or not—do you want him to carry through life the fact that his father was a jail-bird and murderer, just as Jo Byndon carries the scar you made when you threw her against the door?"

"What do you want with me, then?" The man sank slowly and heavily back into the chair.

"There is a way—have you never thought of it? When you threatened others as you did me, and life seemed such a little thing in others—can't you think?"

Bewildered, the man looked around helplessly. In the silence which followed Foyle's words his brain was struggling to see a way out. Foyle's further words seemed to come from a great distance.

"It's not too late to do the decent thing. You'll never repent of all you've done; you'll never do different."

The old reckless, irresponsible spirit revived in the man; he had both courage and bravado, he was not hopeless yet of finding an escape from the net. He would not beg, he would struggle.

"I've lived as I meant to, and I'm not going to snivel or repent now. It's all a rotten business, anyhow," he rejoined.

With a sudden resolution the ex-sergeant put his own pistol in his pocket, then pushed Halbeck's pistol over towards him on the table. Halbeck's eyes lighted eagerly, grew red with excitement, then a change passed over them. They now settled on the pistol, and stayed.

He heard Foyle's voice. "It's with you to do what you ought to do. Of course you can kill me. My pistol's in my pocket. But I don't think you will. You've murdered one man. You won't load your soul up with another. Besides, if you kill me, you will never get away from Kowatin alive. But it's with you —take your choice. It's me or you."

Halbeck's fingers crept out and found the pistol.

"Do your duty, Dorl," said the ex-sergeant as he turned his back on his brother.

The door of the room opened, and Goatry stepped inside softly. He had work to do, if need be, and his face showed it. Halbeck did not see him.

There was a demon in Halbeck's eyes, as his brother stood,

his back turned, taking his chances. A large mirror hung on the wall opposite Halbeck. Goatry was watching Halbeck's face in the glass, and saw the danger. He measured his distance.

All at once Halbeck caught Goatry's face in the mirror. The dark devilry faded out of his eyes. His lips moved in a whispered oath. Every way was blocked.

With a sudden wild resolution he raised the pistol to his head. It cracked, and he fell back heavily in the chair. There was a red trickle at his temple.

He had chosen the best way out.

"He had the pluck," said Goatry, as Foyle swung round with a face of misery.

A moment afterwards came a rush of people. Goatry kept them back.

"Sergeant Foyle arrested Halbeck, and Halbeck's shot himself," Goatry explained to them.

A white-faced girl with a scar on her temple made her way into the room.

"Come away—come away, Jo," said the voice of the man she loved; and he did not let her see the lifeless figure in the chair.

Three days later the plains swallowed them, as they made their way with Billy Goatry to the headquarters of the Riders of the Plains, where Sergeant Foyle was asked to reconsider his resignation: which he did.

The Sun-Dance in the File Hills

from *Sage Brush Stories*
by Frederick Niven

It is unusual for a Mounted Police story to suggest, as Niven's does, that the savage way of life had a seductive appeal for the young men of good breeding who enlisted in the NWMP. In fiction of the Canadian West generally there is little sign of that lure of savage freedom and elemental union with nature which draws fictional heroes to the American West. Niven very appropriately ends his story by showing Harry Verdon's attraction to the Sun-Dance to be a childish delusion. Frederick Niven was already an established novelist when he emigrated from Scotland to the Canadian West in 1920. He is now best known for three novels set on the prairies and in the British Columbia interior: The Flying Years (*London: Collins, 1935*), Mine Inheritance (*London: Collins, 1940*), *and* The Transplanted (*Toronto: Collins, 1944*). *The present story was published in Niven's* Sagebrush Stories (*London: Eveleigh Nash, 1917*).

It was in the days when the settlers in the neighbourhood of what is now Saskatoon were wont to make up parties to sleigh their wheat down to the main—and only—line of railway in the country. It was, as the word is wont to be used, only yesterday for all that—in spite of the spider's web appearance of the map now, with all its railway lines; for a man does not need to be at all old to recall the days when there were no arrival-and-departure blackboards even in Winnipeg, the days when men at the depôt asked only for news of the Eastbound or the Westbound. I remember it all myself, and it will be long,

I hope, ere I ask the elevator boy in the department store, bending over him, paternal, which is the floor for skull-caps. It was after the Riel Rebellion had become history, and before the prairie chickens sniffed and said: "What in thunder is that?" and an old bird, that had flown west, attending easily to a wing-feather, trying to hide the "dog" he wanted to put on, nonchalantly answered: "Petrol!" The last scream of the Red River carts, with their wibblety wheels and ungreased axles, was still heard in the land, had not yet quit, hopeless, drowned out by the kettledrum-like rub-a-dub of the exhausts of the cars that now bob like boats all up and down the prairie rolls bearing land-wise folk making "cities."

It was, then, in these days that Harry Verdon, on his lonesome, rode up into the File Hill country to discover why several Indian trails heading in that direction showed fresh and popular. He was young enough to see life as always a game. He looked on at it. It may be even said that he looked on at Harry Verdon, immensely bucked on all that Harry Verdon was seeing and doing in the game. At Regina they had licked him into shape and discovered that his Cheltenham accent (excessive) had probably been forced upon him against his will because he had an acute ear and couldn't help catching it, rather than because he had practised it hard so as to seem lofty and tin-god like. Don't judge a man always by his accent, or his surface manner. Accents are sometimes like clothes, and a man often wears what his tailor tells him to wear; finds the duds uncomfortable too, if you only knew.

Verdon had friends in the Force, and among the settlers too, even among the sprinkling of men from the Western States not partial to lackadaisical accents, who had, even then, drifted up across Montana into Her (as it was of course called then) Majesty's Dominions. He was "right there" in a prairie fire that threatened the Qu'Appelle district once. He could be greatly interested in such mundane, very mundane, matters, with no spice of danger, as helping to haul a wagon out of a slough. After all it doesn't matter with what kind of accent a man curses a wagon so long as he has his lariat taut between it and his saddle-horn.

127

As for the Indians—Harry had found them different even from Ballantyne's in some respects. "The Crees," he wrote easily to his aged aunt, and one can detect the lackadaisical note in the letter—and the banter, "are not always clean; but then neither are we sometimes. I had to do some patrol work in connection with a branch of the C.P.R." (the Crow's Nest that would be; he was stationed some time at Pincher Creek), "and consider that the camps of the construction gangs are not of much service as models to the Indians." I mention this to show that he was not a kid open to prejudice, and to give you a further notion of the kid who came into the File Hills alone because his partner had gone off with a man who was bug-house through living solitary on a most sequestered quarter section. All kinds of jobs they get, these fellows. Harry Verdon saw the departure of that bug-house individual, and it moved him. All alone now, riding north-east, he seemed still to see him.

"Poor devil," he said.

That was the one kind of job he personally did not like. He would rather arrest a tough whisky-smuggler any day than bring in some locoed person. He sympathised too much with the "poor devils." He would never turn whisky-smuggler. He had no inclination that way. He would never try to ride into a bar-room, in some jerk-water or one-horse place of the plains, loudly crying out that he was It, and that the city was scared of him. With such people he lacked sympathy. He lifted them with enthusiasm. But men who had passed from meditation to brooding, or men who, instead of meditating in the big loneliness to which they had come, were overcome by it—these men he could, if he allowed himself, sympathise with as well as pity. Pity is safer.

He felt so now, for as he rode the effect of the plains round him was as of a saucer to the fly in the centre. The horizon seemed to rise, he to sink. It was as if he floundered in a spread green-brown blanket, not quite taut. Wherever his pony stepped, there were the bottoms of the slopes; such was the optical illusion. It was a relief to see, far off, a blue something above the plains—and to know it was not a cloud; to know it was the hills, to know that by next day they would show better with serrated bits here and there signifying trees on the ridges. There were no grangers in that section. Wheat (the limit of it) was down south, a couple of days' good ride—and then no more again till you rode north-west for a week.

Cattle was the stand-by of the country. A few head of steers helped to relieve the monotony next day, also a ranch house, with talk—for men don't go loco on cattle ranches. You may not always agree with your friends, but you can argue with them. A man all alone in a shack had no one even to disagree with. When he starts in arguing about himself—about why he's there, about what it all means, about the poor job he's made of his life in the past, about whether he's to have a hereafter or not, and so forth—the sky looks at him so complacently that it's worse than if he was dumped down for life on a little bit of rock opposite the Sphinx. From such thoughts, and from doing a trifle more than pitying that locoed fellow his partner had gone off with, Harry Verdon welcomed the sight of the corral bars, and the long, low collection of ranch houses with a wisp of smoke rising up. It was as good to see as the pillar of cloud that you may recall in ancient history or myth.

At this ranch there was word for him regarding his Indians, and suggestion as to their goal and occupation there. The guess was that they were sun-dancing. Now, in those days, sun-dancing was considered bad. Smithsonian Institutes and other kindred inquirers have shed new light on sun-dances, and it is pretty generally admitted that if the powers of darkness are not actually out of the matter altogether, at least the powers of light do have some say in it. Those who care to look it up can find it all in Dorsey's *Arapahoe Sun-Dance*—Vol. IV., to be precise, of the Field Columbian Museum Anthropological Series. But perhaps it was as well, in those days, to discountenance it. It gathered bands of tribes together, and the young men did doubtless often get their heads together and ask why they didn't, feeling good, let somebody see what they were so feeling—put their feeling of vigour to the test!

Yes, the Indians had been passing up into the hills some

numerous, so Harry was told. They were "all right." None of the boys had reason to suspect that any of the range steers had served them for rations on the way. Harry stopped over there that night, and was pulling out next day when the southern neighbour arrived. He also had news of Indians heading for the File Hills. He also had no complaints to make. He had, indeed, spoken to some of them. They were not Crees. For the only Indian language he knew was Sioux; he had treked up here from Dakota some years before and could make himself understood in Sioux. He assured Harry they were Sioux, some Manitoba reservation Sioux he thought. They were not, he guessed, from south of the border. He too had his "guess," and although the Indians did not admit it, he guessed it was sun-dancing, not bear-hunting, that took them up there. This man from Dakota said, laughing, for one does not suggest these things too seriously, that Harry should have a deputy with him—if not a posse.

Harry thought he had better push on. He might be in time to stop the dance. The ranchman here was going into town next day—they had no telephone at that time—and would tell the corporal, if he was back again, where Harry was heading. So Harry thanked him, and passed on. About noon next day he heard, in the great silence, a sound that might have been the blood in his veins, a throbbing sound. He listened. Sound is a difficult thing to locate. If there is a flash of light somewhere the eye leaps to it, locates it; with sound, unless you know what it is, you are puzzled sometimes. For example —a door slams in the house, and you wonder if it is a door in the house that slammed or the powder magazine ten miles away that blew up.

This throbbing sound puzzled Harry for a spell. It grew louder, however, and as the hills ahead began to show green as well as blue he decided, advancing on them, that it was thence the sound came. By late afternoon there was no doubt. Now Harry knew enough to realise that here was a business different from bagging whisky smugglers, from getting the drop on a gentleman whose aim was to terrorise a bar-room, or even from representing law and order at a round-up when little disputes regarding calves might arise. In the first two cases the point is to arrive unseen and sudden; in the last the notion is just to be there. In this case he knew that he would be seen arriving, whether he rode up all free and open, or tried to advance under cover. The Crees, and the handful of Sioux, might not always be clean as a house doctor would wish to see cleanliness, but Harry knew that in some things the Indian could not be given tips by the white. Once, on a survey party, he had seen how the Indians with them spared ammunition— and also, more to the purpose, prevented the scaring of the duck—by creeping through the reeds and hitting the birds with an adroitly flung stick.

He knew that the Indians in the hills, if they were up to mischief, would have scouts posted. He knew that they would see him anyhow. He knew that the red-coat advancing open and easily might put a stop to trouble much more promptly than the red-coat advancing surreptitiously. He relied on the Indian's wisdom not to draw a bead on his red coat; but he surmised that if he advanced skulking, the temptation might arise to do so. Wherefore he advanced to the hills, whence came the beat of the tom-toms, as easily as he would have advanced to a round-up to which he had not only been sent by his superior, but of the holding of which that officer had been apprised by the secretary of the Stock Association.

No feelings now of unutterable loneliness trying to whisper things to him! No thoughts now of that locoed homesteader who was like a child and a demon all in one—and you never knew which might have the ascendancy, "poor devil." Now, instead, there was a queer feeling of wonder, wonder if he had already been spotted by many eyes. The trail was clear, and recently travelled. From south and north other trails converged into it. But to this youth, as to the one in the ballad, came the shades of night, falling fast—and so, coming to a creek he made camp, open and undismayed.

On the morrow he would be up early and ride into the Indians' hill-camp, looking for the master of the ceremonies, and would warn him that the camp must be disbanded, and the men all go back to their reserves. He lit a fire; if they saw it, if they scouted down and discovered a red-coat, well—his job would be executed that way. The red coat was to do the trick anyhow, not by virtue of the one young man under it, but by virtue of all it signified to the Indian of the other men behind it, and the power behind them again—a power that, after all, allowed them a great deal of freedom, of home rule; a power that protected them too from many things; if it gave them a few rules and regulations to get fixed firm in their minds.

As he surmised was probable, so it befel. He was seen. About an hour after he made camp there arrived in the Indian way—whether the Indian wears a breech clout and feathers, or an old black tail coat and dungaree pants—nay, not *arrived* so much as was just there, an Indian; and the moment Harry cocked his head and looked up (and did *not* grab a gun) the Indian, who had probably tramped on the warning twig intentionally, held up his hand and said: "How, Shemogenes!" which being interpreted means: "Greeting, Red-Coat!"

Harry looked at him easily and answered, after a long silence: "How!"—and then recognised him for a sub-chief, one called "Wounds" who had once astonished Harry greatly. It was during that survey trip and Harry had wanted to buy from him, or trade from him, a stone-bowled calumet. Wounds would neither sell for golden eagles nor trade for colt or saddle the desired calumet—intended, by Harry, to grace some drawing-room table of back-home relation. But when the survey was over, and the three red-coats and the two chainmen were pulling out, Wounds gave a parcel to Harry saying: "You open bye-m-bye." For some reason unknown, the kid had found favour in the eyes of Wounds; for when he eventually opened the parcel he found the calumet in it. Since then they had met but once—a pleasant meeting. And now here was Wounds again, in troublous time.

"How are you, Chief?" said Harry. "You bully?"

"Me bully. You feeling good?"

"Yap."

Harry produced his tobacco, and Wounds accepted the hospitality, squatting down. The tom-toming had ceased at sunset, and Harry opined that sunset ended it, not a rumour of his advance. Everything was very quiet. They drew on their pipes a spell, the little fire flickering, the staked horse tearing grass. Red man and Red-coat sat looking at the flames, puffing for some time, and it was the Indian who first spoke after that long silence in which each, in some queer way, had been measuring the other, wondering about the other, less of his war-strength than of himself and his people.

"You come stop dance?" asked Wounds.

Harry looked up slowly from the fire.

"I guess that's my job," he said.

There was a pause again.

"I guess," said Wounds.

"Why you dance?" asked Harry.

"Why? What for?"

"Yap."

The Indian looked in the fire again, as if trying to select from his small vocabulary of white words the "what for." And, as he considered, a throbbing began in the night, and ever and again, in its rising, its growing, came a queer keening of voices with a high note, a note that stirred Harry in a new way. It suddenly struck him that these voices, in that special way, so foreign to a white man's ears, were of *the soil*. Prairie nights had blent with them for ages. Some of the notes, far-carried in the quiet, high and presumably triumphant, were yet full of pathos to him. They were sad as plovers' cries on the moors at home. And at last—"What for?" Harry asked again, and Wounds tried to tell him.

Now it happened that the patrol wagon came over for that locoed man after all, and so Corporal Reid did not have to go to Qu'Appelle. And with the patrol wagon there were three men to support Reid and Harry, with orders for all to go up into the File Hills and break up a dance reported to be forming there. From somewhere down Wolseley and Grenfell way word had come of Indians slipping off from reserves, and going north to Beaver Hills or File Hills. It was to be a big camp, and rumour had it that even some Assiniboine from south had crossed the railway on the way to join.

Back came Corporal Reid, having delivered his "poor devil" to the patrol wagon, left his rig at the post, and set off with the three new arrivals on the trail of Harry Verdon, leaving the other policeman to look after his work and Harry's till the sun dance in the File Hills should be broken up, and the dancers sent wending home.

For their arrival no look-out was kept by the Indians. They were not expected. The assembled dancers believed that Harry was the only Shemogenes on the job; and, with no hilarious triumph—with thanksgiving rather, with, perhaps it may be said, naïf joy in a convert—they were rejoicing over him. For he had reverted. The beat of the tom-toms, the "Hah! hah! hah! hee!"—he had "tumbled" to these sounds. He had heard them not as mere noise. Indians say that our pianos, when first heard, give them but the impression of little hammers hitting wires. But though tom-toms and "Hah! hah! hah! hee!" are not complicated as a pianoforte, doubtless the other way enlightenment, or realisation, can also come. In the simpler noise there is music too—and Harry had succumbed.

Perhaps, too, the "what for" of the sun-dance as told by Wounds last night, blowing smoke and talking in his low voice, had wakened sympathy in that sympathetic kid. At any rate what Reid saw—he having left his three men in a gulch below the camp and advanced, marvelling that the tom-toms kept on, with him so near, and Harry probably arrived—what Reid saw, cresting the hill and looking down on the tipis and the central dance, gave him a shock. All afternoon they had heard the throbbing of the tom-toms as they drew near. It was now well on towards the evening shadow again. And there was Harry Verdon, Kid Verdon, leaning backward as a man leans when he walks before a heavy wind. He was in his blue regulation pants, but his red coat was off, his shirt was open. He had little pieces of wood, like skewers, in his chest, and from them to the top of a lithe pole stretched a cord. Kid Verdon leant back with his weight on the cord, looking at the sun, a great determination on his face. He was having a new experience. He had, as the French say, thrown his cap over the windmills. He might not write of this to his aged aunt later on, but he would remember it to his dying day. All looked at him—all the collected Sioux, Assiniboine, Cree were rejoicing over the convert; and the tom-toms thrilled to aid him.

Reid drew rein and looked on. It seemed to him as if he looked on for ages before any saw him. Then shouts and counter shouts broke out. Some were for flight, some were for fight, some were hopeful of another convert; soon there might be no more missionaries telling them to have a white man's religion, no more missionaries telling them that there were errors in their creeds, but white men coming along to be brothers and take part in their ceremonials. Reid considered the position and, holding up his hand, rode down to the camp.

"Don't cut the strings!" said Harry, in a voice of staying-with-it.

Wounds came up to Reid, and other chiefs too, with him. They were anxious. They wanted to see how the tide set with him. The tom-toms, that had slackened, broke out with new hope. Reid spoke Cree, and in Cree he asked how long Kid Verdon had still to go.

"You can arrest me after!" gulped Harry. "I'll stay with it till the skewers break through—or till sunset."

Reid, with carbine in crook of arm, leant forward in the saddle and listened. He felt that too many were all trying to talk at once. When a lull came he held up his hand, in a very Indian gesture, for quiet to talk. He explained that he had come to stop the dance. He explained that Harry Verdon was a young buck whose head could be turned, and that if he reported this dereliction from duty, the young buck would be cast out of the white man's soldier camps and disgraced. There was a murmur of disapproval. To some of the young red bucks crowding behind the chiefs the obvious way out was to put an end to Reid, seeing that he spoke thus, and was not at all like the younger red-coat. But the chiefs told

Smoke

by Z. M. Hamilton

Hamilton's main character is modelled on a Blood Indian named "Charcoal" who, in October of 1896, shot another of his tribe for making love to his wife, Pretty Wolverine. Charcoal, like "Smoke," terrorized the district and evaded capture for about a month. The killing of Sergeant Major Churchill in this story corresponds closely to Charcoal's shooting of Sergeant William Wilde. Hamilton does not, of course, bind himself to all of the historical particulars. Charcoal actually fled with all four of his wives, and while he took pot-shots at a farm instructor and a Corporal at the Cardston Detachment, and threatened the lives of the local Indian Agent and the Blood Chief Red Crow, he killed only two men. The quality of Hamilton's story and its appearance in an ephemeral 39 page publication entitled Christmas in Regina *(Regina: Roper, 1919), suggest that there may be much readable Mountie fiction hidden in very obscure places. Hamilton, a Regina journalist, published a volume of reminiscences with his wife, Marie, entitled* These Are the Prairies *(Regina: School Aids and Textbook Publishing Co., 1954). For historical treatments of the Charcoal incident, see R. C. McLeod's,* The North West Mounted Police and Law Enforcement, 1873-1905) *(Toronto: University of Toronto Press, 1976), Ernest J. Chambers,* The North West Mounted Police *(1906; rpt, Toronto: Coles, 1972), Ronald Atkin,* Maintain the Right *(London: Macmillan, 1973).*

Smoke was of the Bloods, a powerful sept of the great Blackfoot nation, which in days gone by had held sway over the vast rolling country which ran north from the upper reaches of the Missouri to the forks of the Red Deer River.

He was a good Indian, and ranked high in the estimation of the Indian agent. He was in active middle life, and as a young man had ridden in marauding war parties and joined in the clamorous and barbaric buffalo hunt.

There is no doubt that he stifled many a hungering memory of the old free life of the plains; but he was an Indian of excellent perception, and quickly made up his mind that the new order which arrived with the Mounted Police had changed the complexion of western life, and that intelligence counselled its adoption by the native people.

Accordingly he exchanged his war ponies for a good yoke of oxen, sent his children to the Industrial School, and adapted himself—if somewhat awkwardly—to the restrictions of the trousers issued from the agency store house. He obtained an allotment on the fertile reserve which lay south of the Belly River, did a little cultivation, and proceeded to raise some stock. He also essayed to dig coal from a seam that cropped out on the river bank in his pasture; and on occasion would make a comfortable dollar by hauling it in his brightly painted Chatham wagon to certain of the neighboring ranches, and receiving in exchange what appeared to him considerable sums of ready money.

Whilst the erstwhile brave was thus peacefully following the paths of the white man, he took to himself a new wife of his own people. She was not in any sense the wife of his youth, which in all likelihood had been a polygamous period. She was young and, according to tribal standards, good looking, and Smoke, after administering to her in a rather half hearted way the disciplinary beatings which according to the Indian habit, usually ushered in married life, fell a victim to the uxoriousness not uncommon when male middle age unites with female youth and beauty.

Smoke was well content in his new found domesticity, and

pursued the daily round of his activities, which was yielding
fruit in the way of sleek steers and good white man's money.

The Adventure of the Corrals

Gay youth and douce middle age seldom go well together, and
it was not long until the sober endearments of her spouse
began to be rather wearisome to Mrs. Smoke. Her inclinations
turned in another direction, and she developed rather a contempt for her elderly husband. Furthermore, she did not
have the fear of him before her eyes which she would have
had in the savage old days. His devotion to the ways of the
white man had tempered his blood. He had cast his Indian
sting, when he donned the trousers of civilization.

At least so thought his wife, although her conclusions were
inclined to be hasty.

Accordingly she conceived some sort of an attachment
for a young buck of the tribe, and during the absence of her
husband she philandered with her new love, along the bank
of the brawling river or in the cottonwood groves that bor-
dered the rim of the valley.

Gossip is nowhere more universal than in an Indian community, and soon Smoke heard whispers of what was going
on. During a temporary reversion to strain he gave her a
good beating and concluded that the incident was closed.

It wasn't, however, and events began to move with considerable rapidity.

One fall evening, Smoke returned to his humble domicile
after a somewhat strenuous and irksome day spent hauling
coal, and found his hearth cold and his helpmate absent.

He was hungry, so he composedly cooked some food and
prepared his rawhide quirt against her return.

Darkness fell, and he sallied forth to gather news of her.

An ancient squaw with nutcracker features and a skin like
an old parchment, scarred with a thousand wrinkles, cackled
at him in derision.

"You won't find her along the white man's trail. Will not
your white man's wisdom show you her lover?" she said.

He shook her until her old bones rattled and menaced her with the quirt which he still carried.

"Keep your blows for your own woman," she continued, drawing her blanket around her. "If your eyes are still good look for her among the cattle corrals at the Lower Camp."

Turning away from the old woman, Smoke's civilization fell from him like the casting away of a cumbrous garment.

He returned soberly and quietly to his shack. His movements were unhurried but he went about his preparations with a manner that was certain and inexorable. He gathered the dying poplar embers on the hearth together and fanned them into a blaze that sent fantastic shadows leaping up and down in the dark places.

Glancing around he noted the answering gleam to the firelight of the bright brass tacks which studded the butt of the Winchester carbine, resting in a murky corner. It had not been used much of late, but its care had never been neglected. As he picked it up, it fell smoothly to his hand like the familiar tool of the craftsman. He pumped the lever and noted with satisfaction the run of the brass cartridges to the oiled groove of the chamber. He buckled a leather belt studded with shining cases around his waist, and sweeping up his saddle gear, he cast one glance about the tawdry interior that had served him for home, and bearing his plenishings with him, vanished in the direction of the horse corral. He had added no knife to his equipment. He always carried one in its studded sheath beneath his outer garments.

A few minutes later, the shadowy outlines of a man and horse flew out of the corral and with drumming hoof beats took the trail down the valley.

Down by the Cattle Corrals at the lower camp it was dark and still. The sombre shadows of the bosky ravines threw a pall of inky blackness about the muddled and trampled enclosures. There was no cheerful noice of tenancy, either from human or beast. A circling night bird was betrayed by the curious sibilancy of its wings; and twice a mallard drake, on a river pool, voiced fretfully an uneasy sense of human nearness.

To Smoke's Indian perception the signs were plain. He tied his horse to a young poplar at the edge of a bluff, and rifle in the slope of his arm, came swiftly among the corrals, as nebulous as a flickering shadow.

No one ever explained the details of what happened down there that night. The gay young buck who knew, greeted the cold glimmers of the dawn with wide sightless eyes. Smoke and his wife could also have furnished some information about the happenings in that sinister place of turbulent love and quick, inevitable death: but they were not presently available as witnesses.

About half an hour after Smoke had entered those pitchy corrals, he stalked silently and proudly back to his horse, and his wife walked at his heels. Without any attempt at concealment he swung himself to the saddle and took the track to the agency at the lope. His wife ran free and strong like a native wild thing at his stirrup. She had cast the calico skirt of the trading store for freedom, and her young dusky limbs were naked to the night.

Smoke, following the wisdom of the white man, was only the object of her contempt, but when he tore her, strong, wrathful and barbarous, from the arms of her light o'love, and pausing a moment to kill, as an Indian, her hot, savage blood leaped in response. She did not waste a second thought on the poor carrion that so lately had been her lover.

Smoke was under no illusions as to the justice of the white man. He knew what would follow. Daylight would tell its tale and the red-coated riders would travel hot on his trail. At one stroke he had cast off civilization. He knew he would be harried and hunted like a beast; but he was conscious of no feeling of fear or depression.

On the contrary, he exulted in what he had done. He bestrode a good horse, his belt was full of cartridges, the country swept wide and free with many a lurking place, and his woman was his own again.

Every Indian instinct was awakened and he rode once more in fancy with the war parties of his youth. Let the troopers take him if they could, he would at the worst pass as a warrior fighting. That would be better than a slow old age in a wooden house, and the camp jeering at him for the infidelities of his woman.

*   *   *

The Escape

There was however, several hours to daylight, and prudence counselled the forehanded use of them.

I do not think that a word was spoken between the couple during the five mile run to the agency, near which Smoke's shack was situated. He eased his pony when occasion demanded, and his wife slowed up in accordance. She displayed no sign of distress, and seemed as enduring as the horse. Smoke paid her no attention but was pleasantly and acutely aware of her presence and devotion.

The pair came silently to their own place and instantly fell to preparations for a journey.

Darkness still had some hours to run when they pulled out for the foothills.

Smoke rode a little in advance, his belted blanket about him, and the rifle snug in the hollow of his right arm. He was mounted on a tall, upstanding buckskin, which he bestrode with the native grace of an instinctive horseman. His wife followed on a sturdy pinto, and she trailed a pack horse after her.

In the first clean freshness of a windy dawn the little cavalcade came to the edge of the last terrace before the climbing foothills merged into the forest of the Eastern slopes of the Rockies.

Smoke drew rein, while the woman passed onward and out of sight.

The gusty western wind escaping with the morning from its pent house in a great mountain defile, rustled through the dry prairie grass; the Eastern sky paled and lightened; and the deep dull glow of the coming sun was reflected from the summit of Chief Mountain, which from its isolation has looked down on the country of the Blackfoot people since their history began.

Silent and immovable as a graven statue Smoke sat on his horse, and threw an eagle glance of pride and power over the country that had been his fathers'. From his elevated position he could see a great swelling vista of rolling land—of table land and valley, and hill and fertile plain. With his horse and his weapons and his bearing of a warrior, he looked like the very apothesis of the ancient spirit of the plains.

Then as the sun sent its first red heralds over the rim of the sky line, he wheeled his buckskin and galloped on out of the scene.

Of course when news of the killing was brought to the officer of the Mounted Police at Fort MacLeod, the plains and valleys were beaten for the fugitives. Everything pointed to Smoke as the offender, but the dead man had been a bad Indian, a trouble maker, and all the camps knew of his relations with the woman. The Indian agent, a Scotchman of discernment, appreciated Smoke and had cordially detested his victim. Perhaps therefore, after the first hue and cry, the search was not kept up with any great degree of enthusiasm. Indeed, it is quite probable that had Smoke been taken at that time he might not have been very severely dealt with. At any rate he was not then captured.

He knew a secure place away up one of the defiles of the Swift Current Canyon, and there he passed the winter. Food there was aplenty. The stately elk came out in bands in the parks between the jack pine trees; beavers were on mountain, lake and river; and the ravines were full of prairie chicken that called to each other gregariously from the tree tops on frosty mornings. The grassy sides of the coulee were wind swept bare of snow and the horses wintered well in their hobbles.

Smoke for some time kept a vigilant watch for pursuers, but none came, and he devoted himself to a belated honeymoon. His wife yielded herself his slave. It was the native tradition and she wanted her man to be her master.

*   *   *

The Hidden Valley

The spring came, and when the horses grew smooth sided and sleek with the young tender grass, Smoke's wandering instinct stirred within him. The hunt had died down; and he looked from his eyrie on the sweeping prairie with hungry longing; for the Blackfeet are a plains people, and the mountains stifle them. Besides he wanted converse with his own folk; they would never betray him.

But he listened to the counselling of his woman, and they turned their backs on their native region, and penetrated farther through the defiles of the Rockies.

They found lonely valleys, cloven in the sides of the tumbled ranges, where there was sweet grass for the horses; where the elk came out in stately bands; where the big horn crossed at dawn on their way from mountain to mountain; and where there was neither human presence nor habitation.

Smoke still carried intact the fifty or more shining cartridges which had glittered in his leather belt, the night of his flight. They were kept with forethought for the day of danger and although the carbine was cared for carefully, it was never fired.

He used for a firearm a long, single barrelled, smooth bore which he loaded with shot for the ducks and wild fowl and with round balls for bigger game. Indians are economical hunters, and the big powder horn, with the wooden stopper, he had brought away with him was still three parts full.

After a summer spent in these happy and remote hunting grounds, the approach of snow warned the wanderers to the lower levels; and they came back to the place where they had passed the previous winter.

They reached their old camping ground late one menacing evening. It was unseasonably cold, and a bitter wind with particles of sharp snow stung them as they came along the mountain wall and down the pass. It was a hard journey, and humans and animals alike were glad when they found harborage in the grassy basin which, surrounded by timber and wallsided rocks, provided shelter from the snow laden wind, which boomed in the rocky fissures of the canyon.

Smoke, despite his years, seemed made of iron, and showed no sign of fatigue. His wife was wearied, and did not go about the task of making camp with her usual activity. Smoke spoke little to her but helped her hobble the horses and chop firewood; no small concession on the part of an old time Indian.

They rested snugly enough; but in the morning Smoke saw signs that disturbed him. Cattle had been in the little valley, and that recently. They had been followed by men who rode shod horses. There were the cold remains of little fires about, and Smoke knew that the running iron had been most unlawfully in use. Some one else had found the secret lurking place.

However, there was no one in sight now. Strangers could only approach from the plains, and Smoke from his vantage point so high up could spy anyone coming long before their arrival. Then winter was coming down and they might be left unmolested until spring.

So they made themselves comfortable.

During their wanderings they had relapsed into the old Indian customs. I think Smoke prided himself upon this. He had left the road of the white man, and he and his woman were roving along the ancient trail of their people.

One ominous day, when the sky was leaden and low, and the wind in uneven chilly gusts was sending the tops of the pine trees tossing in scurrying waves, Smoke came down from his eyrie that commanded the plains, and the lower opening of the pass. He cast a quick look at the woman, who was walking heavily backwards and forwards in the glade, her head shrouded in her blanket. He stepped silently to the shelter which they had raised, and, picking up the Winchester carbine, commenced to fill the magazine with shells from his belt.

The woman's time was hard on her, and whilst her man was looking to his arms, she walked out of the clearing into the woods. According to the ancient custom of her people, and like the other wild creatures, she was looking for a solitary place.

She did not come back.

Smoke brought in the horses, gathered the camp gear, and made up the pack. This done, he saddled the horses, led them some distance through the timber where he tied them; then he came back and destroyed as far as possible all evidences of the camp.

During the work he never laid aside the rifle.

Then he betook himself to his vantage point.

Evening was falling gloomy and tempestous. Two men were riding up the pass, and they were urging their laggard horses with many a look to the rear. Smoke hid behind a boulder, and they passed quite close. They went by the little opening of the secret valley, and pressed on into the storm and gloom. Smoke let them go; and he strained his eyes down the pass for the FEAR that he knew rode at their heels.

Very soon he heard the ring of shod horses on the rocky way, and the jingle of arms and accoutrements. Five riders were coming, and they leaned and looked ahead.

The Indian did not need an interpreter for the drama. The first horsemen were rustlers—robbers of the range—and they were riding far and fast before an armed party of ranchers whose herds they had plundered.

As they came opposite the mountain creek that made the opening to the little valley, the cavalcade halted.

A big man in a high stetson and short buffalo riding coat, spoke with authority. Smoke could hear every word. He knew the man. He was big Ed Pearson, the detective of the Stock Growers' Association, and he had the authority of a special of the North-West Mounted Police.

"There is a place hereabouts," he said, "where they may have been holding a bunch. I think I lamped them with my glasses farther up the pass, but it won't do to take a chance. Do any of you boys know the way into the draw?"

Apparently none of them did, and the big range rider swore vigorously.

"Fine bunch you are!" he said disgustedly. "You're not on to your own ranges, although you've been in the country since Chief Mountain was a hole in the ground. Anyway, we can't pass it up. Keep moving up the canyon, I'll take a look in here and then follow you. I think I know the way."

Almost before he had finished speaking, he had leaned his

bridle hand on the neck of his powerful horse, and clattered up the draw.

The other men bunched together, and with the intent onward look, which always distinguishes man-hunters proceeded on their way.

Quick as Pearson's decision had been, Smoke was before him into the hidden valley. He crouched at the edge of the timber, and quietly and with infinite precaution ran a shell from the magazine into the chamber of the rifle.

Pearson rode evenly into the amphitheatre, and cast a keen cool eye around. He was a big stout man, but he sat deep in his saddle as if he had been moulded to it. He held the loose ends of his reins long and high in his left hand and guided his horse by almost imperceptible neck pressure. The animal seemed to respond to his lightest movement. On coming into shelter, he had loosened the lower fastenings of his short buffalo coat, and his right hand was resting easily on his hip close to the butt of his pistol.

Smoke watched his every movement intently.

The gloom of a lowering day was rapidly merging into darkness, but there was still sufficient light for Pearson to observe the signs of recent human tenancy. His keen and trained observation soon convinced him that he had struck a recent Indian camp, and he was not out hunting Indians. Furthermore, the Indian signs were a pretty good indication that the white men he was after had not made their hide in that place.

He had turned his horse about and was ready to ride away when he heard a movement in the trees. Instantly he wheeled and froze to stillness. His right hand came away from his hip and the big forty-five was in it.

He listened intently. It was eerie in the silence there. The wind for the moment had died away, and everything was listening. Nothing stirred, and Pearson was about to resume his way under the impression that the movement had been made by a wolf or deer, or some other wild denizen of the wilderness.

At that moment a wind squall whirled through the little glen, making the rocks and tunnels vocal with its crying.

Then clear and unmistakable, out of the heart of the gust, came a thrilling human cry. It started low at first, and seemed to gather with vital agony; then it was cut off as with a mighty effort.

Pearson was brave as men of his kind are but the place, the gloom, and that high quavering note, unlike anything he had ever heard, all combined to make his flesh creep. He waited a moment for something to happen, then, pistol in hand, he sent his spurs home and bounded his horse forward in the direction of the sound.

Smoke crouched in the trees before him. He was the primitive Blackfoot—the wanderer of the wilderness—defending his female in the hour of her agony from approach and intrusion.

Had Pearson understood the situation it is likely that he would have gone on his way. With all his boldness, he was not without a native sense of propriety, and he respected the prejudices of the Indians. As it was, he only knew that a strange human sound had come from the dark recesses of the trees, and he wanted its interpretation. He leaped from his horse, and leaving it standing with outflung reins and drooping head, advanced into the timber.

Smoke knew this big man was like lightning with a gun, so he did not show himself. He cried a warning from his cover in the Blackfoot tongue; but Pearson either did not understand or care, and strode on through the trees. The Indian waited very composedly until his bulky body showed against a patch of waning light, and then shot him through the middle. As he fell, the stricken man fired twice, but his bullets went wide.

As the big stock man lay huddled on the frozen ground Smoke fired two more shots into him. Then he went swiftly in the direction of the horses.

When it was dark, they moved slowly down the watercourse, and took a meagre cattle track down to the plains. Smoke rode ahead leading the pack horse, his rifle in the crook of his arm, the very personification of vigilance. The woman was behind on her single footing pinto with her man child held close from the cold beneath her blanket next her skin.

* * *

The Killing of the Sergeant

Of course the whole country was up at the news of the killing. Ed Pearson had been a person of consequence in the cattle country, and was besides well esteemed and popular.

He was dead and cold when his men found him. They were experienced and could read the signs. No white man's work this, and the killing was attributed to the proper quarter. Smoke had done it; that was all; and the hue and cry was raised.

When the news was brought to Fort MacLeod, the "boot and saddle" rang through the barracks of the Royal North-West Mounted Police. It was near midnight but Sergeant Major Churchill ran though the men's barrack room kicking up the troopers.

In almost less time than it takes to tell, various parties were riding hot foot through the barrack gates.

There was nothing perfunctory about the search. The word of the Commanding Officer had gone forth that Smoke must be taken, alive if possible, but if that could not be done, then dead. Not the youngest trooper of the force thought of doubting it. It was an order to get their man and must be accomplished.

For a day or so Smoke and his family lay hid and the woman gained back her strength. Smoke most of the time stood watch; but sometimes contemplated the child that had come to him amidst these turmoils and alarms.

Then the search came too close and they fared forth again, travelling vast distances in a night to place their pursuers at fault.

The baby had been bedded in a native mossbag, strapped with rawhide thongs to his mother's saddle.

The police were everywhere. Morning would show their

red coats, and the gleam of their weapons on some ridge that rolled up like a giant wave to the mountains; all day they rode the plains and searched each draw and watercourse. Every party had a Blackfoot scout that could follow a cold trail at the lope, and could read like big print the tale of trampled grass or broken twigs.

Still Smoke was not taken, although there were rumours of his presence everywhere. A rancher at Standoff called out by the barking of his dogs, had seen a shadowy horseman thunder past at the gallop, and in the stream of light from the open door was certain he recognized the buckskin. He saddled up and brought his news to the barracks at Fort MacLeod but in a few hours came the story of a Mormon's wife at Lee's Creek fifty miles away, who had seen the strange company of three pass silently along the trail at the corner of the corral. She was not mistaken. She had gone out in the night to minister to a sick animal and was standing in the stable door with her lantern when that weird procession went by.

She was afraid; but they never looked at her; just passed on like dark mysterious things of the night. Smoke, as always, rode in advance with the rifle; his wife led the pack horse; and the child slept in the moss bag at the saddle horn.

The weather kept them out of the mountains, where there was game; and now the remains of many a good steer began to be found on the range. The hand of civilization was against the Indian, and its goods were fair spoil.

Once the police almost had him. A small patrol was crossing the St. Mary's River opposite a little peninsula, that covered with tangled bush merged its landward side in several ravines coming down from the cut banks. They were halted by a rifle bullet from this lurking place. They took cover and opened fire, but they had no mark to shoot at and it is not likely they did any damage. A bullet from the ambush killed a police horse and ripped the strap from the shoulder of the officer in command of the party.

At length after drawing no more fire they rushed the place, but found nothing except the remains of a camp.

153

The officer in command at MacLeod swore long and bitterly at them for a tenderfoot bunch. Ottawa and Regina were aroused and bitter telegrams were keeping the wires hot. No wonder the unfortunate man stormed. One Indian with a squaw and baby was defying the whole force.

After this it became known that Smoke was riding on some solitary raids. He must have found a safe hiding place for his woman and child.

Sergeant Major Churchill of the North-West Mounted Police was one of these splendid specimens of manhood who have made that wonderful force famous. He stood six foot one in his bare feet, was lean and wide and as straight as a dart. He was a time expired Life Guards man, whom the Commissioner had brought with him from England; and he wore the blue ribbon of Egypt. For the rest he was good looking and debonair and all the girls at Fort MacLeod were proud to have him for a partner at the monthly dances at the barracks.

Like so many men of the force he had its honour at heart and he made up his mind that Smoke was to be captured. He picked two or three of the best troopers and a Peigan half-breed who acted as scout and incessantly scoured the country.

One late afternoon the party was rather perfunctorily beating up the sides of a dry watercourse. They had experienced a long day following up rumours that led to nothing and were saddle galled and weary.

Suddenly a long moving shadow flickered across the side hill, and the thrush, thrush of a horse's feet in the withered grass told them that they had flushed their game unawares.

In an instant in response to quirt and spur the horses of the police party bounded forward in pursuit. As the big broncho of the Sergeant took the lead, and he settled down in the saddle he shouted:

"Take no chances, boys, shoot on range."

But Smoke had got a good start, and when they reached the summit of the draw, he was a quarter of a mile away lying low on the buckskin and urging him with drumming heels. Steadily the fine horse of the sergeant carried him away from his companions and drew up on the fugitive.

Smoke rode very quietly and did not seem to have any fear. Once, when Churchill was drawing close to him, he cast that wary look over his shoulder peculiar to plains Indians and coyotes, but gave no sign of perturbation. The rest of the party had fallen hopelessly to the rear, but they were witnesses of what followed.

Smoke was racing up a long acclivity when the sergeant closed in upon him. He called to the fugitive but got no response, and those following saw him reach out and try to seize the Indian by his long hair. Smoke simply moved his carbine with the muzzle backwards into the crook of his left arm and pulled the trigger. Then the two men continued to gallop side by side so fast that the little curl of smoke from the shot remained in the rear. In a minute the sergeant's horse pulled ahead; he swayed in his seat and fell to the ground, his horse leaping sideways as he cleared the saddle. Instantly Smoke stopped the buckskin and dismounted. He approached the figure of the policeman, which lay face down in a queer hunched up heap, and fired a shot into his back. It made a little round hole and soon the blood oozed out and spread on the tunic like red ink on blotting paper.

Without haste Smoke caught the dead man's horse (there was a fine Lee–Metford carbine in its scabbard under the stirrup), unbuckled the bandolier of cartridges; adjusted it to his own body; and, leaping to the saddle, galloped out of sight, unmindful of the bullets from the police party which were pecking at the prairie all about him. He was pretty safe, however, for Winchester carbines of the old police model do not make very good practice at five hundred yards.

Now, indeed, were the police aroused. Almost every daily paper in Canada told of the tragedy, and carried double column pictures of the dead man. Headquarters was furious and the officer in command at Fort MacLeod was harried until he nearly went mad. A lone Indian was holding at bay one of the most important detachments of the most famous constabulary corps in the world. It was incredible, unthinkable, impossible. Yet nevertheless it was a fact.

The best frontiersmen of the force were summoned to Fort

MacLeod to aid in the chase, and men from the detachments at Calgary, Edmonton, Regina and Prince Albert arrived by every train. The prairie was combed but the fugitive was on his native plains, and they couldn't catch him. Rumours led them everywhere. He had been seen in the next valley; a steer was killed just over that hill, but he was never there when the police arrived. He became a phantom to them a sort of prairie "Flying Dutchman," with no real presence, only a very real capacity for dealing death.

For a time it was easy for the Indian scouts to follow the trail of the iron shod police horse and Smoke covered incredible distances. It was, however, not difficult to get fresh mounts, for there were plenty of good horses on the range and Smoke was familiar with the use of a lariat. He rode the sergeant's horse to a standstill, and then abandoned it, apparently getting away on a fresh one he had picked up on the prairie. The police found it foundered, and spent, with the sweat still wet; but there was no sign of the rider.

At this stage the Indian Agent took a hand. He was a shrewd Scotchman, who understood his people and who had a remarkable reputation amongst them for fair dealing.

It was plain to him that Smoke was receiving aid and comfort from some of the Indian folks. He instituted careful inquiries, and, although he learned nothing directly of the fugitive, he discovered that a woman answering the description of Smoke's wife with a baby, had been seen at the lodge of an Indian who was related to the fugitive.

One day he drove over to this man's place, and invited him to accompany him to MacLeod. When he arrived there he told him that he knew that he had been helping Smoke. The Blackfoot denied the charge vigorously.

"All right," said the agent, "then I am going to put you in jail until he is captured, or you tell me all about him."

The Indian was vehement in his protestation but he was promptly locked up.

Now confinement to a Blackfoot is worse than death. An Indian who will face danger without a tremor will break down at the sight of prison walls.

After two weeks of the guardroom this man sent for the agent and told him if he would only let him free he would unburden his soul to him.

He said that Smoke had been at his home; and so had his wife and child.

"I only gave him food and shelter; it is the law of our people from the ancient time," he said piteously. "He was of my father's folk, what else could I do?"

"I have a good mind to send you to jail for the rest of your life," said the agent, "but you have been a pretty good Indian, and I will let you go back home if you do what I tell you. You are to remain quietly at your place and tell no one what I say to you. Then when Smoke comes, as come he will now that winter is here you are to seize and hold him and send for me or the police."

The Indian was not very sanguine about his ability to capture an armed man who had already three killings to his score, but he promised he would do his best.

*   *   *

The End of the Tragedy

And so it befell that Smoke was taken, not by the police, whom he baffled so long, but by his own people.

A fall of snow had come, tracks were easy to follow, and he was kept incessantly on the move. He traveled incredible distances. At nightfall there were traces of him at one place; in the first glimmers of dawn he was sixty miles away. The police rode relays, sweating and sweating, and foundering their horses; but he fled from place to place as immaterial as a shadow.

Perhaps, however they pressed him harder than they knew.

One night when it was very cold and windy, and the drift was covering up all tracks in the snow, he walked into the house of his kinsman, who had been in jail at MacLeod.

There were several Indians around the open fire and the embers glowed with friendly warmth, making a deep tinge on those impassive faces.

He came as if he were amongst friends, and put the carbine of the dead sergeant against the wall. He was cold and pressed close to the fire, and not a word was passed. He was a poor wrecked figure of a man. His face and upper body was thin and emaciated; but his lower limbs were swollen from long ridings. Some one brought him food, and he ate but sparingly, standing up and turning himself about to the fire.

"I will rest here awhile," he said.

A blanket was brought and he lay down on it, beside the hearth. He was far spent and never looked towards his rifle.

At first he found it difficult to lie from the pain in his body, but at last he slept.

There was no light except from the fire in that place, and the impassive heads and faces of the watching Indians gleamed with a rich dullness.

They looked silently on the sleeping figure for awhile, and then with one accord they seized and bound him with rawhide ropes. He was very weak and did not struggle. They were surprised that one who had done so much should not be stronger. They fastened him very tightly and the cords hurt his poor tortured limbs.

After he was secured he lay very still, whilst an Indian rode to carry the news to the agent. I think if the ropes had not hurt him so much that he—even he, wild wanderer of the plains that he was—was glad he was now at rest.

When the agent came he ordered that his bonds be eased. Smoke asked what they would do to his woman and child.

"Nothing" said the agent, "they will be given a place on the Reserve, and food and treaty money, but you will be punished for what you have done against the law of the Queen."

Smoke was manifestly relieved, and whilst they were waiting for the police, asked for tobacco, and smoked with much satisfaction. He gave directions to the Indian agent where to find his wife and child, and asked that he might see them before he died. Compliance with his request was promised.

He was far gone with suffering, and it was considered advisable to have a doctor attend to his limbs before he was removed.

The trial was hurried on. There was no doubt of his guilt, but the law in its majesty had to be served, and an example to be made for the edification of the Indians who had been growing excited and restless as the news of his exploits were told in the lodges and around the camp fires.

It was all rather mysterious to him. He had become a weak, sick old man. His long winter rides had given rise to an affliction of the lower limbs that was very painful, but he never complained. He knew that he had to die, and he was mildly curious about the law of the white man. He had only killed to protect his woman, and when he was attacked. It was all so strange.

He was sentenced to death, with much circumstance, and he was so weak that he had to be supported by two troopers to listen to what the judge had to say.

At the last he was sinking rapidly, and efforts were made to keep him alive for execution so that the warning might not be lost on his kindred.

The morning he was to die his wife and child were brought in to see him. He lay, a feeble old man, on a pallet bed, and there seemed something monstrous and cruel in invoking all that circumstance to take a life that hung by such a feeble thread. He spoke little to the woman, but seemed well content. She looked very proud, and held her child close.

He could not walk, and had to be carried to the gallows, but he suffered from infirmity, not fear; I do not think he knew what fear meant.

He was hanged very effectively to the edification of a number of Indians brought from the reserve to learn a potent lesson. I think he cared less about the process than anyone else present.

The Gold Rush
and the
North

Routine Patrol

by James B. Hendryx

It is ironic that "Routine Patrol" should have been published in a book called Great Tales of the American West, *ed.* Harry E. Maule (*New York: Modern Library, 1945*). *It is set in the Yukon, and while some of the American "stampeders" may have started out believing the Klondike was on U.S. soil, the gold fields were one area in which Mounted Police law decisively asserted itself over the loose assortment of miners' committees which threatened to impose a kind of ad hoc frontier justice on the Klondike. The Mounties' enforcement of peace, order, and good government, under the direction of (who else?) Sam Steele, remains one of the most remarkable achievements in the history of the Force. Hendryx was another of the most prolific writers of Mounted Police fiction from the 1920s to the 1950s, and in this story the commonplaces of northern life are especially vivid and convincing. The history of the Klondike can be found in Sam Steele,* Forty Years in Canada (*1915; rpt.* Toronto: Coles, 1973), Morris Zaslow, The Opening of the Canadian North, 1870-1914 (*Toronto: McClelland and Stewart, 1971*), *and Pierre Berton,* Klondike: The Last Great Gold Rush, 1896-1899 (*Toronto: McClelland and Stewart, 1972*). Hendryx *published a series of stories about Corporal Downey in the North, including* At the Foot of the Rainbow (*New York: Putnams, 1924*), Blood on the Yukon Trail (*Toronto: Doubleday Doran and Grundy, 1930*), Outlaws of Halfaday

Creek (*Garden City: Doubleday Doran, 1935*), and others too numerous to mention.

Corporal Downey, ace of the North-West Mounted Police non-coms in the Yukon, glanced uneasily at the glittering, distorted sun, low-hung in the sky to the southward. There was an unfamiliar, unreal look to it; and an unnatural feel to the dead, still air. Before him stretched the unending windings of the river, flanked to the northward by high sparsely timbered hills, and to the southward by flat tundra and low rolling prairie, even more sparsely timbered.

At late sunrise the wind had died and it had grown steadily colder. For two days past his Government map had been useless, vague dottings showing the supposed course of the river. His working map, hand-drawn in Dawson by a breed who had helped Stan Braddock pack his stock of trade goods and liquor to the new camp of Good Luck, had been doubted at Selkirk. Two men who professed to have been to Good Luck insisted that the breed had located the camp on the wrong branch of the Pelly. They drew Downey a new map. Another argued that the breed's map might be right, but doubted that anyone could cover the ground in eight days even on the hard, wind-packed snow. An old Indian, who had trapped the country to the eastward a dozen years before, drew a crude map that coincided with neither of the others. In disgust Downey had pulled out of Selkirk, leaving those knowing ones wrangling among themselves.

The dogs slowed. Even Topek, the lead dog, was traveling listlessly, his muzzle low to the unbroken snow. Tight-curled tails had lost their gimp, and breath plumes frosted shaggy coats. Downey, himself, was conscious of a growing lassitude. He swore unconvincingly at the dogs, but the long-lashed whip remained coiled in his mittened hand, and the dogs paid no heed.

Somewhere on the heights to the left a tree exploded with the frost. Again Downey glanced across the rolling prairie toward the sun. White specks danced before his eyes—specks that resolved themselves into false suns that danced their silent mockery in the ice-green sky above the cold dead waste of snow.

In a dull, detached way, he estimated that it was one o'clock. The conclusion seemed of no importance, and of no importance seemed the slow pace of the dogs as he walked on and on behind the sled. Vaguely his mind reverted to his maps—the breed's map, and the others. He shivered with a chill not born of the cold—for he realized that, to his dulled senses, the maps, too, seemed of no importance. Pulling himself together with an effort, he cracked his whip and swore loudly at the dogs. His voice sounded curiously flat and unfamiliar, and the animals plodded on without increasing their pace, proud tails at half-cock. Downey, too, plodded on without bothering to coil his whip, the long walrus lash dragging behind him, his eyes on the unbroken snow that covered the river ice. Since leaving Selkirk he had seen no tracks. No moose, nor caribou —not even a wolf nor a fox had crossed the river. And this fact, too, seemed of no importance even though he was low on meat—for himself, and for his dogs. Tonight they would get the last of the frozen fish—then no more till Good Luck. Perhaps they would never reach Good Luck. The matter seemed of no importance beyond being a good joke on the dogs. Downey realized that he was chuckling inanely.

The lopsided, brassy sun touched the horizon and as the officer looked, the false suns leaped and danced—a dance of hideous mockery on the rim of the frozen world. "I've heard of it," he mumbled, striving to control his brain—"the white death—it comes in the strong cold—but it ain't the cold—the air goes dead, or somethin'—some of the old timers claim it's a lie—but others claim a man dies or goes crazy.... Well, if a man goes crazy, or dies, what the hell?" A delicious lassitude permeated his brain—a pleasant, warming numbness— and he slogged on.

The leader swung abruptly from the river and headed up a small feeder that emerged from a notch in the hills. "Hey, you, Topek! Gee, Topek, gee!" But the leader paid no slightest heed to the command, and Downey grasped the tail-rope as the superb brute threw his weight into the collar, tightening the traces. By his very strength and power he dragged his lagging team mates into a faster pace. "Whoa, Topek! Down! Damn you—down!"

Ignoring the command, the big dog plunged on, head up, ears cocked expectantly ahead. Tightening his grip on the tail-rope, the officer followed. He glanced over his shoulder toward the southward. The brief March sun had set. No false suns danced crazily before his eyes—only long plumes of blue-green light were visible, radiating from a bright spot on the horizon to the zenith above his head. His glance shifted to Topek. Topek, the best lead dog in the police service, deserting the trail! Ignoring commands! What did it mean? Downey heard his own voice babbling foolishly: "Gone crazy—crazy with the white death—dogs and men both—they go crazy or die, if they don't camp. Or, maybe Topek knows a new trail—no one else knows this damn country—maybe Topek knows. Might as well die up one crick as another. Hi, Topek —mush!"

The high hills closed in abruptly, shutting out the weird light of the blue-green plumes. Naked rock walls rose sheer to jagged rims outlined high above against the sky. The canyon, a mere cleft in the living rock, was scarce fifty feet from wall to wall. The new snow was softer, here—protected from the sweep of the wind by the high walls. Dully Downey realized that, despite the shifty footing, and the increased drag of the sled in the softer snow, the pace was fast. Drooping tails once more curled over shaggy backs as each dog threw his weight into the collar. Gone was the languor that had marked the brief daylight hours of travel. It was as though Topek had inspired his team—was inspiring Corporal Downey, too. Slowly, but consciously, as one awakening from a horrible dream, the officer realized that the dangerous brain lethargy that had gripped him on the river was losing its hold. He shook his head to clear it of the last remnant of fogginess, and his voice rang sharp and hard through the narrow corridor as he shouted words of encouragement to the dogs.

One mile—two—and the canyon suddenly widened to a

hundred yards and terminated abruptly in a dead end—a sheer rock wall at the base of which stood a grove of stunted spruce.

"Fire-wood, anyway," the officer muttered, as he glanced about him in the semi-darkness. Topek headed straight for the copse and disappeared, his team mates following, pulling the sled which came to a halt partially within the timber a few yards from where Downey stood. Rumbling, throaty growls issued from the copse, and the officer hurried forward to see the huge lead dog, his muzzle low against the door of a small pole-and-mud cabin, lips curled back to expose gleaming white fangs as growl after growl issued from the depths of the mighty chest.

Making his way around the sled, Downey was about to speak to the dog when the great brute settled back on his haunches, pointed his sharp muzzle to the sky, and howled. Loud and eerie the ululation rose until as if at a signal, each of the other six dogs of the team followed the example of their leader until the horrid cacophony rolled and reverberated in an all-engulfing hullabaloo of strident noise. Then, as suddenly as it had begun, the deafening hubbub ceased, and at a word of command, the dogs sank onto their bellies, reaching out here and there to snap up mouthfuls of snow.

For some moments the officer stood peering into the gathering darkness. A neatly piled rank of firewood, an ax standing against the wall beside the door, a pair of snowshoes hanging from a peg driven into the wall all spoke of occupany. Yet—not a track was to be seen. No one had passed in or out of the cabin since the latest fall of snow.

Pulling the thong that raised the crude wooden latch bar, Downey pushed the door open and stepped into the absolute blackness of the room. Shaking off a mitten, he shuddered slightly as he groped in his pocket for a match—the interior seemed colder even than the outside air, seemed fraught with a deadly chill that struck to the very marrow of his bones. Closing the door, he scratched the match upon its inner surface, and as the light flared up he started back in horror at sight of the dead man who lay upon his back in the middle of

have been inflicted by a pistol held in the man's right hand. Blood had flowed from it, trickling down just in front of the ear, and had dripped from the stained white beard, freezing as it fell, to form a tiny red pyramid, or inverted cone upon the floor. "Done it when the strong cold was on," Downey muttered, "or that blood wouldn't have froze as it dripped. But not this spell of the strong cold. He hasn't left the shack since the last snow—an' that must be a week, or more."

Picking up the revolver, he noted that it was of .41 caliber, and that it held five loaded cartridges and an empty shell. "Funny he'd shoot himself with plenty of grub on hand, an' enough giant, an' caps, an' fuse to last him quite a while," he mused aloud, as is the wont of lone men. "Might be he got just one disappointment too many. But them old timers is used to disappointments. They've got a sort of hopelessly hopeful faith that they'll hit it next week, er next month, er next year. It's what keeps 'em goin'—that faith in the mother lode."

Clearing a space along the wall near the stove, Downey stooped to lift the corpse. As he raised the outflung right arm from the floor a low exclamation escaped his lips. He lowered the body, and for long moments knelt there—staring. For, gripped between the thumb and finger of that iron-hard right hand was an unlighted match! "A man can't shoot himself in the right temple with a gun held in his left hand," he murmured slowly. "An' he can't hold a gun in his right hand— when that hand is grippin' a match." His glance strayed to the face of the corpse, and he started nervously. For, as a drop of grease guttered down the length of the candle, the flame flared, and in the flickering light the frozen left eye seemed to wink knowingly. The officer grinned into the glassily staring eyes. "I get you, old timer," he said. "You sure put it acrost— what you wanted to tell me. This ain't suicide—it's murder!"

Arranging the body close against the wall, Downey turned his attention to a more minute examination of the room. An hour later he fried the caribou steaks, seated himself at the table, and devoured a hearty meal. "Things had a wrong look, in the first place," he mused. "What with a revolver, an' no extry shells for it. An' some rifle shells on the shelf, an' no rifle.

An' that pair of mukluks—one all covered with dust, an' the other without no dust on it to speak of. But I guess, now, I've got the picture—someone comes along, an' the old timer invites him in. He lays his fire, an' just as he's about to light it, the other shoves the revolver almost against his head an' pulls the trigger. Then he makes a quick search an' finds the old man's cache of gold in one of them mukluks—the one without the dust. There'd be seven pokes of it, accordin' to that caribou hide—maybe eight, ten thousand dollars. Then he beat it without lightin' the fire. He wasn't takin' no chances in bein' caught in this box canyon if someone should come along. A man can't never tell what he's goin' to run up against on one of these routine patrols."

In the morning Downey inventoried the old man's effects, lifted his body to the bunk and covered it with a blanket, requisitioned a quarter of caribou meat to augment his meager supply of dog food, and struck off down the canyon. The strong cold persisted, but the curious dead feel was gone from the air, and the dogs bent to their work with a will. Later in the day a light breeze sprang up and the temperature moderated considerably.

On the third day thereafter the outfit pulled into the camp of Good Luck, situated at the precise location the breed had indicated on his map. Stepping into Stan Braddock's saloon, Downey was greeted by Old Bettles and Camillo Bill, two sourdoughs who had thrown in with the Good Luck stampede.

"Hello, Downey!" cried Bettles, "yer just in time to have one on me! What in hell fetches you up to Good Luck? So fer, we've got along fine without no police."

Corporal Downey winked at Camillo Bill as he filled the glass Stan Braddock spun toward him with professional accuracy. "The inspector sent me up here to see why two able-bodied men would be hangin' around a saloon in the daytime, instead of workin' their claim," he replied.

"Well, ain't a man got a right to celebrate his birthday?" grinned the oldster.

Camillo Bill laughed: "Bettles, he celebrates his birthday every month."

171

"Shore I do! Every month except Feb'ry. Why wouldn't I? It was a damn important day fer me. I was born on the thirtieth —so every time the thirtieth comes around, I celebrate. What I claim—a man overlooks a lot of bets if he don't celebrate his birthday only onct a year."

"Guess that's right," Downey agreed. "How's things goin'?"

"Oh, not so bad. Good Luck ain't no Bonanza nor Hunker. But she's a damn sight better'n a lot of other cricks men are stickin' to. Most of the boys's takin' out a lot better'n wages."

"Heard any complaints? Any cache robbin', or claim jumpin' goin' on?"

Stan Braddock shook his head: "Nope. Here it is damn near April, an' we've gone through the winter without no crime that anyone knows of—an' I'd have heard it in here, if anythin' out of the way had be'n goin' on. Some of the boys is in here every night."

"They's be'n three deaths," supplemented Bettles, "but they was all of 'em common ones. A rock squushed one fella where it fell on him, an' the other two died of some sickness they got. There ain't no doctor in camp, but we figger it was their guts went back on 'em, er mebbe their heart. We buried 'em decent, an' saved their names an' their stuff fer the public administrator. Two of 'em didn't have much, but one done pretty well fer hisself. It's all in Stan's safe, there—he'll turn it over to you."

"How many men do you figure wintered in Good Luck?"

"Couple hundred wouldn't miss it far," Braddock replied.

"Mostly chechakos, I s'pose."

"Yeah," said Camillo Bill, "Good Luck's jest like all the other camps. What with the damn chechakos crowdin' into the country, it's gittin' so us old timers can't hardly git enough of us together no more fer a decent stud game."

"Speakin' of old timers," said Downey, casually, "who's the old fella that located in a box canyon about three days back down the river?"

"He must mean old Tom Whipple," Bettles opined. "This here canyon runs in from the north, an' dead ends a couple of mile up, don't it?"

172

"That's the one."

"Yeah, that's old Tom. He's kinda batty—like all them hard-rock men—allus huntin' the mother lode. I know'd Tom first, must be fifteen, sixteen year ago—on Birch Crick, over on the American side. He wouldn't pay no 'tention to the placer stuff in the crick beds. Stuck to the hard rock—shootin' an peckin'—peckin' an' shootin'—pryin' a little flake gold out of his samples with the p'int of his belt knife. He passed up all the good cricks—Forty Mile—Bonanza—Hunker—Dominion. We tried to git him to quit foolin' around amongst the rocks an' git in on some of the cricks—but it wasn't no use. He was old, then—too old, I guess, to learn him new tricks. He'd look at us like we didn't have all our buttons—like he was kinda takin' pity on us, er somethin'. 'That damn stuff in the crick beds ain't worth nothing but float,' he'd say. 'I wouldn't fool away my time on it. It's all got to come from the mother lode. Find the mother lode—that's where the gold is,' he'd tell us. 'An' the mother lode's in the hills—not in the crick beds.'

"There can't no one claim old Tom ain't got faith. He stuck to his idee when we was pannin' out two, three dollars to the pan on Birch Crick, an' up to seven, eight dollars on Forty Mile, an' then twenty an' a hundred on Bonanza. He watched us gittin' rich right in under his nose—but he wouldn't fool with it. An' he's stickin' to the same idee yet, up on the head of that canyon."

"A damn sight more faith than sense—that's what he's got, if you ask me," opined Camillo Bill. "Gold's where you find it, whether it's in the cricks, er on the hills."

"Didn't he ever make a strike," Downey asked.

Bettles shook his head: "Nope. Jest keeps on shootin' down rock, an' peckin' with his pick, an' pryin' with his knife. Don't cost him nothin' much to live. Never has nothin' to do with wimmin er licker—never blow'd an ounce in his life. Beans, an' tea, an' flour, an' sugar—a little chawin' terbacer, an' ca'tridges fer that old rifle of his—that's all he needs."

"But, keepin' at it long as he has, an' not spendin' no more'n what he spends, he'd be bound to have some dust cached away somewheres, wouldn't he?"

173

"Oh, chances is, he's got some—prob'ly enough to keep him the rest of his life, when he gits too old to fight the rocks. I doubt an' he kin show ten thousan' in dust fer God knows how many years he's worked."

"You spoke of an old rifle," said Downey. "Would you know that gun if you saw it?"

"Shore, I'd know it. So would Camillo, here, an' Moosehide Charlie, an' Swiftwater Bill. It's a Marlin. He bust the stock, one time on Birch Crick, an' we wired it up fer him with some wire we ontwisted out of a chunk of cable. But—what you so int'rested in old Tom Whipple fer?"

"Didn't own a revolver that you know of?" persisted Downey, ignoring the question. "A forty-one calibre six-gun?"

"Hell, no! What would old Tom be doin' with a revolver? He allus travelled light. I seen him 'long about Christmas. Come up here draggin' a hand-sled after a load of grub an' giant. I kidded him about not havin' no dogs, an' he claimed it cost too much to feed 'em, an' he didn't need none. Claimed he sold off all his dogs two year back, when he located where he's at. There wasn't no Good Luck then—Tom had the country all to hisself. Claimed he's right up agin the mother lode, this time, an' would never have to make another move. Told me he'd be into it, come spring, fer shore—an' then he'd show us what damn fools we was fer muckin' around in the gravel. Pore old cuss—he'll keep on huntin' the mother lode till the last day he kin stand on his legs—an' allus it'll be jest ahead of him. If he'd throw'd in on the stampedes, like we done, he could of had as much dust as the best of us—more, 'cause he's a hard worker, an' he don't never spend nothin'. It's too damn bad. A fella with faith like that ort to win."

Stan Braddock smiled, and set out a fresh bottle. "I don't look at it that way, Bettles," he said, as the glasses were filled. "A man like that wouldn't never be satisfied with placer gold— no matter how much he took out. He'd always figure he was a fool fer passin' up the mother lode. An' what good would a lot of dust do him, anyhow—livin' like he does? I'm telling you, he's a damn sight happier'n the most of us. He's got enough to keep him, an' he's got his faith—an' he'll have it till he dies. If a man knows he's goin' to be the richest man in the world next week, er next month, er next year, he's bound to be happy. What happens to him in the meantime don't matter. Ain't that so, Corporal?"

Corporal Downey nodded slowly, as he toyed with his glass on the bar: "Yes," he said, "I guess maybe yer right."

Men began to drift into the saloon, and Braddock became busy with bottles and glasses. The officer turned to Bettles: "This last snow—when did it come?"

"'Bout a week ago. It snowed fer two days."

"An' before that you'd had a spell of the strong cold?"

"I'll tell the world we did! Worst I ever seen. She hit fifty below fer twelve days, hand runnin'." He paused and indicated a man who had just entered and was limping painfully to the bar. "There's a bird kin tell you more about it than me. It ketched him comin' in—froze all his toes an' one of his heels. He's in a hell of a shape, without no doctor in camp. Them toes had ort to come off."

"Chechako?"

"Yeah—rawer'n hell. Claims he come in over the White Pass an' split off from his pals at Selkirk, when he heard about this strike."

Corporal Downey regarded the man intently as he hobbled to the bar and elevated a clumsily swathed foot to the rail. He was a large man, unprepossessing and ill-kempt, with a month's growth of beard. He called for whiskey without inviting others to join him, and when Braddock set out the bottle, he filled his glass to the brim and emptied it at a gulp. He repeated the performance and tossed a pouch to the bar.

"He ain't be'n able to do much work since he got here, has he?" Downey asked. "Ain't taken out much dust?"

"Hell, no!" Camillo Bill replied. "He moved into Bill Davis's shack—it was Bill got squushed by the rock. Me an' Bettles went down there yesterday to see if we could do somethin' fer him, an' the stink in there was somethin' fierce. Them toes of his has started to rot. We offered to cut 'em off fer him— but the damn fool wouldn't let us. By God, if they was my toes they'd come off—if I had to do it myself with an ax! But,

175

that's the way with a damn chechako. They don't know nothin'
—an' never will. He cussed the hell out of us when we told
him he'd be dead in a month with the blood pizen."

Corporal Downey watched Stan Braddock pick up the
sack the man had tossed onto the bar and shake a few yellow
flakes of gold into the scales. "Kind of queer, ain't it?" he
observed, "that a chechako jest in over the pass an' not in shape
to take out any dust after he got here, should be spendin' dust?"

Old Bettles looked up quickly. "Why—why—shore it is!"
he agreed.

"Damn if it ain't," said Camillo Bill. "Where would he git it?"

"I believe," replied Downey, "that I know."

The man had turned from the bar and hobbled to a chair
on the opposite side of the room as Downey slipped to the
scales just as Braddock lifted the little pan to transfer the gold
to the till. He thrust out his hand, palm up. "Pour it in there,
Braddock. I want to have a look at it," he ordered, and when
the man complied, he returned to where Bettles and Camillo
Bill waited under one of the big swinging lamps. Eagerly, the
three examined the yellow grains, as the officer prodded them
about with a forefinger. "Ever see any stuff like it?" he asked,
abruptly.

"Them flakes is sort of sharp edged," ventured Camillo Bill.
"They don't show no water wear."

"That," replied Downey, "is because they didn't come out
of a crick bed. They was pried out of rock samples—with
the point of a belt knife, maybe."

"You mean!" exclaimed Bettles, his eyes suddenly widening,
"that—"

The officer silenced him with a wink, and a glance toward
the chechako who sat sprawled in his chair, his eyes on his
bandaged foot. "Yeah," he replied, in an undertone. "Old Tom
Whipple was murdered an' robbed in his cabin in that box
canyon. It happened durin' the last spell of the strong cold—
there was no tracks in the new snow. Whoever done it stole
Whipple's dust, an' his rifle. The three of us'll jest sift down
to this chechako's shack, now. Besides, Whipple's old rifle
I think we'll find his dust, in caribou-hide sacks—six of 'em,

besides the one the chechako's packin' on him. An' when we rip 'em apart, I think we'll find that the pieces was cut out of a hide I fetched along out of Whipple's shack. We'd ort to find some forty-one-caliber revolver ammunition, too. Forty-ones ain't common. It's the gun the murderer left to make it look like Whipple killed himself. When we find them things, I'll arrest that bird—an' I'll have enough evidence to hang him higher than hell."

"It'll be all right with me," growled Camillo Bill, as the three stepped out onto the hard-packed snow, "if we can't find no evidence whatever in his shack. Hangin's too good fer a damn cuss that would murder old Tom Whipple—which Tom had prob'ly took him in to save him from the strong cold. I'd ruther see him left here to rot from his toes clean up to his chin!"

"How come you turned up that canyon, if there wasn't no tracks in the snow?" queried Bettles, as Downey spoke to his dogs who had lain down in the harness, wrapped snugly in their bushy tails.

"That was pure accident," the officer replied. "The air had gone dead. There was a peculiar feel to it, an' there was false suns dancin' in the sky. I felt sort of weak an' light headed—like nothin' mattered—an' I guess the dogs felt it, too. Anyhow, my lead dog turned off up this canyon, an' I couldn't head him off. Like I said—nothin' seemed to matter—one crick seemed as good as any other—so I let 'em go."

Old Bettles nodded: "The white death reachin' fer you, eh? Some claim it's a lie—that there ain't no sech thing. But don't you believe 'em, Downey. I know."

"You tellin' me?"

"Where'd you git that lead dog?" the oldster asked, after a moment's pause, his eyes on the great brute who stood alert, awaiting the word of command.

"Down in Dawson, a year ago. Best lead dog in the country. It's funny he'd leave the trail for a side crick."

"Not so damn funny as you think," Bettles replied. "I know that dog. He's Topek. Old Tom Whipple raised him from a pup."

177

The Law versus the Man

from *Steele of the Royal Mounted*
by James Oliver Curwood

This chapter from Curwood's novel is aptly named, because the action raises a crucial question when it brings Philip Steele's private sense of justice into direct opposition with established law. Curwood was an American writer, so of course gives the American answer to the question: men, or at least men of heroic stature, are superior to the law. Curwood wrote at least three novels and numerous short stories about the Force, but his Mounties remain U.S. Marshals in red tunics. The present chapter is not only absorbing adventure narrative; it is a classic of the Americanization of the Mountie. Curwood featured Mounties in a number of his novels, including Steele of the Royal Mounted *(Montreal: Pocketbooks, 1946 [1911]),* Isobel *(New York: Grosset and Dunlap, 1913),* The River's End *(Philadelphia: Blakiston, 1919),* The Flaming Forest *(Toronto: Copp Clark, 1921), and others. There are also Mounties in his short story collection,* Back to Gods Country *(New York: McKinlay, Stone and MacKenzie, 1920), which was the basis for one of the first Canadian feature films.*

Suddenly a great thrill shot through Philip, and for an instant he stood rigid. What was that he saw out in the gray gloom of Arctic desolation, creeping up, up, up, almost black at its beginning, and dying away like a ghostly winding-sheet? A gurgling cry rose in his throat, and he went on, panting now like a broken-winded beast in his excitement. It grew near, blacker, warmer. He fancied that he could feel its heat, which was the new fire of life blazing within him.

He went down between two great drifts into a pit which seemed bottomless. He crawled to the top of the second, using his pulseless hands like sticks in the snow, and at the top something rose from the other side of the drift to meet him.

It was a face, a fierce, bearded face, the gaunt starvation in it hidden by his own blindness. It seemed like the face of an ogre, terrible, threatening, and he knew that it was the face of William DeBar, the seventh brother.

He launched himself forward, and the other launched himself forward, and they met in a struggle which was pathetic in its weakness, and rolled together to the bottom of the drift. Yet the struggle was no less terrible because of that weakness. It was a struggle between two lingering sparks of human life and when these two sparks had flickered and blazed and died down, the two men lay gasping, an arm's reach from each other.

Philip's eyes went to the fire. It was a small fire, burning more brightly as he looked, and he longed to throw himself upon it so that the flames might eat into his flesh. He had mumbled something about police, arrest and murder during the struggle, but DeBar spoke for the first time now.

"You're cold," he said.

"I'm freezing to death," said Philip.

"And I'm—starving."

DeBar rose to his feet. Philip drew himself together, as if expecting an attack, but in place of it DeBar held out a warmly mittened hand.

"You've got to get those clothes off—quick—or you'll die," he said. "Here!"

Mechanically Philip reached up his hand, and DeBar took him to his sledge behind the fire and wrapped about him a thick blanket. Then he drew out a sheath knife and ripped the frozen legs of his trousers up and the sleeves of his coat down, cut the string of his shoe-packs and slit his heavy German socks, and after that he rubbed his feet and legs and arms until Philip began to feel a sting like the prickly bite of nettles.

"Ten minutes more and you'd been gone," said DeBar.

He wrapped a second blanket around Philip and dragged the sledge on which he was lying still nearer to the fire. Then he threw on a fresh armful of dry sticks and from a pocket of his coat drew forth something small and red and frozen, which was the carcass of a bird about the size of a robin. DeBar held it up between his forefinger and thumb, and looking at Philip, the flash of a smile passed for an instant over his grizzled face.

"Dinner," he said, and Philip could not fail to catch the low chuckling note of humor in his voice. "It's a Whisky Jack, man, an he's the first and last living thing I've seen in the way of fowl between here and Fond du Lac. He weighs four ounces if he weighs an ounce, and we'll feast on him shortly. I haven't had a full mouth of grub since day before yesterday morning, but you're welcome to a half of him, if you're hungry enough."

"Where'd your chuck go?" asked Philip.

He was conscious of a new warmth and comfort in his veins, but it was not this that sent a heat into his face at the outlaw's offer. DeBar had saved his life, and now, when DeBar might have killed him, he was offering him food. The man was spitting the bird on the sharpened end of a stick, and when he had done this he pointed to the big Mackenzie hound, tied to the broken stub of a dead sapling.

"I brought enough bannock to carry me to Chippewayan, but he got into it the first night, and what he left was crumbs. You lost yours in the lake, eh?"

"Dogs and everything," said Philip. "Even matches."

"Those ice-traps are bad," said DeBar companionably, slowly turning the bird. "You always want to test the lakes in this country. Most of 'em come from bog springs, and after they freeze, the water drops. Guess you'd had me pretty soon if it hadn't been for the lake, wouldn't you?"

He grinned, and to his own astonishment Philip grinned.

"I was tight after you, Bill."

"Ho! ho! ho!" laughed the outlaw. "That sounds good! I've gone by another name, of course, and that's the first time I've heard my own since—"

He stopped suddenly, and the laugh left his voice and face. "It sounds—homelike," he added more gently. "What's yours, pardner?"

"Steele—Philip Steele, of the R.N.W.M.P.," said Philip.

"Used to know a Steele once," went on DeBar. "That was back—where it happened. He was one of my friends."

For a moment he turned his eyes on Philip. They were deep gray eyes, set well apart in a face that among a hundred others Philip would have picked out for its frankness and courage. He knew that the man before him was not much more than his own age, yet he appeared ten years older.

He sat up on his sledge as DeBar left his bird to thrust sticks into the snow, on the ends of which he hung Philip's frozen garments close to the fire. From the man Philip's eyes traveled to the dog. The hound yawned in the heat and he saw that one of his fangs was gone.

"If you're starving, why don't you kill the dog?" he asked.

DeBar turned quickly, his white teeth gleaming through his beard.

"Because he's the best friend I've got on earth, or next to the best," he said warmly. He's stuck to me through thick and thin for ten years. He starved with me, and fought with me, and half died with me, and he's going to live with me as long as I live. Would you eat the flesh of your brother, Steele? He's my brother—the last that your glorious law has left to me. Would you kill him if you were me?"

Something stuck hard and fast in Philip's throat, and he made no reply. DeBar came toward him with the hot bird on the end of his stick. With his knife the outlaw cut the bird into two equal parts, and one of these parts he cut into quarters. One of the smaller pieces he tossed to the hound, who devoured it at a gulp. The half he stuck on the end of his knife and offered to his companion.

"No," said Philip. "I can't."

The eyes of the two men met, and DeBar, on his knees, slowly settled back, still gazing at the other. In the eyes of one there was understanding, in those of the other stern determination.

"See here," said DeBar, after a moment, "don't be a fool, Steele. Let's forget, for a little while. God knows what's going to happen to both of us to-morrow or next day, and it'll be easier to die with company than alone, won't it? Let's forget that you're the Law and I'm the Man, and that I've killed one or two. We're both in the same boat, and we might as well be a little bit friendly for a few hours, and shake hands, and be at peace when the last minute comes. If we get out of this, and find grub, we'll fight fair and square, and the best man wins. Be square with me, old man, and I'll be square with you, s'elp me God!"

He reached out a hand, gnarled, knotted, covered with callouses and scars, and with a strange sound in his throat Philip caught it tightly in his own.

"I'll be square, Bill!" he cried. "I swear that I'll be square— on those conditions. If we find grub, and live, we'll fight it out —alone—and the best man wins. But I've had food today, and you're starving. Eat that and I'll still be in better condition than you. Eat it, and we'll smoke. Praise God I've got my pipe and tobacco!"

They settled back close in the lee of the drift, and the wind swirled white clouds of snow-mist over their heads, while DeBar ate his bird and Philip smoked. The food that went down DeBar's throat was only a morsel, but it put new life into him, and he gathered fresh armfuls of sticks and sapling boughs until the fire burned Philip's face and his drying clothes sent up clouds of steam. Once, a hundred yards out in the plain, Philip heard the outlaw burst into a snatch of wild forest song as he pulled down a dead stub.

"Seems good to have comp'ny," he said, when he came back with his load. "My God, do you know I've never felt quite like this—so easy and happy like, since years and years? I wonder if it is because I know the end is near?"

"There's still hope," replied Philip.

"Hope!" cried DeBar. "It's more than hope, man. It's a certainty for me—the end, I mean. Don't you see, Phil—" He came and sat down close to the other on the sledge, and spoke as if he had known him for years. "It's got to be the end for me, and I guess that's what makes me cheerful like. I'm going to tell you about it, if you don't mind."

"I don't mind; I want to hear," said Philip, and he edged a little nearer, until they sat shoulder to shoulder.

"It's got to be the end," repeated DeBar, in a low voice. "If we get out of this, and fight, and you win, it'll be because I'm dead, Phil. D'ye understand? I'll be dead when the fight ends, if you win. That'll be one end."

"But if you win, Bill."

A flash of joy shot into DeBar's eyes.

"Then that'll be the other end," he said more softly still. He pointed to the big Mackenzie hound. "I said he was next to my best friend on earth, Phil. The other—is a girl—who lived back there—when it happened, years and years ago. She's thirty now, and she's stuck to me, and prayed for me, and believed in me for—a'most since we were kids together, an' she's written to me—'Frank Symmonds'—once a month for ten years. God bless her heart! That is what's kept me alive, and in every letter she's begged me to let her come to me, wherever I was. But—I guess the devil didn't get quite all of me, for I couldn't, 'n' wouldn't. But I've give in now, and we've fixed it up between us. By this time she's on her way to my brothers in South America, and if I win—when we fight—I'm going where she is. And that's the other end, Phil, so you see why I'm happy. There's sure to be an end of it for me—soon."

He bowed his wild, unshorn head in his mittened hands, and for a time there was silence between them.

Philip broke it, almost in a whisper.

"Why don't you kill me—here—now—while I'm sitting helpless beside you, and you've a knife in your belt?"

DeBar lifted his head slowly and looked with astonishment into his companion's face.

"I'm not a murderer!" he said.

"But you've killed other men," persisted Philip.

"Three, besides those we hung," replied DeBar calmly. "One at Moose Factory, when I tried to help John, and the other two up here. They were like you—hunting me down, and I killed 'em in fair fight. Was that murder? Should I stand

183

by and be shot like an animal just because it's the law that's doing it? Would you?"

He rose without waiting for an answer and felt of the clothes beside the fire.

"Dry enough," he said. "Put 'em on and we'll be hiking."

Philip dressed, and looked at his compass.

"Still north?" he asked. "Chippewayan is south and west."

"North," said DeBar. "I know of a breed who lives on Red Porcupine Creek, which runs into the Slave. If we can find him we'll get grub, and if we don't—"

He laughed openly into the other's face.

"We won't fight," said Philip, understanding him.

"No, we won't fight, but we'll wrap up in the same blankets, and die, with Woonga, there, keeping our backs warm until the last. Eh, Woonga, will you do that?"

He turned cheerily to the dog, and Woonga rose slowly and with unmistakable stiffness of limb, and was fastened in the sledge traces.

They went on through the desolate gloom of afternoon, which in late winter is, above the sixtieth, all but night. Ahead of them there seemed to rise billow upon billow of snow-mountains, which dwarfed themselves into drifted dunes when they approached, and the heaven above them, and the horizon on all sides of them were shut out from their vision by a white mist which was intangible and without substance and yet which rose like a wall before their eyes. It was one chaos of white mingling with another chaos of white, a chaos of white earth smothered and torn by the Arctic wind under a chaos of white sky; and through it all, saplings that one might have twisted and broken over his knee were magnified into giants at a distance of half a hundred paces, and men and dog looked like huge specters moving with bowed heads through a world that was no longer a world of life, but of dead and silent things. And up out of this, after a time, rose DeBar's voice, chanting in tones filled with the savagery of the North, a wild song that was half breed and half French, which the forest men sing in their joy when coming very near to home.

They went on, hour after hour, until day gloom thickened

into night, and night drifted upward to give place to gray dawn, plodding steadily north, resting now and then, fighting each mile of the way to the Red Porcupine against the stinging lashes of the Arctic wind. And through it all was DeBar's voice that rose in encouragement to the dog limping behind him and to the man limping behind the dog—now in song, now in the wild shouting of the sledge-driver, his face thin and gaunt in its starved whiteness, but his eyes alive with a strange fire. And it was DeBar who lifted his mittened hands to the leaden chaos of sky when they came to the frozen streak that was the Red Porcupine, and said, in a voice through which there ran a strange thrill of something deep and mighty, "God in Heaven be praised, this is the end!"

He started into a trot now, and the dog trotted behind him, and behind the dog trotted Philip, wondering, as he had wondered a dozen times before that night, if DeBar were going mad. Five hundred yards down the stream DeBar stopped in his tracks, stared for a moment into the breaking gloom of the shore, and turned to Philip. He spoke in a voice low and trembling, as if overcome for the moment by some strong emotion.

"See—see there!" he whispered. "I've hit it, Philip Steele, and what does it mean? I've come over seventy miles of barren, through night an' storm, an' I've hit Pierre Thoreau's cabin as fair as a shot! Oh man, man, I couldn't do it once in ten thousand times!" He gripped Philip's arm, and his voice rose in excited triumph. "I tell 'ee, it means that—that God—'r something—must be with me!"

"With us," said Philip, staring hard.

"With me," replied DeBar so fiercely that the other started involuntarily. "It's a miracle, an omen, and it means that I'm going to win!" His fingers gripped deeper, and he said more gently, "Phil, I've grown to like you, and if you believe in God as we believe in Him up here—if you believe He tells things in the stars, the winds and things like this, if you're afraid of death—take some grub and go back! I mean it, Phil, for if you stay, an' fight, there is going to be but one end. I will kill you!"

We Generally Don't

from *The Law-Bringers*
by G. B. Lancaster

*"G. B. Lancaster" was actually Edith Lyttleton,
a feminine counterpart of British writers like
R. M. Ballantyne and Roger Pocock who travelled the Empire in search of romantic settings
for their adventure stories. Lyttleton's novels
are set anywhere from Halifax to Tasmania.
The Law-Bringers (New York: Doran, 1913)
takes place in the North, and we know that Miss
Lyttleton did travel at least as far as Peace
River, but her strength is in portraying people
rather than places. Her hero, in the best imperial
tradition, carries the code of the British public
school into the world of snowshoes and sleigh-
dogs, and in "We Generally Don't" he is teach-
ing his young assistant, Kennedy, not only the
lore of the trail, but the sort of behaviour that
befits a gentleman.*

"I guess that'll take him goin' some to figure it out," said Poley
in a pious content.

Kennedy straightened from pulling up the last sled-strap;
breathed heavily on his hands to make them bend sufficiently
to go back into the fur gloves; beat them together, and said:

"Well, *I* guess Dick'll be handin' out trouble to you in a
minit, all right, all right."

Poley peered sulkily over the collar of his mangy bearskin
coat at the snarling knot of giddés in the traces.

"Teach him ter make picters o' me," he said. "Wait till he
starts bossin' that hound a bit. That'll larn him."

The dog-teams at Grey Wolf were drawn from "any kind
o' dog as'll work," and the barrack-teams were Poley's the

full summer through, descending to Tempest and Dick when work began. Poley knew them intimately; mysteriously. He communicated his opinion on the universe and his fellows to them, and last night he had told them—so far as words would go—exactly what he thought of Dick for a certain sketch of himself which was just now circulating Grey Wolf. This morning he had improved the lesson by harnessing one team in wrong order when Dick left the work half-done to go in at Tempest's call; and now he stood with Kennedy, who was over-young for skilled labour, and waited results. Dick came out briskly, pulling on his gloves. He glanced from the tangle of yelping dogs to Poley, and his smile was soft.

"Who treated you at Grange's last night, Poley?" he asked. "For I'll swear you never got as bad as this out of your own pocket."

Because Poley was known to be over-careful of his private purse Kennedy choked with laughter as Dick sprang in among the dogs; cuffing and kicking in a good-humoured savagery such as they loved. The huge short-haired Mackenzie hound was buckled into his rightful place in the lead, where he proclaimed his content with head up. Sharkey, the one husky of the team, backed his vigorously-curled tail against the sled, and along the traces between Dick strung the mongrels, quick and certainly. They stood motionless as Tempest brought the second team round the corner at a run. And then Dick slipped his feet into the snow-shoe thongs.

"Get busy," he said to Kennedy. "Mush, boys. Mush along."

He cracked the long whip once, and at the yard gate he wheeled to send Poley a parting word of cheer.

"I gave Alice another sketch of you last night, Poley," he shouted.

On the lip of the forest Dick sprang ahead to break trail; swinging his weight on alternate feet and jerking up the heel of the long shoe with the kick born of much practice. The new-fallen snow packed in the shoe-lacings and before the runners, and all Dick's endurance and great muscle-power were sternly taxed before he halted, taking heavy breaths through his nostrils, and reached his coat from the sled.

"Get down to it," he said.

Kennedy hesitated. This was his first winter trail, and he was soft.

"Suppose I get cramp, or the snow-shoe heel?" he suggested.

"Suppose you don't," said Dick with meaning, and dropped into place beside the sleds.

This trip promised all the elements that were good for Dick. There was danger, there was unusualness, there was likely to be sufficient bodily discomfort to flog quiet in him the restless passions that grew during stagnation. Early in the fall a handful of men and women had come from the States and up the water-ways, calling themselves a lost tribe of Israel, and thrusting through the wilderness in the certain expectation of finding the land of Canaan at the North Pole. Remembering a recent march of the Doukhobors in "the altogether," when the Mounted Police chased them with underclothing and much tact, Tempest had picked apart this tribe more than once. But always they had drawn together again as an eddy draws straws, drifting north all the while. Yesterday word had come through by the Indian telegraph which flashes from mouth to mouth with curious speed that Abraham, the patriarch of the tribe, was sharpening knives and preparing to offer up some Isaacs to the God who walked the sky in the coloured Northern Lights which were to lead them into Canaan.

It was for Dick to discourage Abraham, and, what would probably be much more difficult, the tribe, and to bring back such members as he thought fit. Privately he sorrowed that the process could not be left to work itself to a legitimate conclusion by means of Abraham's knives; publicly he agreed with Tempest that there might be a big force to contend with; for the wild, hairy father of Israel had that quality which brought men to obey and follow him, and a khaki tunic and a few shiny buttons were not likely to prove of much weight there. But to Kennedy when he asked questions Dick said one thing only.

"When you've lived as long as I have you won't try to jump your fence till you come up right to it—and if you don't limber your ankles you'll get that stiff tendon before you know it."

Kennedy knew it that night when he hobbled in sharp agony through the hour of stern, breathless work, done in the eye and the teeth of the inclosing frost. Both men were red with hot young blood and sweating with labour; both wrenched from the dying day and the living cold every ounce they could get. But dark had shut down and the keen-toothed frost was on them before the tent had been pitched in the clearing shovelled out by the snowshoes, and the big fire lit, and the rawhide lacings, now rigid as iron, beaten and bent from the sledge-covers, and the outfit brought in, and the frozen whitefish, threaded six on a stick, hung in the heat to thaw out for the dogs.

Dick took kettle and frying-pan and got supper, whistling softly, with his shadow treading about him like a giant with its head against the wall of black beyond the fire-circle. On the snowy rim of the circle sat the dogs, slavering, motionless, with savage eyes drawn to pin-points that never left their master. Dick reached for the whitefish, and in a flash the welter of dogs was about him, hunger-mad. Kennedy saw the gleam of white teeth and the red of many eyes against the tall man's shoulder, and he sat still, with a sudden thrill in him that he did not care to name. But Dick beat and kicked and swore unemotionally; doling out the fish to each, and hammering the brutes apart that they might slink aside, each with his own, to bolt it with growling throat and back-looking, suspicious eyes. Then he cast away the whip, and poured the tea.

"That boar-hound is a sure enough devil," he said. "What does Poley call him?"

"Okimow," said Kennedy, continuing to rub liniment into his tendon Achilles.

"Um-m," said Dick. " 'Chief,' is he?" He looked at the hound where it snuffed round the edge of things with long ears flapping. "My lad," he told it, "there isn't going to be but one chief in this outfit, and I guess that is yours truly." And then he looked at Kennedy. "I've shown you how to wrap your feet before," he said. "But I'll swear you've got your instep chafed right now. Let up and have supper. I'll fix you after."

He did, with scrupulous exactness and plain words. For a

189

man's feet on the long trail are of infinitely more value to him than his soul or anything else. Besides, in Kennedy's case, they did not belong to him at all, but to that great organisation of which he was such a very minor part, and all this Dick made clear to him without pity or evasion. Then the fire was rebuilt, huge and glowing, with the night rounding it like a black basin full of blood; and the dogs slunk from dark to light and from light to dark again, restless as a weaver's shuttle, and unsatisfied still.

The men hung their outer clothes around the fire. Then, in their dry rough furs they lay down and slept, forgetful of the frost that was at its stealthy work about them; splitting the sappy trees where their trail would pass; making brittle the steel knives at their belts; stiffening the cover-lacings and the harness, and creeping near to snatch with icy grip at the fire itself.

Twice in the night Dark rose to fling on more wood and to see the Northern Lights chasing across the sky like merry children at play. The long months at Grey Wolf had been bad for Dick. They had cramped him back into the old desires which had been too strong for him all his life. Among men he fell on men's sins instantly, and desired nothing else. But here, with the great call of the unsubdued North-West, whose colours he wore vibrating through all his senses, he paused a moment on the threshold while the stars went by, and the black pines peaked their tops to point where their feet could not follow.

Dick had no desire to follow. He had no wish to be good. But he knew, with a wide-awake, grim amusement, that the delight of bringing a certain man to justice was shortly going to be weighed against the pain of hurting a certain woman.

The North Star that the sailors love swung high in the glittering night. Dick had never kept but one star true all his days, and that was the star of his own wild will. He dropped his eyes and crept back to his skins with their rough, coarse hair and their animal smell. But they were good to Dick, for they were Nature's own way of pulling him back to the verities past all the subtle creeds of yea and nay.

On the fourth night Dick bought more whitefish at a clump of tepees on the rim of a snow-spread lake that ran to the forest lip. He gave in exchange a memorandum-form where, above his scrawled name, he had set this request: "To the Hudson Bay Company. Please pay to Kewasis Eusta the sum of two dollars, and charge to general acct."

That paper would hold good all over the North-West and the old chief knew it, folding it with stiff fingers that yet had not lost cunning at trap and trigger.

"Perhaps I go to Peace River Landing," he said. "And perhaps to St. John. Ne totam goes west?"

Dick's knowledge of Cree would not string a sentence. But his hand-language presently brought him out an interpreter; a middle-aged half-breed with tangled hair lank on his shoulders and mangy skins close to his throat. The whole camp smelt badly; it was poor and desolate, and at Dick's feet a couple of children gnawed together on a last-year's moose-bone dug out of the snow. The breed looked down on them with pride.

"Mine," he said, in the French of the half-breed West. "I have a brother who is un homme blanc."

He explained further than his brother lived in a white-man house "outside" and drank and swore after the manner that white-men use. He clung to that piece of civilisation as Randel clung to his battery-key and Jennifer to her silk portières, and Dick nodded.

"You're belly-pinched, my friend," he said. "And you're old before your time. But you are a happier man than your brother. Your social problems don't keep you awake o' nights, I imagine. Now, tell me what you know of that lost tribe of Israel which has gone up into the Clear Hills to find a picturesque place to sacrifice Isaac in."

What the breed told, Dick afterwards translated to Kennedy in the tent.

"They're camped some place where they expect to make out for the winter. But they can't be hunters, for they have already traded most of their clothing here for food. I'm taking dried moosemeat along, and we can give 'em some skins if they'll

191

wear them. But I'd like to know why nakedness and certain phases of religion go together, and I'd like to know what we're to do with that nursery when we find it."

Kennedy was rubbing his knotted calves where the last hour's cramp had caught him. But three days with Dick had taught him to endure his pains without comment, and the agonising snow-shoe ache was eased since he had learned to grease the instep and properly lace the thongs.

"Will we have to bring all the beggars in?" he demanded.

"The Lord forbid," said Dick, and laughed. "There should be four men and eleven women and six children. But we'll leave that puzzle till we come to it, I think."

On the second afternoon they came to the puzzle, where a crazy knot of branch-made shacks, helped out by slabs of snow, crouched under the flank of a cliff where the spruces brooded with their wide-winged branches, snow-spread, for a roof above all.

"If they last the winter out the first Chinook will drown them," said Dick. Then he called Kennedy forward as the first dog in the camp gave tongue.

"I'm out for Abraham," he said. "But you're to look after his wives, Kennedy—as many of them as you can manage. Leave me the men."

"B-but—what can I do with 'em?" said Kennedy in his nervous youth.

"Anything. Kiss 'em. But keep them off me. Abraham will likely show fight, and I can't be mussed up with other things."

The dogs drew into the camp and dropped panting, each where he stood. But Okimow the hound watched Dick with his red-rimmed, sagging eyes. One night those two had met for victory, even as Poley had predicted, and the dog now gave the man that proud obedience which one lord may yield another. Dick rubbed the wet nose as he passed Okimow.

"Good boy," he said, and strode up to a shapeless muddle of sticks and snow sealed by a wooden door that had once been the floor of a wagon. His knock on the door woke the silent camp as a bee-hive wakes at a kick. Unseen children screamed; a woman ran out of a near-by shack and dived back. More dogs barked, and sound went calling through all the crazy structures where no man appeared to stand against these two who carried their errand in their very tread.

"Saints send that Abraham has offered up himself," said Dick, and burst the door down with his shoulder and went in.

A damp air breathed at him; fetid, and chill and horrible. He struck a match and held it up, looking round. Then his blood suddenly ran slow. The smoke-blackened place was empty, swept naked of all that made it human habitation. And yet human habitation was there, stretched on a piece of sacking at his feet; a still body, small and young, and but partly covered. Dick dropped on his knee with his heart thumping. He struck another match, and sought with swift eyes and fingers. There was no blood; no mark of the knife anywhere at all. And yet the boy lay there very truly as a sacrifice; offered up to the madness of man's beliefs as surely as though he had died by the steel on the wind-swept hill.

Dick stepped out again with his lips close and eyes dangerous. Any little mercy that might have been in him was dead, and he kicked in the brush-and-snow shelters with slight ceremony, unearthing the remaining children and all the women. The women cried, clamouring to Kennedy in an unknown tongue. They were drawn by his fresh cheeks and his young eyes, and Dick laughed, watching.

"Keep your head and keep your temper," he said. I suppose Abraham and the other bucks have gone hunting. We'll wait for them."

Kennedy never forgot that hour when Dick inspected everything in the camp that would bear inspection and much that would not. The children followed him; dark-eyed little shaggy creatures, hopping from one foot to the other to warm their half-clad misery. The women stood apart with sullen mutterings, and their eyes were suspicious under the close-drawn shawls. Dick pushed his investigations through to the bitter end, unembarrassed. Then he came to Kennedy.

"They live like beasts," he said. "But they likely can make out. They have food and warmth. I guess I'll have to pluck the patriarch, though. His doings savour mildly of insanity."

193

He flung up his head, with the listening look in his eyes. "Here they come," he said. "And—Lord, they've got a battle-chant like the South Sea Islanders."

Down the narrow trail that gave to the naked woods four men swung into the clearing with the white spray breaking from their snow-shoes. Moose-meat hung from their shoulders in great lumps; grey coarse stuff, dark with its blood. Two were weedy weaklings who shambled, looking sideways. The third walked like a hunter, with a Winchester crooked in his arm, and his keen eyes glancing. Abraham led, chanting what was probably an Old Testament war-song. His grey beard, stiffened by frost, blew into points over each shoulder; the moose-pelt girded about him, trailed, congealing in bloody lumps of fat. His eyes were wild, the toss of his great arms was wild, and Dick slid the revolver round in his belt, speaking curtly to Kennedy.

"Keep your head *and* your temper. And don't shoot till you know there's no other way."

The Mounted Policeman who brings his prisoner in dead has to suffer for it. Kennedy remembered, with the apple swelling in his throat, as the men neared. His mind was under fire for the first time, and he began to realise that it is possible for a man to do less than make good. He sat down on the sled nervously; stood up again, and heard the hound growl where it lay with muzzle on stretched paws.

Dick walked three steps and saluted; made another step, and the barrel of a second Winchester shone among the folds of the moose-pelt. Kennedy began to feel sick, for he knew that ten-shot automatic rifle, and he saw Dick walk straight up to it with unflinching feet. But then he could not see, as Dick saw, the wavering in those red eyes of insanity. Abraham quivered; swerved; made a break for the woods, and Dick swung like a flash and leapt after him.

"Hold the others," he shouted. And the raw, sappy youth jerked forward his revolver and covered the three with shaking hand and heart that quailed as sound died out in the forest.

It was the first searing in the boy's soul of the claims made on manhood, and he stood alone in the sudden dumb silence, striving to make his face look bold. The two weaklings dropped in the snow. The third stood, holding him eye to eye, and the rifle was flung forward along his wrist. The women whimpered, afraid to scream; but the children crawled up to the hunters, dragging at the raw meat. And out of the forest where the grey of dusk drifted there came no sound.

Kennedy's breath caught in great gulps. An insane man occasionally has the strength of ten, and if that maniac came back alone—something at the back of his head said eternally: "I won't run. By ——, I won't run."

Then he looked down at the hound, straining in the harness. With a gasp of understanding he loosed him, holding the steel menace still, and Okimow shot across the clearing like a brown log launched into space. The grip of numb dread lessened in Kennedy, and he realised that the cold was eating into his bones, and that, in the frosty metallic light, the held-up men looked grey.

By signs he got them moving, and the four took the treadmill trail over the narrow clearing, round after round; the white boy with the blue scared eyes driving the swarthy, shaggy men of alien tongue and breed.

Shivering and complaining the women made fires, and presently the smell of roast moose-flesh stirred Kennedy's vitals until he shut his nostrils against it. And the tension of fear and hunger and weariness grew. It had grown to the edge of hysteria when Dick came back, walking heavily. He was half-stripped in the bitter cold, and he staggered as he swung up his fur artiki from the sled and bisected Kennedy's march.

"Okimow's watching Abraham," he said. "I left him most of my dunnage. Get those men over to the fires and feed. Sharp! We've got to go after him."

Kennedy asked one question as his teeth met in the smoking meat.

"Did Okimow help any?" he said. And Dick answered, sitting with Abraham's rifle across his knees:

"Just about saved my life, I guess."

That was all that Kennedy ever knew in words of the struggle in the forest; but imagination told him a little more when they lifted the bound man on to the sled in the dark, and Dick's clipped tones of exhaustion bade him stand clear of the snapping jaws and the writhing, taloned hands. All that had been man in Abraham had given way, and he foamed like an animal in a trap; raving in an unknown tongue, and glaring with starting eyes.

Dick showed neither pity nor horror. He engineered the burdened sled into a shack; covered it warm for the night, and left it. Then he and Kennedy took sentry-go in turns until the dawn broke. And at dawn they buried the Isaac of a later history; baring the ground of snow and building the body in against wolf and coyote with rocks brought with great labour. For the earth rang like iron, denying entrance to the earth that lay placid above it. Then Dick straightened, wiping the sweat from his face.

"Time we pulled out," he said. "They've got one *man*, and he's a hunter. They'll do till we can get 'em out in spring."

But Kennedy halted shamefaced by the grave.

"Perhaps you wouldn't want ter say somethin'," he mumbled.

"What?" Dick stared. Then humorous contempt twitched in his lips.

"Say anything you feel like, son," he said. "And take your time. I imagine it would come better from you than me."
Abraham and the remainder of the lost tribe of Israel watched the hound and listened to the whirling words of the pinioned man. And an hour later began that long nightmare that walked with them through the eight days into Grey Wolf; days that two men remembered long after the third had gone to find his senses again in another world.

There were hours when the man on the sled turned livid from cold, and Dick had to let him up to keep life in him, locking the handcuffs to his own belt for safety. There were hours when Abraham lay rigid, with clenched teeth through which they struggled to force food in vain. There were hours too when the blizzard caught them; so that men and dogs bowed to its might, and crouched under the half-pitched tent with the raving man at their ears until the storm was spent and they rose again, recounting their lessening food-kit.

But to Kennedy the edge of all horror was reached in the times when Dick set the maniac on his feet, and ran beside him, or struggled against him, or whirled with him in a drunken, hideous dance, according to Abraham's whim, in order that life might be kept in this huge creature whom earth did not want and dared not lose. Dick's own life was often in danger from the sheer brute strength of the man. He was worn from sleeplessness and exhaustion and cold, and, in later days, from hunger. A spot on his chin had been bitten black in an hour when he had no time to give thought to it. Abraham's teeth had met once in the fleshy part of his hand, and the incoming frost threatened a long, painful healing. His nerves were strong as a man's need be, but the tension was unslackening; food ran short, and bad weather made trail-breaking needful for three ghastly days on end. Kennedy worked well and uncomplainingly; but his mental and physical fibres were not yet set, and the burden of all fell on Dick.

And then came the last night out from Grey Wolf, in an empty freighter's shack by the river. For fifty hours Abraham had refused food. He lay weak as a child by the fire, moaning until Dick loosed the rawhide that had wound him about through his last fit of violence, and left him at ease with the handcuffs only. He fell asleep then, and Dick looked with sunken eyes on Kennedy.

"I must sleep right now, if we all die for it," he said. "You can have Okimow help you; but I believe he's fagged out. Give me two hours, and then call me."

Within two hours another than Kennedy very nearly called Dick, when a gasping smother of human hair pressed down on him, and somewhere in the dark he heard the mad jaws clashing. He was full awake and alert with all the instinct of self-preservation; and, like reality piercing through a nightmare, the click of Kennedy's revolver-hammer came to him.

"Don't shoot," he shouted, and fumbled for the throat-grip with his maimed hand as Kennedy flung himself on the two.

Dick said nothing when Abraham was laid at last like a moss-baby on the earth, and the fire was made up, and Okimow's bristles quieted. But when Kennedy floundered into self-accusation he swore impatiently.

"Sit up and make out the report of this capture," he said. "That'll keep you awake."

"I don't guess I know how——"

"You've seen a Blue Book, haven't you? Get busy and shut up."

The shack fell silent. Outside, the world was infinitely quiet and far in its sweeping wastes of snow. The wood wheewed and crackled, spitting suddenly when a lump of snow in a broken fork caught the heat. Abraham lay still, breathing thickly. Kennedy, with his heavily-stockinged feet thrust out to the fire, wrote laboriously and lengthily, and Dick watched the flames and remembered this game which he was playing with Ducane as goal. He spoke at last abruptly.

"Give me that paper, Kennedy. I'll put it in my pocketbook."

"I'm not through yet——"

"Holy smoke! What are you writing? A book? How much have you got?"

"Only four pages and a bit."

"It'll go into four lines. Tear that stuff out and chuck it on the fire. Now, write as I tell you. 'Sir,—I have the honour to report that the maniac Abraham—surname unknown—who headed the company of fanatics calling themselves a lost tribe of Israel, was lately captured by Constable Kennedy and myself at their settlement in the Clear Hills. Constable Kennedy, who has recently joined, behaved with commendable coolness under rather trying circumstances. I have the honour to be, Sir, your obedient servant——'"

"Lord!" said Kennedy sharply. "You don't want to rub it in like that."

"You'll make a man all right when you grow up," said Dick. "And then you will understand that a man only talks about the things he doesn't do. What were you going to make out of this little game home in Grey Wolf?"

Under the quizzical eyes Kennedy burned with the red of shame.

"All right," said Dick, and laughed. "But I guess I wouldn't. We generally don't, you know."

O'Brien's Doom

by Joseph Gollomb

Some of the best stories about the Mounties were not intended as fiction. In "O'Brien's doom," for example, Joseph Gollomb was obviously intent on telling the truth about a real murder investigation in the Klondike, but his way of fleshing out the bare bones of official records gives the narrative all the appeal of a good detective story. In the process he also contributes to the almost legendary character of Constable Pennecuick, a detective the Force relied upon for years to solve their most difficult cases. Gollomb's story appeared in the RCMP veteran's magazine, Scarlet and Gold vol. XVIII (1937), and represents the best of a type of documentary fiction which the magazine has published frequently over the years. Detail as exhaustive as Gollomb uses could be verified only by consulting Mounted Police records, especially the NWMP Annual Reports to Parliament published for that period.

One Christmas morning at Minto on the Yukon River began with mildness and a thaw, exceptional weather for such a time and place. At Fussell's Roadhouse in Minto three men breakfasted early and at 9 o'clock set out on foot for Hootchiku, also on the river, which they should have reached easily in time to eat their Christmas dinner. They were William Clayton, a young Seattle merchant who was carrying with him a considerable amount of money; Linn Relfe, who had been doing well in Dawson; and Ole Olsen, a lineman who had to see to it that the telegraph wires in the region stayed up. They left Minto in high spirits and set out on the river ice along a trail that followed the right bank of the Yukon.

Four days passed. Nothing was heard of the three men. Accordingly a detachment of the Royal Canadian Mounted Police began a search. But the heavy snow which had fallen since Christmas had covered all tracks. Mounties and others thoroughly scoured the country between Minto and Hootchiku but could find no trace or clue. One possibility was that the travellers had fallen through the ice on the river trail, but the river was solid now. Another theory was that not the hazards of the trail but man was the cause of their strange disappearance. Constable Pennecuick of the Mounted was assigned to look into the matter.

The Search Begins

Pennecuick was an Englishman, as much at home in the wilderness as any Indian could be; and how much he supplemented his woodcraft with gifts as a detective we shall see. He set out from Fussell's Roadhouse just as the three missing men had done, and took the river bank trail that led to Hootchiku. Only instead of a traveller's usual outfit, Pennecuick took with him a shovel and a broom.

Six miles from Fussell's Roadhouse the river makes a sharp bend, and to save distance, travellers reaching that point sometimes choose to climb the steep bank there, cut across the jut of land and reach the river again by a trail ten miles long and more or less straight. Half way between the two ends of the cut-off is a high hilltop.

Pennecuick closely scrutinized the snow at every step of the river trail and stuck to it instead of taking to the cut-off at the bend of the river. But minute as was his study of the snow he saw not the slightest thing of interest to him until he came to the tip of the headland equidistant between the two ends of the cut-off.

Snow lay smoothly everywhere over the bank and to an ordinary observer there would have been nothing unusual here to notice. But Pennecuick remarked ever so shallow a depression in the snow at this point and ventured a deduction. It might be that under the fresh snow that had fallen since Christmas there was a similar depression. If so he wanted to know about it.

With shovel and broom Pennecuick carefully swept away the top snow until he came to a harder layer. It will be remembered that the snow partly melted by the Christmas thaw froze hard that night, and Pennecuick found in it what he had hoped for, signs that someone on Christmas Day had taken to the bank from the river at that point, or had come down from the hill to the river. Also he read in the uncovered trail more than foot tracks: it looked to him as if something heavy had been dragged along it. He followed the depression and it led him to the top of the hill.

The River Lookout

Here he looked about. I have said that the cut-off began at one side of the headland and ran in an almost straight line to the river at the other side. But no foot trail made by travellers through the wilderness is perfectly straight; here a clump of growth, there a rock, elsewhere rough going underfoot makes the track deviate from the straight line. And on a thickly wooded stretch such as that cut-off, the deviation would make it unlikely that one could see along the trail for more than a comparatively short distance.

But Pennecuick was surprised to find that, narrow as the cut-off was, when he got to the top of the hill he could see five miles in each direction down to the river. In other words the cut-off had been made remarkably straight, so much so that Pennecuick wondered.

Then he saw that someone had gone to considerable labor to straighten the trail. Twenty-three cottonwoods had been chopped down and there they lay. The Mountie knew of no public-spirited effort expended to make that cut-off geometrically straight. Such labor would have been wasted if its purpose were only to make travel easier across the headland, for the original footpath was practically as convenient.

If, then, those trees were cut down not to help travellers, what other purpose was served thereby? Pennecuick concluded that whoever had put in so much work on that trail did it because he wanted a clear view down to the river. And as the landscape here was in no way striking, that view must have been desired certainly not for its esthetic value but for some practical end.

Anyone standing on the top of that hill would see travellers on the river passing the cut-off without himself being seen by them. A man so watching could head off those using the river trail, especially if he got down by the path Pennecuick's broom had discovered. But why should anyone go to all that trouble unless his object was to waylay travellers?

Pennecuick now adopted a double role; he was both the manhunter and the suppositous highwayman of his theory. As a highwayman he imagined himself seeing Clayton, Relfe and Olsen pass the Minto end of the cut-off. He hurried down to the river by the path he as manhunter had uncovered.

In his imagination he waited hidden until the three men came up, then confronted them. Alone or even with accomplices the highwayman would have to act fast and drastically to make three Yukon sojourners stop when they did not want to stop. The chances were that Clayton, Relfe and Olsen would have to be shot down as soon as they reached the ambush.

As a highwayman Pennecuick shot down his three victims. Whoever prepared the elaborate ambush would have made a perfect score. Then there would be the bodies to dispose of. There, in Pennecuick's imagination, they lay, either on the river or on the bank near it if any of the three victims had tried to make a run for it.

The river then would be the first place to look for the bodies. With shovel and broom Pennecuick, now the manhunter again, went to work on the snow until he had uncovered the ice for some distance about the spot of the hypothetical ambush.

He toiled for hours before he found his reward. Some yards from the shore he saw a patch of ice several feet across, which for two reasons interested him. It was more recently frozen than the ice about it, and it gave all the appearance of a hole that had been chopped there.

Pennecuick knew there was little use in opening that hole again. If bodies had gone that way the river by now had taken them downstream and it would be spring before an effective search could be made. He turned with renewed interest to the path he had uncovered.

Where Are the Bodies?

But now that he examined it with new vision he found a new puzzle. The path looked as if something heavy had been dragged over it just before the snow froze after the Christmas thaw. By close examination Pennecuick now found signs that whatever that something was, it had been dragged along that path from the river up.

Were they bodies, any or all of the three Pennecuick supposed were under the river ice? If so, there must have been some imperative reason for the burdensome procedure. Again Pennecuick turned highwayman and as such found that he needed some leisure in which to loot his victims with care; more time than he dared allow himself on a trail where others might come along at any moment.

For it was not enough simply to rifle his victims of their valuables and let the river have everything else. One could not take too many precautions in a triple murder and when those bodies turned up in the spring thaw there had better be as few clues as possible as to who they were. To dipose of such clues was a job that had to be done out of sight of the river trail.

Up the hill again therefore Pennecuick toiled with his imaginary burden of dead, or possibly only wounded, victims. But he also had to ply his shovel and broom to see how far the uncovered trail would take him, the detective, to new discoveries.

Beyond the top of the hill he lay down and squinted along the surface of the snow. In this way subtle differences in the looks of the snow crust became visible to an eye as sensitive as Pennecuick's. He found a spot that differed from the rest of the crust as delicately—in his own words—"as the copper film of an electrotype differs from the rest of the plate."

Brushing away the snow at this spot Pennecuick got down to the frozen crust underneath. It was dark with blood.

With his shovel he broke the ground carefully and piece by piece crumbled each chunk of frozen earth between his fingers. An hour of such prospecting brought him a rich yield. Item one was the bullet of a .45 calibre rifle. Not far from it was another bullet, this time from a .32 calibre revolver.

They were there apparently because they had missed their intended targets. Which would indicate that one or more of the victims reached the top of that hill still alive though probably badly wounded, and had to be quieted there.

Pennecuick noted the furrows each bullet had made. Following the directions they indicated he came to a point where the trajectories of the two bullets converged—the place where the two assassins must have stood when they fired.

The short winter day was coming to a close and with the waning daylight Pennecuick found himself, at least for the time, at the end of his trail as manhunter. Reluctantly he was about to go back to the settlement for the night when he heard a sound, the panting and sniffing of a dog.

It was one of those happenings some would describe as pure luck; it would be more fair to call it opportunely, seeing what inspired use Pennecuick made of it. He recognized the dog as belonging to someone who had been sent to jail in Tagish; Pennecuick racked his memory for the name of the owner.

He asked himself what had brought the dog so far from town? Was he lost? Or had he come there from habit, returning to ground once familiar?

Pennecuick called the dog to him, took off the cord on which a Mountie's revolver is hung and tied it for a leash about the dog's neck. Then on an impulse that must have come straight from inspiration he snapped:

"Home, sir! Go home!"

He uttered the command not in his own characteristically kind tone but harshly as would a brutal master. The dog

205

cringed before him, then turned and started, not toward the settlement from which he had come, but deeper into the woods.

No fisherman could have felt a more poignant thrill than Pennecuick at the tug of the leash. Through deep snow the man floundered in the wake of the dog. For a quarter of a mile there was nothing to see but trees and virgin snow. Pennecuick began to wonder whether the dog was not after all only aimlessly running away from a harsh stranger.

Tent in the Trees

Then in the last glimmer of daylight the dog began to strain forward eagerly and Pennecuick's heart must have jumped a beat faster at the sight ahead of him. Across the silhouettes of several tree trunks was a triangle of darkness—a tent.

It was hardly likely that anyone would select that deserted site as a dwelling place except for very special and temporary use. Yet here was the dog behaving as if had been home to him, and not so long ago.

Pennecuick entered the tent. He had to strike a match now to see. The only furnishing was a small steel camping stove, an empty bunk, and behind it against the tent wall leaned a .45 calibre rifle.

Pennecuick was now as eager to go ahead as a beagle on a warm trail, but the Yukon night was upon him and reluctantly he had to give up his search. With the dog still on the leash he went back to the cut-off, reached Minto and reported to his superior, Sergt. Holmes.

To him Pennecuick turned over the dog and set on foot an enquiry as to its master.

Then he went to bed for a brief rest, and was up so early that when he got back to the tent he had found in the wilderness it was still barely light. On the way he had again as highwayman re-enacted the hypothetical crime and its preparations, now in the light of his latest findings as manhunter.

As X, the unknown, Pennecuick brought the tent and its scanty furniture to the lonely spot; took an axe and cut down the cottonwoods to make a clear view, and lay in wait for victims.

With Pennecuick, the highwayman was a shadowy figure, an accomplice, indicated by the two kinds of bullets Pennecuick had found the day before. Again, the highwayman shot and killed at least one of the victims, dragged the three up the hill, dispatched the living, removed their clothes for leisurely looting, and dropped their bodies through the hole in the river ice.

Then their clothing and effects were taken to the tent, where Pennecuick now took up his twofold role again, manhunter and highwayman.

As detective he became interested in a small snow mound a few yards away from the tent.

Buried Clues Revealed

Digging into it he came on a bed of half-burned logs and ashes. Why a fire outdoors when there was a camp stove in the tent? As a man with a crime to hide, Pennecuick answered his own question. There were clothes to be burned and it would be sensible to do the job outside where the ashes and what remained could be more easily taken care of.

In the ashes Pennecuick found several trouser buttons; some with the stamp of a Seattle tailor, others of metal such as are used on overalls. Gathering these up as if they were nuggets of gold Pennecuick entered the tent.

For an hour he made himself as much at home—in a special sense of expression—as any man but the actual owner could be. He accomplished it, thanks to his excellent imagination, and did it in furtherance of a peculiar device to which he now resorted. He lay down in the bunk. He puttered around the stove. He used the tent in every way he could imagine the owner using it.

Bit by bit there was pieced together in his mind the ways of the owner in his use of the tent. This is how he would stand when at work at the stove. Here is where he would take up his position by the light of day. There is where he would rest his

207

carbine, or put down some other article of habitual use. With this sensitive reconstruction to guide him Pennecuick went out and re-entered the tent, bringing with him—in imagination—the clothes of his victims.

First in pantomime he went through the pockets of the garments for valuables. Whatever these were he put into his own pockets. Then there must have been an assortment of small objects of little value among the loot, which a highwayman would throw carelessly away.

His acquired sense of how the owner of the tent would do things therein made Pennecuick stand just inside the entrance as he looted the dead men's pockets. He came to the point where he had a handful of valueless small objects to throw away. Pennecuick did not leave entirely to his imagination how this would be done.

Robber's Acts Reviewed

Taking out of his own pocket a handful of coins he waited till he achieved an approximation of the mood in which the man he was imitating must have been about to throw away the part of his loot he did not want. Much as an accomplished actor carries out a role he had studied well Pennecuick flung away his handful of coins.

A moment later he changed roles again and getting down on his hands and knees he noted where his coins had fallen. If his re-creation of the highwayman down to the action he had just imitated was correct, where his coins had fallen there should be promise of other objects to be found.

Where Pennecuick had sown he reaped almost at once an interesting if limited harvest. He found an English coin, such as a man in Canada would use only as a keepsake; and he found a key from which he deduced a lock of a kind little used in the Yukon region.

He spent half the day in and about the tent before he was forced to give up that trail for the time being; his utmost efforts had brought him not another strand for the noose he was preparing for X, the unknown.

He went back to the straightened trail on the cut-off. Here he looked at the stumps of the cottonwoods that had been chopped down by the man who wanted a view of the river.

Modern manhunting organizations like Scotland Yard make telling use, as clues, of the traces which a burglar's chisel or jimmy leaves on wood or metal in his effort to get at his loot. For every tool has its own teeth—minute nicks and notches in the cutting edge—and from the looks of the bite one can tell what teeth made it, if one compares the two. In most cases, however, it takes a lens of high power to detect such traces and identify the tool that left them.

It was this bit of detective technique that made Pennecuick study the stumps of the cottonwoods. He studied the bite of the axe with which they had been cut. He had no powerful lens wherewith to make this examination, only his excellent eyes.

Stranger Avoids Police

Fortunately, an axe has a coarser cutting edge than a wood chisel, and this particular axe must have been rather the worse for wear even before it was used on the cottonwoods. Pennecuick read in the cut wood that one of the corners of the axe was blunt; there were three bad notches along the edge, and the other corner must have struck a stone in its previous career.

With a mental picture of the working end of this axe, Pennecuick went from one cut cottonwood to another, and concluded that either one man had cut all the trees down, or, if he had help, the same axe was used.

This was the last clue Pennecuick found in the wilderness, and he returned to Minto to see what there was to be found in the town.

His fellow Mounties meanwhile had been making good use of what Pennecuick had brought back the day before. They had a man under arrest and a story to piece out whatever Pennecuick could tell them.

The previous winter a stranger riding a sorrel was seen

209

coming along the trail that should have taken him past the door of the Tagish post of the Mounted Police guardhouse. But instead of staying on the trail, this man gave the guardhouse a wide berth; his detour even took him to the other bank of the frozen river. This was such curious behavior for an honest man that a Mountie went after the stranger to find out why he so obviously avoided a police post.

The stranger tried to escape, but the sorrel struck a bad stretch of snow and sank up to his haunches. The suspect was taken back to the post for investigation. It developed that he was Thomas O'Brien, recently released from jail at Dawson. He was short, dark, tough of body and sullen of temper. His small brown eyes were keen but furtive. When pressed hard by questions, he would refuse to answer.

It was known that he left Dawson jail with only $10 in his pocket. Where, then, did he get his horse? O'Brien refused to answer; so he was charged with vagrancy and sentenced to six months in jail at Tagish.

The police took care of his dog and a few belongings, which included an axe. The dog was more or less adopted by the Mounties at Tagish while his master was in jail, and was restored to O'Brien when he came out some time in the fall of the year.

The dog was the one that had led Pennecuick to the tent in the wilderness. The axe, which originally belonged to O'Brien, became mislaid during his term in jail, and when he came out the Mounties gave him another in its place. Pennecuick found it among O'Brien's belongings and took it back with him to the cottonwood stumps. But the trip was only a matter of conscientious routine. The moment Pennecuick looked at O'Brien's axe, he recognized the teeth that had bitten into trees on the cut-off.

Found in O'Brien's possession when he was again arrested was a curious nugget of gold. It was of the size of a baby's hand and roughly like one, round and at five places the edge curled until the nugget looked like an almost closed fist. Inside was another nugget, loose, but retained by the fingers of the larger nugget.

O'Brien said he had found it in a strike he had made along the river. But on investigation it was shown that this curious nugget formerly belonged to Relfe, one of the three missing men.

The pocket piece which Pennecuick found in the tent in the wilderness was also identified as Relfe's. The key found near it fitted the lock of Clayton's strongbox in Seattle. The buttons Pennecuick unearthed in the ashes near the tent were eventually traced to the overalls of Ole Olsen, the third of the missing men.

Spring unlocked what the river held of the triple murder. With the bodies of the three men recovered, the case against O'Brien was ready for trial.

But it was fully two years before all the circumstantial evidence needed to hang a man was assembled and presented to a jury. Then the story of the crime came out.

Details of the Murder

O'Brien had conceived his scheme as far back as his sojourn in jail at Dawson. He tried to get "Kid" West, a fellow jailbird, to join him in carrying it out. West refused and O'Brien got "Little Tommy" Graves, another criminal, to help him.

They erected the tent back of the cut-off. They chopped down the cottonwoods with O'Brien's axe. With unconscious cynicism O'Brien chose Christmas Day for the crime. When the three men bound for Hootchiku reached the bend in the river, O'Brien shot them from ambush. Clayton and Olsen fell, shot through the heart, Relfe was only wounded.

The two murderers dragged their three victims up the bank to the top of the hill. Here O'Brien with his .45 rifle and Graves with his revolver killed Relfe. The bodies were dropped through a hole in the frozen river. The clothing of the men was taken to the tent and the loot divided.

O'Brien told Graves to burn the garments outside of the tent, and while Graves was at work O'Brien shot him dead from behind, on the principle that dead men tell no tales. The body of Graves joined his victims in the river.

211

O'Brien was hanged.

And the trial judge, in summing up the work of Pennecuick and his colleagues, spoke of the Royal Canadian Mounted Police as "the pride of Canada and the envy of the world."

PART FOUR
The Twentieth Century

The Wolfer

by Wallace Stegner

Set in the Cypress Hills area in the notorious winter of 1906–07, "The Wolfer" is a very vivid evocation of the savagery of the prairie winter. Stegner, a distinguished American novelist, spent several years of his childhood in that part of southern Saskatchewan. There is probably an historical original for the wolfer, Schulz, because he is mentioned again in Stegner's Wolf Willow (*New York: Viking, 1962*). "The Wolfer" *first appeared in* Harpers *in October, 1959.*

Yes, I saw a good deal of it, and I knew them all. It was my business to, and in those days it wasn't hard to know nearly every man between Willow Bunch and Fort Walsh, even the drifters; the women you could count on your two thumbs. One was Molly Henry at the T-Down Bar, the other was Amy Schulz, living with a reformed whiskey trader named Frost up on Oxarart Creek. I knew Schulz, too, and his miserable boy. At least I had seen him a good many times, and stopped with him a half-dozen times at one or another shack when I was out on patrol, and at least that many times had come within an ace of being eaten by his hound. Probably I knew him better than most people did, actually. Friends—that's another matter. He was about as easy to be friendly with as a wolverine.

Summers, he camped around in the Cypress Hills, hunting, but in winter he used the shacks that the cattle outfits maintained out along the Whitemud, on the patrol trail between the Hills and Wood Mountain. Two of them, at Stonepile and Pinto Horse Butte, were abandoned Mounted Police patrol posts—abandoned in the sense that no constables were stationed there, though we kept the barracks stocked with emergency supplies and always cut and stacked a few tons of prairie wool there in the fall. Both Schulz and I used the barracks now and then, for he as a wolfer and I as a Mountie covered pretty much the same territory. If the truth were known, I kept pretty close tab on him in my patrol book, because I was never entirely sure, after Amy left him, that he wouldn't go back up on Oxarart Creek and shoot Frost.

Probably I wronged him. I think he was glad to get rid of Amy; it freed him to be as wild as the wolves he hunted, with his snuffling adenoidal boy for a slave and daily killing for occupation and his staghound for friend and confidant. They were a pair: each was the only living thing that liked the other, I guess, and it was a question which had the edge in savagery. Yet love, too, of a kind. I have heard him croon and mutter to that thing, baby-talk, in a way to give you the creeps.

Whenever I found Schulz at Stonepile or Pinto Horse I picked an upper bunk; if the hound got drooling for my blood in the night I wanted to be where he'd at least have to climb to get at me. There was no making up to him—he was Schulz's, body and soul. He looked at every other human being with yellow eyes as steady as a snake's, the hackles lifting between his shoulders and a rumble going away down in his chest. I'd hear him moving in the dark shack, soft and heavy, with his nails clicking on the boards. He wore a fighting collar studded with brass spikes, he stood as high as a doorknob at the shoulder, and he weighed a hundred and forty pounds. Schulz bragged that he had killed wolves single-handed. The rest of the pack, Russian wolfhounds and Russian-greyhound crosses, slept in the stable and were just dogs, but this staghound thing, which Schulz called Puma, was the physical shape of his own savagery: hostile, suspicious, deadly, unwinking. I have seen him stand with a foolish, passive smile on his face while that monster put his paws up on his shoulders and lapped mouth and chin and eyes with a tongue the size of a coal shovel.

He was a savage, a wild man. He hated civilization—which

meant maybe two hundred cowpunchers and Mounties scattered over ten thousand square miles of prairie—but it was not civilization that did him in. It was the wild, the very savagery he trusted and thought he controlled. I know about that too, because I followed the last tracks he and his hound made in this country.

My patrol books would show the date. As I remember, it was toward the end of March 1907. The patrol was routine—Eastend, Bates Camp, Stonepile, the Warholes, Pinto Horse Butte, Wood Mountain, and return—but nothing else was routine that winter. With a month still to go, it was already a disaster.

Since November there had been nothing but blizzards, freezing fogs, and cold snaps down to forty below. One Chinook—and that lasted only long enough to melt everything to mush, whereupon another cold snap came on and locked the country in a four-inch shell of ice. A lot of cattle that lay down that night never got up: froze in and starved there.

That time, just about Christmas, I passed the Warholes on a patrol and found a *métis* named Big Antoine and twenty of his Indian relatives trapped and half-starved. They had made a run for it from Wood Mountain toward Big Stick Lake when the Chinook blew up, and got caught out. When I found them they hadn't eaten anything in two weeks except skin-and-bone beef that had died in the snow; they were seasoning it with fat from coyotes, the only thing besides the wolves that throve.

A police freighter got them out before I came back on my next trip. But the cowpunchers out in the range shacks were by that time just about as bad off. For weeks they had been out every day roping steers frozen into the drifts, and dragging them free; or they had been floundering around chasing cattle out of the deep snow of the bottoms and out onto the benches where the wind kept a little feed bare. They had got them up there several times, but they hadn't kept them there. The wind came across those flats loaded with buckshot, and the cattle turned their tails to it and came right back down to starve. At one point the two Turkey Track boys stationed at Pinto

Horse had even tried to make a drag of poles, and drag bare a patch of hillside for the cattle to feed on. All they did was kill off their ponies. When I came by in March they had given up and were conducting a non-stop blackjack game in the barracks, and laying bets whether the winter would last till August, or whether it would go right on through and start over.

We had a little poker game that night. Whenever the talk died we could hear, through the logs and sod of the shack, the heavy hunting song of wolves drawn down from the hills for the big barbecue. It was a gloomy thing to hear. Say what you want about cowpunchers, they don't like failing at a job any better than other people. And they were sure failing. In November there had been close to 70,000 head of cattle on that Whitemud range. At a conservative guess, half of them were dead already. If we didn't get a Chinook in the next week, there wouldn't be a cow alive come spring.

I quit the game early to get some sleep, and for a joke pushed the deck over toward Curly Withers for a cut. "Cut a Chinook," I said. He turned over the jack of diamonds. Then we went to the door for a look-see, and everything was wooled up in freezing fog, what nowadays they call a whiteout. You could have cut sheep out of the air with tin shears. "Some Chinook," Curly said.

In the morning there was still no wind, but the air was clear. As I turned Dude down the trail and looked back to wave at the Turkey Track boys I had the feeling they were only six inches high, like carved figures in a German toy scene. The shack was braced from eaves to ground with icicles; the sky behind the quiver of heat from the stovepipe jiggled like melting glass. Away down in the southeast, low and heatless, the sun was only a small painted dazzle.

It seemed mean and cowardly to leave those boys out there. Or maybe it was just that I hated to start another day of hard cold riding through all that death, with nobody to talk to. You can feel mighty small and lonesome riding through that country in winter, after a light snowfall that muffles noises.

220

I was leading a packhorse, and ordinarily there is a good deal of jingle and creak and sound of company with two ponies, but that morning it didn't seem my noises carried ten feet. Down in the river trough everything was still and white. Mainly the channel had a fur of frozen snow on it, but here and there were patches of black slick ice full of air bubbles like quarters and silver dollars. Depending on how the bends swung, drifts sloped up to the cutbanks or up to bars overgrown with snow-smothered rose bushes and willows. I crossed the tracks of three wolves angling upriver, side by side and bunched in clusters of four: galloping. They must have been running just for the hell of it, or else they had sighted an antelope or deer. They didn't have to gallop to eat beef.

Without wind, it wasn't bad riding, though when I breathed through my mouth the aching of my teeth reminded me that under the Christmas frosting the world was made of ice and iron. Now a dead steer among the rose bushes, untouched by wolves or coyotes. I cut a notch in a tally stick, curious about how many I would pass between Pinto Horse and Eastend. Farther on, a bunch of whitefaces lying and standing so close together they had breathed frost all over one another. If they hadn't been such skeletons they would have looked like farmyard beasts in a crèche. They weren't trapped or frozen in, but they were making no move to get out—only bawled at me hopelessly as I passed. Two were dead and half drifted over. I cut two more notches.

In three hours I cut a good many more, one of them at a big wallow and scramble near the mouth of Snake Creek where wolves had pulled down a steer since the last snowfall. The blood frozen into the snow was bright as paint, as if it had been spilled only minutes before. Parts of the carcass had been dragged in every direction.

Those wolves rubbed it in, pulling down a beef within a half mile of where Schulz and his boy were camped at Stonepile. I wondered if he had had any luck yet—he hadn't had any at all last time I saw him—and I debated whether to stop with him or go on to Bates and heat up a cold shack. The decision was for Bates. It was no big blowout to spend a night with the

Schulzes, who were a long way from being the company the
T-Down and Turkey Track boys were, and who besides were
dirtier than Indians. Also I thought I would sleep better at
Bates than I would at Stonepile, in an upper bunk with my
hand on a gun while that hound prowled around in the dark
and rumbled every time I rolled over. Sure Schulz had it
trained, but all he had hold of it with was his voice; I would
have liked a chain better.

Just to make a check on Stonepile for the patrol book, I turned
up Snake Creek, and a little after noon I came up the pitch
from the bottoms and surprised the Schulz boy standing bare-
armed before the barracks door with a dishpan hanging from
his hand. The dishpan steamed, his arm steamed, the sunken
snow where he had flung the dishwater steamed. I was quite
pleased with him, just then; I hadn't known he and his old man
ever washed their dishes. He stood looking at me with his
sullen, droop-lipped watchful face, one finger absent-mind-
edly up his nose. Down in the stable the wolfhounds began
to bark and whine and howl. I saw nothing of Schulz or the
big hound.

"Howdy, Bud," I said. "How's tricks?"

He was sure no chocolate-box picture. His gray flannel shirt
was shiny with grease, his face was pimply, long black hair
hung from under the muskrat cap that I had never seen off his
head. I think he slept in it, and I'll guarantee it was crawling.
He never could meet a man's eyes. He took his finger out of his
nose and said, looking past me, "Hello, constable."

I creaked down. Dude pushed me from behind, rubbing the
icicles off his nose. "Pa not around?" I said.

Something flickered in his eyes, a wet gray gleam. One eye-
socket and temple, I saw, were puffy and discolored—about
a three-day-old black eye. He touched one cracked red wrist
to his chapped mouth and burst out, "Pa went out yesterday
and ain't come back!" With a long drag he blew his nose
through his mouth and spit sideways into the snow. His eyes
hunted mine and ducked away instantly. "And Puma got out!"
he said—wailed, almost.

222

At that moment I wouldn't have trusted him a rope-length out of my sight. He looked sneakily guilty, he had that black eye which could only be a souvenir from Daddy, he had fifteen years of good reasons for hating his old man. If Schulz and his hound were really missing, I had the conviction that I would find them dry-gulched and stuffed through the ice somewhere. Not that I could have blamed young Schulz too much. In the best seasons his old man must have been a bearcat to live with. In this one, when he had hunted and trapped all winter and never got a single wolf, he was a crazy man. The wolves walked around his traps laughing—they fed much too well to be tempted. They sat just out of rifle shot and watched him waste ammunition. And though he had the best pack of dogs in that country, he hadn't been able to run them for months because of the weather and the deep snow. Out on the flats the dogs could have run, but there were no wolves there; they were all down in the bottoms hobnobbing with the cattle. The last time I had passed through, Schulz had talked to me half the night like a man half-crazed with rage; red-faced, jerky-voiced, glassy-eyed. To make his troubles worse, he had headaches, he said; "bunches" on his head. A horse had fallen on him once.

So in a winter of complete hard luck, who made a better whipping boy than that sullen son of his? And who more likely, nursing his black eye and his grievance, to lie behind the cabin or stable and pot his father as he came up the trail?

It was a fine theory. Pity it wasn't sound. I told young Schulz to hold it while I turned the horses into the police haystack, and while I was down there I got a look around the stable and corrals. No bodies, no blood, no signs of a fight. Then up in the barracks, in the hot, close, tallowy-mousy room with muskrat and marten pelts on bows of red willow hanging from the ceiling and coyote and lynx hides tacked on the wall, and three spirals of last-year's flypaper, black with last year's flies, moving in the hot air above the stove, I began asking him questions and undid all my nice imaginary murder.

I even began to doubt that anything would turn out to be wrong with Schulz or his hound, for it became clear at once that if Schulz was in trouble he was in trouble through some accident, and I didn't believe that the Schulzes had accidents. They might get killed, but they didn't have accidents. It was about as likely that he would freeze, or get lost, or fall through a rapid, or hurt himself with a gun, as it was that a wolf would slip and sprain his ankle. And if you bring up those bunches on his head, and the horse that he said fell on him, I'll bet you one thing, I'll bet you the horse got hurt worse than Schulz did.

Still, he was missing, and in that country and that weather it could be serious. He had left the barracks the morning before, on foot but carrying snowshoes, to check on some carcasses he had poisoned down by Bates Camp. Usually he didn't use poison because of the dogs. Now he would have baited traps with his mother, or staked out his snuffling boy, if he could have got wolves that way. He shut the wolfhounds in the stable and the staghound in the barracks and told the boy to keep them locked up. The staghound especially had to be watched. He was used to going everywhere with Schulz, and he might follow him if he were let out.

That was exactly what he did do. Young Schulz kept him in the barracks—it would have been like being caged with a lion—until nearly dark, when he went down to the stable to throw some frozen beef to the other dogs. He slid out and slammed the door ahead of the staghound's rush. But when he came back he wasn't so lucky. The dog was waiting with his nose to the crack, and when it opened he threw his hundred and forty pounds against the door and was gone. No one but Schulz would have blamed the boy—ever try to stop a bronc from coming through a corral gate, when you're there on foot and he's scared and ringy and wants to come? You get out of the way or you get trompled. That hound would have trompled you the same way. But Schulz wouldn't think of that. The boy was scared sick of what his father would do to him if and when he came back.

I thought that since the hound had *not* come back, he obviously must have found Schulz. If he had found him alive and unhurt, they would be back together before long. If he had found him hurt, he would stay with him, and with any luck I could find them simply by following their tracks. I asked the boy if he was afraid to stay alone two or three days, if necessary. He wasn't—it was exactly the opposite he was scared of. Also I told him to stay put, and not get in a panic and take off across a hundred miles of open country for Malta or somewhere; I would see to it that his old man laid off the horsewhip. Somebody—his old man, or me, or somebody— would be back within three days at the latest.

He stood in the doorway with his arms still bare, a tough kid actually, a sort of wild animal himself, though of an unattractive kind, and watched me with those wet little gleaming eyes as I rode off down Snake Creek.

I couldn't have had better trailing. The light snow two nights before had put a nice firm rippled coating over every old track. When I hit the river the channel was perfectly clean except for Schulz' mocassin tracks, and braided in among them the tracks of the hound. A wolf makes a big track, especially with his front feet—I've seen them nearly six inches each way—but that staghound had feet the size of a plate, and he was so heavy that in deep snow, even a packed drift, he sank way down. So there they went, the companionable tracks of a man and his dog out hunting. If I hadn't known otherwise I would have assumed that they had gone upriver together, instead of six hours apart.

The day had got almost warm. Under the north bank the sun had thawed an occasional rooty dark spot. I kneed Dude into a shuffle, the packhorse dragged hard and then came along. I could have followed that trail at a lope.

It led me four miles up the river's meanders before I even had to slow down, though I cut four more notches in the tally stick and saw two thin does and a buck flounder away from the ford below Sucker Creek, and took a snapshot with the carbine at a coyote, fatter than I ever saw a coyote, that stood watching me from a cutbank. My bullet kicked snow at the cutbank's lip and he was gone like smoke. Then a mile above

Sucker Creek I found where Shulz had put on his snowshoes and cut across the neck of a bend. The hound had wallowed after him, leaving a trail like a horse.

The drifts were hard-crusted under the powder, but not hard-crusted enough, and the horses were in to their bellies half the time. They stood heaving while I got off to look at a little tent-like shelter with fresh snow shoveled over it. The hound had messed things up some, sniffing around, but he had not disturbed the set. Looking in, I found a marten in a No. 2 coyote trap, caught around the neck and one front leg. He wasn't warm, but he wasn't quite frozen either. I stuffed marten and trap into a saddlebag and went on.

The trail led out of the river valley and up a side coulee where among thin red willows a spring came warm enough from the ground to stay unfrozen for several feet. The wolfer had made another marten set there, and then had mushed up onto the bench and northwest to a slough where tules whiskered up through the ice and a half-dozen very high muskrat houses rose out of the clear ice farther out.

At the edge of the slough I got off and followed where man and hound had gone out on the ice. Where the ice was clear I could see the paths the rats make along the bottom. For some reason this slough wasn't frozen nearly as deep as the river, maybe because there were springs, or because of organic matter rotting in the water. The Royal Society will have to settle that sometime. All I settled was that Schulz had chopped through the ice in two places and set coyote traps in the paths, and had broken through the tops of three houses to make sets inside. He had a rat in one of the house sets. Since I seemed to be running his trapline for him, I put it in the other saddlebag.

Nothing, surely, had happened to Schulz up to here. The hound had been at every set, sniffing out the trail. That would have been pretty late, well after dark, when the fog had already shut off the half moon. It occurred to me as I got back on Dude and felt the icy saddle under my pants again that I would not have liked to be out there on that bare plain to see a wild animal like that hound go by in the mist, with his nose to his master's track.

From the slough the trail cut back to the river; in fifteen minutes I looked down onto the snowed-over cabin and buried corrals of Bates Camp. There had been nobody stationed in it since the T-Down fed its last hay almost two months before. No smoke from the stovepipe, no sign of life. My hope that I would find the wolfer holed up there, so that I could get out of the saddle and brew a pot of tea and eat fifty pounds or so of supper, went glimmering. Something had drawn him away from here. He would have reached Bates about the same time of day I reached it—between two and three in the afternoon—for though he was a tremendous walker he could not have covered eight miles, some of it on snowshoes, and set seven traps, in less than about four hours. I had then been on his trail more than two hours, and pushing it hard.

I found that he hadn't gone near the shack at all, but had turned down toward the corrals, buried so deep that only the top pole showed. Wading along leading the horses, I followed the web tracks to the carcass of a yearling shorthorn half dug out of the snow.

There were confusing tracks all around—snowshoes, dog, wolf. The shorthorn had died with his tongue out, and a wolf had torn it from his head. The carcass was chewed up some, but not scattered. Schultz had circled it about six feet away, and at one place deep web tracks showed where he had squatted down close. I stood in the tracks and squatted too, and in front of me, half obscured by the dog's prints, I saw where something had been rolled in the snow. Snagged in the crust was a long grey-black hair.

A wolf, then. This was one of the poisoned carcasses, and a wolf that rolled might be sick. Squatting in the quenched afternoon, Schulz would have come to his feet with a fierce grunt, darting his eyes around the deceptive shapes of snow and dusk, and he would not have waited a second to track the wolf to his dying-place. The coyotes he ran or shot, and the marten and muskrat he trapped when nothing better offered, were nothing to him; it was wolves that made his wild blood go, and they had cheated him all winter.

For just a minute I let myself yearn for the cabin and a fire and a hot meal. But I still had an hour and a half of light good enough for trailing—about what Schulz himself had had—and after that maybe another half-hour of deceptive shadows, ghostly moonlight, phosphorescent snow, and gathering mist and dark. If he had got hurt somehow chasing the wolf, he might have survived one night; he couldn't possibly survive two. So I paused only long enough to put the packhorse in the stable and give him a bait of oats, and to light a fire to take a little of the chill out of the icy shack. Then I set the damper and took out on the trail again.

It was like a pursuit game played too long and complicated too far, to the point of the ridiculous—like one of these cartoons of a big fish swallowing a smaller fish swallowing a small fish. There went the sick wolf running from the heat of the strychnine in his own guts, and after him the wolfer, implacable in the blue-white cold, and after him the great hound running silently, hours behind but gaining, loping hard down the river ice or sniffing out the first marten set. There went wildness pursued by hate pursued by love, and after the lot of them me, everybody's rescuer, everybody's nursemaid, the law on a tired horse.

Schulz never did catch up with that wolf. Probably it had never been sick at all, but had rolled in the snow in sassy contempt, the way a dog will kick dirt back over his scats. Up on the bench its track broke into the staggered pairs that showed it was trotting, and after a half mile or so another set of wolf tracks came in from the west, and the two went off together in the one-two-one of an easy lope.

Schulz quit, either because he saw it was hopeless or because the light gave out on him. I could imagine his state of mind. Just possibly, too, he had begun to worry. With darkness and fog and the night cold coming on, that open flat bare of even a scrap of sagebrush was no place to be. In an hour the freak windlessness could give way to a blizzard; a wind right straight off the North Pole, and temperatures to match, could light on him with hardly a warning, and then even a Schulz could be in trouble.

Above me, as I studied his tracks where he broke off the chase, a chip of moon was pale and blurry against a greenish sky; the sun over the Cypress Hills was low and strengthless. It would go out before it went down. And I was puzzled by Schulz. He must have been lost; he must have looked up from his furious pursuit and his furious reading of failure, and seen only misty dusk, without landmarks, moon, stars, anything, for instead of heading back for the river and the cabin he started straight eastward across the plain. So did I, because I had to.

It took him about a mile to realize his mistake, and it was easy to read his mind from his footprints, for there out in the middle of the empty snowflats they milled around a little and made an eloquent right angle toward the south. Probably he had felt out his direction from the drifts, which ran like shallow sea-waves toward the southeast. I turned after him thankfully. But he hadn't gone back to Bates, and he hadn't gone back downriver to Stonepile. So where in hell *had* he gone? I worked the cold out of my stiff cheeks, and flapped my arms to warm my hands, and kicked old Dude into a tired trot across the packed flats.

In twenty minutes I was plowing down into the river valley again. The sun was blurring out, the bottoms were full of shadows the color of a gunbarrel, the snow was scratched with black willows. I judged that I was not more than a mile upriver from Bates. The plowing web tracks and the wallowing trail of the hound went ahead of me through deep drifts and across the bar onto the river ice, and coming after them I saw under the opposite cutbank the black of a dead fire.

I stopped. There was no sign of life, though the snow, I could see, was much tracked. I shouted: "Schulz?" and the sound went out in that white desolation like a match dropped in the snow. This looked like the end of the trail, and because it began to look serious, and I didn't want to track things up until I got a chance to study them, I tied the horse in the willows and circled to come into the bend from below. When I parted the rose bushes to slide down onto the ice, I looked straight down on the body of Schulz's hound.

Dead, he looked absolutely enormous. He lay on his side with his spiked collar up around his ears. I saw that he had been dragged by it from the direction of the fire. He had bled a great deal from the mouth, and had been bleeding as he was dragged, for the snow along the drag mark had a filigree of red. On the back of his head, almost at his neck, was a frozen bloody patch. And along the trough where the body had been dragged came a line of tracks, the unmistakable tracks of Schulz's moccasins. Another set went back. That was all. It was as clear as printing on a page. Schulz had dragged the dead dog to the edge of the bank, under the overhanging bushes, and left him there, and not come back.

I tell you, I was spooked. My hair stood on end, I believe, and I know I looked quickly all around, in a fright that I might be under somebody's eyes or gun. On the frozen river there was not a sound. As I slid down beside the hound I looked both ways in the channel, half expecting to see Schulz's body too, or somebody else's. Nothing. Clean snow.

The hound's body was frozen rock hard. His mouth was full of frozen blood, and the crusted patch on the back of his neck turned out to be a bullet hole, a big one. He had been shot in the mouth, apparently by a soft-nosed bullet that had torn the back of his head off. And no tracks, there or anywhere, except those of Schulz himself. I knew that Schulz never used any gun but a .22, in which he shot long rifle cartridges notched so they would mushroom and tear a big internal hole and stop without making a second puncture in the hide. If he had shot the hound—and that was totally incredible, but who else could have?—a .22 bullet like that would not have gone clear through brain and skull and blown a big hole out the other side unless it had been fired at close range, so close that even in fog or half-dark the wolfer must have known what he was shooting at.

But I refused to believe what my eyes told me must be true. I could conceive of Schulz shooting his son, and I had already that day suspected his son of shooting *him*. But I could not believe that he would ever, unless by accident, shoot that dog. Since it didn't seem he could have shot it accidentally, someone else must have shot it.

It took me ten minutes to prove to myself that there were no tracks around except the wolfer's. I found those, in fact, leading on upriver, and since I had looked at every footprint he made from Stonepile on, I knew these must be the ones he made going out. Instead of going home, he went on. Why?

Under the cutbank, in front of the fire, I found a hard path beaten in the snow where Schulz had walked up and down many times. The fire itself had never been large, but it had burned a long time; the coals were sunk deeply into the snow and frozen in their own melt. Schulz had evidently stayed many hours, perhaps all night, keeping the little fire going and walking up and down to keep from freezing. But why hadn't he walked a mile downriver and slept warm at Bates?

I might have followed to try to find out, but the light was beginning to go, and I was too tired to think of riding any more of that crooked river that night. Still, just thinking about it gave me an idea. In any mile, the Whitemud ran toward every point of the compass, swinging and returning on itself. If Schulz had hit it after the fog closed in thick, he would have known that Bates lay downriver, but how would he know which way was downriver? There were no rapids in that stretch. There would have been no landmarks but bends and bars endlessly repeating, changing places, now on the right and now on the left. Some of the bends were bowknots that completely reversed their direction.

That might answer one question, but only one. I put myself in the path he had made, and walked up and down trying to see everything just as he had. I found the mark where he had stuck his rifle butt-down in the snow, probably to leave his arms free for swinging against the cold. There were hound tracks on the path and alongside it, as if the dog had walked up and down with him. At two places it had lain down in the snow off to the side.

That answered another question, or corroborated what I had guessed before: Schulz couldn't have shot the hound not knowing what it was; it had been there with him for some time.

Standing by the fire, I looked back at the deep tracks where Schulz, and after him the hound, had broken down off the bar onto the ice. The hound's tracks led directly to the fire and the path. I walked the path again, searching every foot of it. I found only one thing more: just where the path went along a streak of clear ice, where ice and snow joined in a thin crust, there were the deep parallel gouges of claws, two sets of them, close together. Would a heavy hound, rearing to put its front paws on a man's shoulders and its happy tongue in a man's face, dig that way, deeply, with its hind claws? I thought it would.

I stood at the spot where I thought Schultz and the hound might have met, and again studied the tracks and the places where the hound had lain down. In front of one of them was a light scoop, just the rippled surface taken off the new snow. Made by a tongue lapping? Maybe. By pure intensity of imagining I tried to reconstruct what might have happened. Suppose it went this way:

Suppose he fumbled down to the river with the visibility no more than fifty or a hundred feet, and could not tell which way it ran. The fact that he had lost himself up on the bench made that not merely possible, but probable. A fire, then, until daylight let him see. Willows yielded a little thin fuel, the tiny heat along leg or backside or on the turned stiff hands made the night bearable. But caution would have told anyone as experienced as Schulz that the night was long and fuel short —and at Pinto Horse the night before the thermometer had stood at fifteen below. He would have had to keep moving, the rifle stuck in a drift and his arms flailing and the felt cap he wore pulled down to expose only his eyes and mouth—a figure as savage and forlorn as something caught out of its cave at the race's dim beginning.

The sound of hunting wolves would have kept him company as it had kept us company in our social poker game, and it would have been a sound that for many reasons he liked less than we did. Except for that dark monotone howling there would have been no sound in the shrouded bend except the creak of his moccasins and the hiss of the fire threatening always to melt itself out—no other sound unless maybe the grating of anger in his own aching head, an anger lonely, venomous, and incurable, always there like the pressure of those "bunches" on his skull. I could imagine it well enough: too well. For the first time, that day or ever, I felt sorry for Schulz.

Endless walking through frozen hours; endless thinking; endless anger and frustration. And then—maybe?—the noise of something coming, a harsh and terrifying noise smashing in on his aloneness, as something big and fast plowed through the snowy brush and came scraping and sliding down the bank. Schulz would have reached the gun in one leap (I looked, but could find no sign to prove he had). Assuming he did: while he crouched there, a wild man with his finger on the trigger and his nerves humming with panic, here came materializing out of the white darkness a great bony shape whining love.

And been shot as it rushed up to greet Schultz, shot in the moment of fright when the oncoming thing could have been wolf or worse? It would have been plausible if it hadn't been for those hound tracks that went up and down along the path on the ice, and that place where the toenails had dug in as if the hound had reared to put its paws on the wolfer's shoulders. If there was ever a time when Schulz would have welcomed the hound, greeted it, talked to it in his mixture of baby talk, questions, and grunts of endearment, this would have been the time. The coming of the dog should have made the night thirty degrees warmer and hours shorter.

Surely the hound, having pursued him for ten miles or so,

would have stuck close, kept him company in his pacing, stood with him whenever he built up the fire a little and warmed his feet and hands. But it had walked up and down the path only two or three times. Twice it had lain down. Once, perhaps, it had lapped up snow.

And this hound, following Schulz's tracks with blind love— and unfed all day, since it had escaped before the Schulz boy could feed it—had passed, sniffed around, perhaps eaten of, the carcass of the yearling at Bates Camp.

Suppose Schulz had looked up from his stiff pacing and seen the hound rolling, or feverishly gulping snow. Suppose that in the murk, out of the corner of his eye, he had seen it stagger to its feet. Suppose, in the flicker of the fire, its great jaws had been opening and closing and that foam had dripped from its chops. Suppose a tight moment of alarm and disbelief, a tableau of freezing man and crazed hound, the deadliest creature and his deadly pet. Suppose it started toward him. Suppose the wolfer spoke to it, and it came on; yelled his peremptory command of "Charge!" which usually dropped the dog as if it had been poleaxed—and the hound still came on. Suppose he yelled a cracking yell, and the hound lumbered into a gallop, charging him. The spring for the gun, the mitt snatched off between the teeth, the stiffened finger pulling the trigger, a snapshot from the waist: Schulz was a good shot, or a lucky one; he had had to be.

Suppose. I supposed it, I tell you, in a way to give myself gooseflesh. By the vividness of imagination or the freakishness of the fading light, the hound's tracks arranged themselves so that only those decisive, final ones were clear. They led directly from one of the places where it had lain down to the bloody scramble where it had died, and if I read them right they came at a scattering gallop. Standing in the path, Schulz would have fired with the hound no more than thirty feet away. Its momentum had carried it in a rolling plunge twenty feet closer. I stepped it off. When Schulz, with that paralysis in his guts and shaking in his muscles, lowered his gun and went up to the dead pet that his own poison had turned into an enemy, he had only three steps to go.

I went over to the hound and took off his collar, evidence, maybe, or a sort of souvenir. Dude was drooping in the willows with his head down to his knees. It was growing dark, but the fog that threatened was evidently not going to come on; the moon's shape was in the sky.

What Schulz had done after the shooting of the hound was up for guesses. He had had to stay through the night until he knew which way was which. But then he had made those tracks upriver—whether heading for the T-Down for some reason, or wandering out of his head, or simply in disgust and despair, starting on foot out of the country.

I would find out tomorrow. Right now it was time I got back to camp. When I led Dude down onto the ice and climbed on, the moon had swum clear, with a big ring around it. There was no aurora; the sky behind the thin remaining mist was blue-black and polished. Just for a second, when I took off a mitt and reached back to unbuckle the saddlebag and put the hound's collar inside, I laid my hand on the marten, stiff-frozen under soft fur. It gave me an unpleasant shock, somehow. I pulled my hand away as if the marten might have bitten me.

Riding up the channel, I heard the wind beginning to whine under the eaves of the cutbanks, and a flurry of snow came down on me, and a trail of drift blew eastward ahead of me down the middle of the ice. The moon sat up above me like a polished brass cuspidor in a high-class saloon, but that could be deceptive; within minutes the wrack of another storm could be blowing it under.

Then I rode out into an open reach, and something touched my face, brushed it and was gone, then back again. The willows shuddered in a gust. Dude's head came up, and so did mine, because that wind blew out of hundreds of miles of snowy wastes as if it wafted across orange groves straight from Florida: instantly, in its first breath, there was a promise of incredible spring. I have felt the beginnings of many a Chinook; I never felt one that I liked better than that one.

Before I reached Bates I was riding with my earlaps up

235

and my collar open. I had heard a willow or two shed its load of snow and snap upright. The going under Dude's feet was no longer the squeaky dryness of hard cold, but had gone mushy.

By morning the coulees and draws would be full of the sound of water running under the sagged and heavied drifts; the rims of the river valley and patches of watery prairie might be worn bare and brown. There might be cattle on their feet again, learning again to bawl, maybe even working up toward the benches, because this was a wind they could face, and the prairie wool that had been only inches below their feet all winter would be prickling up into sight. Something—not much but something—might yet be saved out of that winter.

That night I went to bed full of the sense of rescue, happy as a boy scenting spring, eased of a long strain, and I never thought until morning, when I looked out with the Chinook still blowing strong and saw the channel of the Whitemud running ten inches of water on top of the ice, that now I wouldn't be able to follow to their end the single line of tracks, by that time pursuing nothing and unpursued, that led upriver into ambiguity. By the time I woke up, Schulz's last tracks were on their way toward the Milk and the Missouri in the spring breakup; and so was his last fire; and so, probably was the body of his great hound; and so, for all I or anyone else ever found out, was he.

Main-teen Luh Droyt

from *The Meadowlark Connection*
by Ken Mitchell

One way of reacting against the romantic image of the Mountie has been with humour, and in "Main-teen Luh Droyt," Ken Mitchell conducts an anti-romantic deflation of the heroic traditions of the Force. Constable Ashenden has set himself the task of uncovering an international drug ring in Meadowlark, Saskatchewan, and Mitchell develops the situation with the same rich sense of absurdity found in his first novel, Wandering Rafferty *(Toronto: Macmillan, 1972). Mitchell teaches at the University of Regina, and has written a number of plays as well as* Rafferty *and* The Meadowlark Connection *(Regina: Pile of Bones Publishing, 1975). He has recently edited an historical anthology of writings about his native prairies entitled* Horizons *(Toronto: Oxford, 1977).*

It was after barely two hours' sleep that Constable Ashenden encountered Ellie Sanders' scrambled-egg-and-fried-tomato breakfast and its horrible aftermath. Well, when he finally cracked the Pules-Feltham case, he would ask for two days' leave to recuperate.

He managed to get the office cleaned up, the prisoner's cell scoured, his hat brushed, and the reports typed before 3:30. But there was no time to clean his vomit-stained tie before going to the Maple Leaf Cafe and Bus Depot to meet the 3:34 bus from Moose Jaw.

As Ashenden briskly marched along Main Street, a black Oldsmobile sedan pulled up behind him, so that he saw neither it nor the driver, a heavy man with his jacket collar turned up and his fedora low over his eyes. As the car eased abreast, the window on the passenger's side slid down, and the man's lumpy face scowled through the opening. "Ashenden!" he barked.

The policeman whirled to face the challenge, his hands thrusting forward to deal with any threat, physical or verbal. It was a reaction thrummed into his muscles by months of tough drilling, preparing him instantly to deliver a karate chop or a finger-waving lecture on disrespect for the law.

"Were you talking to *me?*" he said, peering into the dark interior of the Olds, trying to study the face.

"Just get in."

"Do you know who you're talking to, mister?"

"Yes. Constable Ashenden of the RCMP."

"That's right. And I want to see your operator's licence."

The heavy-faced man stared at him, his tiny blue eyes crinkling with distaste. "I am your inspector, you god-damned moron!" he said finally.

Ashenden's training once again served him in good stead. He leaped to attention with instant reflex action, his polished black boot heels popping together above the hot late-afternoon sidewalk. His hand snapped into a crisp salute that belied his exhausted condition. "Good afternoon, sir! Pleased to see you, sir!" he snapped, his eyes staring straight ahead across the street, where he could see the green and orange awning of the MacLeod's Store flap in the slight breeze. He hoped his stained tie was not showing.

"For Christ's sake, Ashenden! You'll get sunstroke out there. Climb in!"

Ashenden opened the door and slid into the passenger's seat. The cool, dark interior was a relief on a day like this. He noticed, as the window whirred back into place, that the inspector's car had air-conditioning. Maybe after the Pules-Feltham gang was captured and put in jail, he would get air-conditioning in his car too.

"Now what's all this bullshit about a secret mission?"

"Secret mission, sir?"

"That's all I've heard about for the past two hours. Every-

239

body from Earl's Esso station to the waiter in the Ponderosa Beverage Room seems to think I'm here on some 'secret' mission."

Ashenden groaned inwardly, but managed to keep his eyes level with Inspector Heavysides'. "Well, isn't that why you're here in Meadowlark, sir?"

"No, that is *not* why I'm here in Meadowlark, sir!" the inspector roared. "I'm up here to kick your ass up Main Street and around the block for you! How come every sonuvabitch and his dog in this town knows I was coming?"

"I think I can explain, sir. There's a manual telephone exchange here and the operator—well, she's a bit of a gossip."

"Which is *exactly* why we do business by mail in this subdivision, Ashenden!"

"Yes, sir. I considered it an emergency under Regulation 352, Clause 17(d)."

"Don't hand me that crap!" the inspector rasped. "Just tell me what I'm doing up here besides booking you for a demotion!"

Ashenden began to perspire again, despite the air conditioner whirring behind him. "Well, sir, I have reason to suspect there is a drug-trafficking ring being established here, with foreign agents and political connections in Quebec."

"Foreign agents, eh, Ashenden? That's pretty good."

"Thank you, sir."

"*But what the hell are they doing in Podunk, Saskatchewan?*"

"But they could appear *anywhere*, sir. You said so yourself in the Sub-Divisional Memo circulated June 4 of this year. Paragraph 14, clause (e)."

Inspector Heavysides stared at Ashenden a brief moment, his breath hissing from the corner of his mouth. "This had better be good, Ashenden."

"I think I can justify your faith in me, Inspector. At this very moment, I have an agent infiltrating the enemy camp. We are going to meet at suppertime to exchange information. I'm pretty confident you'll give me a complete go-ahead after that time."

"An agent, Constable? We do not hire agents in the RCMP."
"Well, she's a volunteer, sir. I could hardly refuse the help."
"*She?*"
"Yes—there she is now, Inspector." Ashenden pointed to the south end of Main Street, a half-mile distant, where it joined Highway No. 15 to Shakespear. There was a bright yellow flash in the sun, and Sharon's MG swerved off the highway onto the gravel road; its familiar plume of dust rose majestically behind as the distant whine of the accelerating engine reached their ears. She must have hit seventy m.p.h. by the time she reached the hotel, when she geared down with a squeal of tires and a series of backfiring explosions. Ashenden leaned over and beeped the inspector's horn, as she zoomed past them. Sharon waved at them prettily, and in the middle of Main Street took a sharp, skidding U-turn with a violent flip of the steering wheel, her lustrous coppery curls swinging free in the faint breeze. She pulled alongside the big Oldsmobile, revving her engine furiously.

"Ashenden," Inspector Heavysides said, gazing at the girl in the MG. "You're starting to worry me, do you know that?"

"Well—sir—"

"Tell her to park that—thing and get in here. I'm going to get to the bottom of this."

Ashenden did as he was told. When Sharon was safely in the back of the car, the inspector drove to Elm Street, where he parked across from the Legion Hall. Ashenden introduced them.

Sharon leaned forward, her winning smile directed at the Inspector's scowling face. "I'm a writer," she said. "For the CBC."

The inspector's fedora seemed to pop up suddenly off the top of his head, revealing a close-cropped skull with deep fissures running across the forehead. A swollen vessel on the temple pulsed noticeably, and his eyes appeared to bulge from their sockets. He turned his head slowly toward Ashenden, his mouth working, unable to speak.

Ashenden smiled encouragement.

"SHE—WORKS—WHERE?" the inspector bellowed.

241

A couple of faces appeared at the door of the Legion Hall beer parlour across the street to see what all the noise was about.

"Um—CBC, sir." Ashenden knew now that something was definitely wrong. But there had been nothing about the CBC in the memos, and he had just assumed the two federal agencies were working for roughly the same employer: Her Majesty, The Queen.

"Jesus H. Christ! Have you gone right round the *bend?* You're *bushed*, Constable! You must be! CBC!" He shook his head incredulously. "Do you know what I'm going to do to you, Ashenden? Do you know where your next posting's going to be?"

"Baffin Island, sir?"

"Not on your sweet life, Ashenden—Baffin Island's too *cushy* for you. You're going to spend the rest of your life in this police force following the Musical Ride around with a push-broom and dust-pan, sweeping up after the horses. That's where *you're* going!"

Ashenden saluted, his face a study in stoicism. "Very good, Inspector. Thank you, sir."

"Shut up!" He turned to Sharon, who was glowering at him with her luminous green eyes. "Now as for you—you goddam *seductress*—you slink back into that Dinky Toy and get out of town. Stop putting lunatic ideas into this kid's head."

"Inspector Heavysides!" Sharon protested. "You have to listen. This is serious. These people are really up to something. We've got a tape recording!"

"Ashenden, I am holding you responsible for shutting this woman up."

Sharon flared. "*Listen, you—fascist pig!*"

"Constable. If she utters another word. I want her arrested for public mischief. Now get her out of here."

Ashenden jumped out of the car to open the rear door for Sharon.

"Never mind!" she said. "I can get out myself." She stepped out, slammed the door, and flounced up the street, turning once, as Ashenden watched in horror, to give the inspector a long, elegant middle finger. Fortunately the inspector was making notes in his small black book. Ashenden stood at attention beside the car.

"See that she's out of Meadowlark by sundown," Inspector Heavysides said, not looking up from his jotting.

"Today, sir?"

The inspector glared at him. "Every day, Ashenden. Is that understood?"

"Yes, sir."

"I'm giving you one last chance." The inspector looked up at the young officer, his bushy eyebrows nearly concealing his tiny blue eyes. "Let's say you're entitled to a couple of mistakes. But this is conditional upon your clearing up this mess. You have to redeem yourself, Ashenden."

"Thank you, sir."

The inspector's chilly smile was intended to convey compassion. "I was a raw rookie just like you once, Ashenden. I know what it's like. Especially when women get involved."

"But, sir—."

The inspector held up a hand. "Your superior officers have confidence in you, Ashenden. They *have* to have. Or they wouldn't have given you that uniform. And now—good luck."

Inspector Heavysides extended his enormous hand to Ashenden, then pumped the accelerator, apparently anxious to begin the long drive back to Moose Jaw.

"Thank you, sir. Now—about these red FLQ types bringing in the shipment of drugs?"

"Ashenden."

"Yes, sir?"

"There are no reds here. There is no FLQ here. There aren't any drugs *for a hundred miles*! I am hereby issuing you an order—on threat of dismissal from the Force—to get rid of this crazy obsession of yours about a drug conspiracy!"

Ashenden tried to locate the inspector's ice-blue eyes under the shaggy brows. And order had been given; it had to be carried out. A direct order from a superior countermanded all previous orders, all the regulations in the book. It super-

seded individual discretion. "Yes, sir," he said smartly.
"We know what we're doing in Moose Jaw, Constable. And
now, I'm keeping you from your highway patrol duties. So
long."

Ashenden stepped away from the car, forsaking its cool
interior for the mind-numbing heat waves beating upward
from the sidewalk.

"Oh, and get that goddam tie dry-cleaned," the inspector
said, slamming the door shut. Then the black Oldsmobile
was gone, purring down the street and out of Ashenden's life
as ominously as it had entered. He was left on the sidewalk,
gazing after it. His headache was getting worse. He needed
sleep desperately, and he wanted to visit Trooper. The com-
panionship of his horse always lifted his spirits. He glanced
at his watch. Nearly supper-time. Maybe he could slip out for
half an hour before Ellie Sanders rang the little hand-bell in
her dining room.

As though in answer to his yearning for sympathy, a loud
racket burst out behind him, and Sharon's speedy little road-
ster screeched to a halt at his elbow.

"I thought the old fart would never go!" Sharon yelled
above the roar of her engine, waving at him gaily.

He moved toward the car, facing one of the most painful
tasks of his life. He gestured to Sharon to switch off the
engine. "Well, I guess that's it, Sharon. It's all over."

Her dark green eyes stared at him incredulously. "You
don't mean it!" she breathed. "After all we've gone through
to crack this case?"

"I'm afraid so. An order is an order."

"Well, it might be for you, Constable. But I don't take
orders from some brass-hatted ape."

"Duty comes first, Sharon."

She gazed at him, her beautiful face intense with conviction.
"Does it, Jimmy?" she said quietly. "Is duty always first? How
about initiative, and responsibility?"

"Let's not get started talking about *principles*," he replied
shortly.

"Listen to me, Jimmy. Listen to me as you've never listened

to anything I've said before! Those—persons are going to execute Plan G on Saturday. In this *town*, which you have sworn to protect to the best of your ability! Are you going to abandon *that* duty?"

"Sharon, please!"

"I'll tell you what. You won't even have to dirty your hands looking after it. Go back out and *run* your radar trap. I'll do the investigation for you, unofficially. We won't even *tell* them in Moose Jaw."

"No, no, no!"

"And then, when we crack the ring—you'll be a bigger hero than ever—because you did it all yourself. You persisted in your sworn oath in the face of all obstacles!"

"But an order," he groaned. "From Inspector Heavysides!"

"Hah! Inspector Heavysides! What does *he* know, sitting in his plush office in Moose Jaw? I bet it even has an air-conditioner—so he won't get contaminated by the rich, clean dust of the prairies! Why do your superiors want to suppress this investigation?"

"My duty—!"

"Your duty is to the law! To justice! Jimmy, tell me, what is the motto of the Force?"

He could not suppress a quaver of emotion from his voice, as he declaimed the oath he had memorized for the graduation exercises: "Main-teen luh droyt!"

"Yes! *Maintien le droit*! Let it ring, Constable Jimmy Ashenden! Let it ring through the length and breadth of Meadowlark! Don't surrender now!"

Sharon stood on the seat of her MG, her right hand raised in a fist. Her rings glittered in the late afternoon sun. She seemed, silhouetted against the outline of the Legion Hall, like an avenging angel of the law. For the first time in his career, RCMP Constable James Ashenden faltered in the execution of a direct order.

"Sharon, do you know what's going to happen to me if this doesn't work?" He paused, white-faced. "Horse latrine detail with the Musical Ride."

She looked at him with pride. "I knew you wouldn't give up,

Jimmy." Her tanned thighs flashed alarmingly as she vaulted out of the car. She took him by the arm and breathed in his ear, "Do you know what I found out today? Do you know the Wheat Pool elevator Agent?"

"Well, not personally." The grain buyer at the Wheat Pool elevator was the only Oriental in town, a man by the name of Yu Ching with a reputation for quietness. He smiled a lot and nodded, but had never spoken to Ashenden.

"Do you know why he's so quiet? Why he never talks to *anybody*?"

"Well, he's only been here a couple of months, Sharon. Maybe he's very shy. These things take time, you know."

Sharon shook her head triumphantly, her copper hair swinging from side to side. "Not even close. It's because he doesn't speak English! Just Chinese!"

Ashenden stood rooted to the spot. It was as though a blindfold had been ripped from his eyes. The yellow hordes of China were at the gates of Meadowlark!

The Detachment Man

by H. J. MacDonald

H. J. MacDonald's "The Detachment Man"
is also set in a small Saskatchewan town, but
it would be difficult to find a sharper contrast
with Mitchell's light-hearted satire. It might
be argued that this story, like "O'Brien's doom,"
is not, strictly speaking, a fiction, but it belongs
in this collection because every detail of the
author's painstaking anatomy of the life of a
"detachment man" contributes to the essentially
dramatic effect of the plot. Having served on
the Force for twenty years, MacDonald clearly
knew where the heroism of the real Mountie lay.
This story was first published in MacLean's
in July, 1972.

In the prairie village, it is shortly after six on a hot August
morning and Corporal Jack Willow, 38, of the Royal Canadian Mounted Police drives his police car on dusty Fort Street.
Willow grew up in a small Saskatchewan town similar to
this one and he sees things with a native's eye. Already the
morning sun begins to show how hot the day will be. At the
bottom of First Street, Willow passes the old railway station.
As usual no one waits on the decaying platform for the early
train. It probably won't stop for a drop or a pickup again
today. As a raw recruit, almost 17 years ago, Willow had
stepped from a train in another prairie town just like this one.
It had been a brilliant spring day in that thriving village, and
one he had never forgotten. He had stood on the crowded
platform suddenly conscious of the fact that he was a curious
target. He stood in "review order"—stetson hat, scarlet serge,
Sam Browne, yellow-striped navy-blue breeches, boot-camp

polished boots, gleaming brass, nickel spurs, a khaki knap-
sack slung over one shoulder and a new leather crop gripped
in one hand—all in all an immaculate one-man parade. And
people were staring at him, frank stares that seemed to say,
"New Mountie in town...New Mountie in town..." It
unnerved him and the butterflies began. He tried to remember
what a hardened NCO had once told him: "You smile too
easy, son. Slow down. Make 'em earn it."

The daydream ended and he turned the car up Main Street
past the long-neglected Royal Hotel.

Jack Willow was, in the idiom of the RCMP, a "detachment
man." Detachment is the name the force gives its posts or
police stations. Since it acts as the provincial police in all
of the provinces except Ontario and Quebec, several hundred
detachments can be found in the small towns throughout
western Canada, many of them having only one or two men.
This morning, Willow drove straight to the Esso service
station on the other side of town. Later in the day, he had a
patrol to make. The night before, he had arranged with Bill
Smuranski, the mechanic, to give the police car a quick tune-
up before he hit the road. Reaching the service station, he
left the car. Then, on foot, he set off on his way back to the
police detachment.

The village Willow walked through that morning is a village
greying with dust and decline, a prairie village that had seen
better times, like most today. Laid out in the typical prairie
gridiron pattern, the streets run in straight alignment, are
regularly spaced and cross each other at 90-degree angles
with wide rights-of-way. The town seems empty, always, as
if someone had planned a big party and nobody had turned
up. Main Street wears an affronted injured look. The lumber
company Willow passed was boarded up. Above the door of
the closed Grange Café, the neon sign swung uneasily on
one hinge. In a vacant store window, a wrinkled Centennial
poster remained: (*Howdee Podner! Are Ya Attending Thee
Centennial Jubilee Fireworks And Dance On Monday!
Pancake Party! Jubilee Ice Cream And Bake Tables! See
Harry Swert's Grand Champion Bull! Hobbycraft Show!*

COME IN COSTUME OF CANADIAN HISTORICAL FIGURE!) And there on the marquee of the closed-up movie house, the Rialto (with the *i* and the *l* smashed), six letters spelled out THE END.

As the folks in town will tell you, this is the community service centre for a farming district that takes in about 5,000 people spread through some 30 miles square of land encompassing the village (also roughly the area of Willow's detachment jurisdiction), an orderly land of rich black loam. When the local people talk of their village—and they talk of it readily enough—they speak in tones heavy with hope and loyalty.

"We've never had a better year," Lance Hartwell, owner of the clothing store will tell you. "The town's retail sales hit six million dollars—an all-time record!"

But Hartwell had to let his only clerk go last week and ask his wife Ethel to come in to spell him off during the day. Jeff Trasker and his two sons, Ned and Roger, farm the home quarter and the old Morgan sections south of town. "Sure," Jeff Trasker says, "we can't afford the machinery we usta. Can't pay for the stuff we got. And wheat ain't the mighty winner it usta be, I guess, but take a look at the new mink ranch in town and the way most of us here've spread our fields—sunflower crops, cukes, sugar beets, onions, rapeseed . . ."

But the Traskers are storing 40,000 bushels of Number One wheat in their bins and another 15,000 lies dumped under canvas on stubble. Since cash is scarce, they're ready to barter some of their produce for a price one third the going rate to get the things they need.

But the village creek is still running, muddy and sluggish and low, perhaps, but running. It's an honest-to-god stream, where town kids paddle and older dreamers sit with fishing poles out waiting for a miracle to happen. More than 100 years ago the first settlers drifted into this area: Presbyterian farmers from Ontario; peasant Ukrainian stock following in the footsteps of Vasyl Elyniak and Ivan Pylypiw; meticulous Swiss; rugged Danes; canny Americans. How special this creek was to them can be seen in a small neat building beside a stand of silver willow with the date of its erection chiseled into the pebbled stone above the door: BUILT 1910. It's the sewage plant. Many big cities with big rivers don't treasure their water this way even today.

The fact is the human head count of this village district dropped another 14% last year. As fast as they hit 17 or 18 the kids are getting out. Their absence sucks the vitality from village life. Age—old age—dignified and strong sustains this village, this village whose newest building happens to be not a youth centre, not a new school, not a new ice arena, but the Senior Citizen's Home.

Even the Indians and Métis ("breeds" they are still called here) who live on the outskirts of the village in the squalor of poplar-board shacks covered with weathered corrugated paper siding or log hovels caulked with horse manure, the one-room shelters where the animals and youngsters share sleeping space under the bed—even their ranks have been depleted of youth. For that matter, 60% of the town's housing is more than 40 years old, of frame construction, without proper plumbing, lighting and ventilation. Their owners can't afford better conveniences. The mill rate teeters on the horizon ready to drop out of sight.

Yet there is no question that Willow's past and present are contained in this village—more precisely, in places like this one. For, if he had been aware of it, all the years of his adult life awaited him here. Willow was to know, *really know*, no other kind of life, no other kind of place. Everything he was to become would happen in towns and villages related in spirit and purposes to this one.

By the time Willow reached the detachment building his wife had breakfast prepared. The children were up. The walk from the service station through town had taken him about three quarters of an hour.

The detachment sits not far from the ghostly railway station. It is a red brick building with white wood trim, a flag in a stanchion, neat lawn, small flower and vegetable garden at the back. One half of the detachment has two stories, the living quarters for Willow, his wife and his three children, a boy eight, and two girls, 10 and four. The other half is one story and contains the detachment office, and, in a large rear room, a lockup comprising three cells and washroom facilities. The building is government-owned and was constructed five years ago, with hardwood floors, reasonable living space and modern conveniences, one example of the force's long-term plan to make sure its men on detachment have decent, comfortable conditions, perhaps to ease somewhat the other interminable inconveniences their job requires them to put up with. Willow had not always been as lucky. His worst experience had taken place early in his career when he'd been a single man and had been transferred to a temporary detachment up north in the province. He'd lived in a run-down former construction hut with a Quebec heater, a chemical toilet and no running water. When there were prisoners to look after, they lived with him until he could take them south to appear before a magistrate or JP; there was nowhere else to put them. At night, he handcuffed them to his bed. More often than not, they slept and he didn't. Shades of *Rose Marie*.

Detachment life can be a gypsy existence. The men are transferred every two or three or four years, often from one end of the country to the other. They move from hell to hell or heaven to heaven, depending on their temperament, their skills, their ambitions, their luck. Their daily life can become chaotic, a life spun wildly from hour to hour on chance circumstances, unknown conditions, uncertain developments in the form of auto wrecks, smashed bodies, broken spirits, and both savage and ingenious spurts of criminality. It can be an arduous calling. The euphemism uttered by a Depot Division lecturer, "Your situation on detachment will always remain fluid . . ." is perhaps remembered years later and only then appreciated, grimly. In this atmosphere, on detachment, true personalities are hidden or are changed; the brave grow braver; the weak, stronger; only the true misfit falters or stands out.

In Willow's detachment, the walls weren't soundproof enough sometimes to block from the living quarters what went on in the police office or lockup areas. As a result, their lives—Willow's life and each member of his family's—were inevitably touched by, and would often become intertwined with, the incidents taking place "next door."

It was always worse when you knew somebody. They would never forget, for example, the sound of Joe Caroson's sobbing. Everybody in town knew Joe. A farmer, Joe got blind drunk one Saturday night and piled his half-ton truck into a car full of kids coming home from a dance, killing three, one of them his neighbor's.

From the tiny cell Joe's sobs filtered through to the family in their beds for the rest of the night. He hadn't been scratched. But his pain was audible to the Willows. They knew there was no escape from Joe's anguish. But the Willows didn't complain. None of them told Joe Caroson to shut up and go to sleep. And Willow couldn't be fussy whom he invited in. Prisoners snored, got sick, went berserk. They had to be fed special foods, because of ulcers, given insulin shots, had the DTs. Pregnant girls came in out of nowhere, scared, but their running ended, and had to be taken care of. People dropped in to talk their problems over, an alternative to confession, and then went out to become normal people again or, perhaps, to commit suicide. Or came to dip into the old box of clothes Willow kept. The Indians and Métis always seemed to be in need of something.

Marion Willow, a small, wiry, auburn-haired woman with the compassion and simplicity of a nun, became, over the years, a kind of cell mother. She had met Willow in a small town in Manitoba when she was in training to become a registered nurse. She darned prisoners' socks, washed their clothes, helped them write letters, tended their ills. From across the land at Christmas time, cards and presents arrived signed "John" or "Mary" or, as often, with no name at all. One young man had not missed sending her a Mother's Day card in seven years.

Willow had the opportunity to get away from it, to move on up the ladder of the force. Once, they transferred him to plainclothes duty at a division headquarters in Edmonton.

253

In a few months he requested a transfer back to detachment duty. For Willow was one of those rare ones—a born detachment man. Something about the life engaged his interest. He wasn't particularly special or brilliant at his work but a man who didn't seem to mind the long hours and moving constantly in a world where, as Racine observed, "Crime like virtue has its degrees."

Thus Willow landed back in this middle-prairie village, one man who, in some strange way, had unknowingly chosen his own destiny.

"The detachment man is the workhorse of the force," says one RCMP senior officer. "The secret of being a good one is to know how to handle people. That requires a special ability. Because people, no one needs to be told, aren't all the same. Willow had the knack of handling all kinds."

On the other hand, he was among people who really didn't need a lot of "handling."

"Mounties don't live the kind of subculture life out here that I suppose some policemen in the big cities do," says village lawyer Dick Bond, a greying, restless man who moves about his office with a deep frown. "So they haven't got the hang-ups city policemen have. They're respected by the community. And *we* respect them. There isn't one I've dealt with who wasn't up on his Code or Statutes or court procedures better than most lawyers I know. And that included Willow."

And if Willow needed help, he usually got it. "He hadn't had as much as a fight around here, if I remember right," said Bill Smuranski, the service-station mechanic. Smuranski had a way of waving his bruised-looking hands in the air when he talked, giving a certain liveliness to the unvaried pitch of his voice. "But I went out on a posse with him last September. Me and about 20 of the boys. Tramped through that muskie country north of town looking for some crazy breed who'd put a bullet through his girl friend. But that didn't amount to much. Not much at all. The breed shot himself before we got to him. Put a .22 right through the centre of his forehead. The damnedest thing. The hole, she looked just like a pimple."

The farmers respected him. "He'd come out here moseying around when things were quiet," one farmer recalled. "Break a head of my wheat open and run the kernels between his fingers to test for moisture. Maybe tongue up a few to test the hardness. Then he'd say, 'She's ready for cutting, Joe. Ready as ripe can be.' And y'know, most times he'd be dead on." Money rides on a farmer's decision to harvest. He has to guess right, for it takes just the right hardness and moisture to make the finest wheat flour for bread and cereals.

Willow had been stationed here for three years, and was active in the district. He skipped a local curling team. He sat on various planning committees for community projects, took part in youth programs by lecturing and showing films on various aspects of law enforcement. He liked to sing, and sometimes sang with the United Church choir. His favorite singing group was Martien Ferland and his choristers, a group he had on audio tape in the *Le Feu de Camp Chez Soi* school series.

"Willow was just a regular guy," says the corner druggist. "You weren't ever conscious of the fact that he was a policeman. Sure, when we were curling or playing bridge or something he might be called away, because he always left a number with the operator or the baby sitter."

"The only thing he didn't like much," said another friend, "was taking a turn at the skull saw when Doc was doing an autopsy."

After breakfast, Corporal Willow spoke to his son about the poor spelling mark on the boy's report card, promised to pick up the plants his wife had loaned to the school for the Home and Garden Show, and then went next door to the office to catch up on some paperwork.

As a detachment man, Willow had been reprimanded twice in his career: once for allowing men under his command to use a police car for other than service purposes; another time for allowing a prisoner he was escorting to escape. He hadn't solved any sensational crimes, and his record of cases "concluded" wasn't memorable. But he worked conscientiously at trying to clean up the hundreds of commonplace, and often tedious, crimes and quasi-crimes that came his way.

That morning, in his detachment, Willow's "complaint book" contained 40 cases that were SUI (still under investigation). These included theft of wheat from a granary; 15 assorted but minor traffic infractions; one indecent assault; two missing teen-agers; one breaking, entering and theft; a suspected arson case; a possession of a homemade still case; and two manslaughter charges arising out of highway accidents.

For the year, up to that day in August, Willow had investigated more than 700 complaints of one kind or another. Forty percent of them had been reported to him between the hours of midnight and 6 a.m.

The fact is that RCMP detachment men offer one of the few remaining 24-hour services left in the world. Day and night, when the phone rang Willow answered it. Day and night, when somebody came pounding on the door, Willow answered it. If for some reason he wasn't there, the duty fell to Marion Willow—she didn't *have* to do it but she just did it (in the force a Mountie's wife is known as the unpaid second man on detachment).

In the office, Willow made out a requisition for a new set of snow tires for the patrol car and some stationery. Then he typed up a 237 on a crime dealing with a successful investigation that had occupied almost two full days of his time, aided by the dog master and the police dog from his subdivision headquarters. The case concerned the butchering and theft of a calf. The doberman, tracking on a farm belonging to one of the complainant's neighbors, had sniffed out two burlap bags stuffed with about 45 pounds of beef, made up into roasts, and a green Hereford calf hide—the loot—all partly hidden underwater in the dugout behind a clump of tall swamp grass.

Then, shortly after ten, the detachment telephone rang. It was Smuranski, the mechanic. The police car was ready.

Willow went into the house side of the detachment, collected a thermos of coffee and some sandwiches Marion Willow had made up for his lunch. Willow kissed his wife good-bye and left. The parting was routine. It had happened hundreds of times before.

Outside, he started, on foot again, on his way back to the service station. He walked past the railway station, along First, and onto Main Street. He was glad to be out in the sun again, glad to get a little exercise, because, at 38, Willow was no longer trim. He had a round, soft, pleasant-looking face, squinty eyes, and the thousands and thousands of miles riding a police car had bestowed on him a slightly paunchy look and a plodding, heavy step.

At the garage, when he was in the car, he took out his "issue" eyeglasses, which he kept in the glove compartment, and put them on. The plain, plastic-framed glasses made him look more like a kindly schoolteacher than the "rider of the Plains who always gets his man."

Then, over his car radio, he reported his car number and "eight-10, general patrol north," which would be noted at his division headquarters, some 300 miles away, at precisely 10.55 a.m.

His first call that morning was at the home of a farmer named Peter Smithson. A complaint had been made against Smithson by a neighbor who had reported that the man had been taking potshots with a rifle at the man's cows. Willow had decided to drop in and have a talk with Smithson.

It took Willow about a half-hour to reach the Smithson farm. He turned into a narrow rutted laneway, flanked by a double row of stunted Russian poplars, which led up to the house. A single-story frame building, the house was badly run down. The barn had never been painted, and a large patch of the shingled roof had been eaten away by age. At the sound of the car in the laneway, a brown and white mongrel dog had come racing from the field and was setting up a howl.

Willow parked the police vehicle beside a muddied track at the edge of an abused garden. Stepping out, paying no attention to the dog yapping at his heels, he began to walk slowly towards the side door of the farmhouse.

Inside the house, Smithson stood at the kitchen window.

He didn't know Willow, and Willow had never met him. But, that morning, something let loose within Smithson, some inner frustration or deep grudge against the world, either real or imagined, which he'd probably been damming up for years. Smithson poked the ugly snout of a .303 rifle through his kitchen window and took aim at the unsuspecting policeman.

At that time, the RCMP uniform for detachment patrol duties comprised black ankle boots, blue overalls with a broad yellow stripe running down the outside of each pantleg, brown serge jacket, khaki shirt and plain navy-blue tie. Willow's jacket had gold-thread corporal chevrons sewn high on the right sleeve. High on the left sleeve were three yellow-worsted, five-pointed stars, in a little half-moon design, each star representing five years' service. On the same sleeve, but centred six inches from the bottom of the cuff, were yellow-silk crossed revolvers on a black background, noting that Willow was qualified with this weapon. The white lanyard of his brown-leather Sam Browne equipment trailed from around his neck, down the front of his jacket like a long string tie and disappeared into his buttoned-up holster, located waist-high over his right hip; out of sight, the end of the lanyard was knotted to the ring hook of his .38 Smith and Wesson police special revolver. Willow wore a forage cap: navy-blue top, black peak, with a bright sunflower yellow band centred by a brilliantly polished brass badge, with the RCMP motto, *Maintiens Le Droit*, stamped into the metal.

Willow would not hear the report of the rifle whose bullet smashed into his body to end his life.